STAY FREE!

[signature]

JAMES 2:24

THROUGH SACRIFICE : FREEDOM

The Incredible Life Story of Angelo Flaim

TOM FLAIM

Copyright © 2024 by Tom Flaim.
All rights reserved.

Second Edition

First Original Publishing by Page Publishing, 2022

No part of this publication may be reproduced, stored in a retrieval system, or transmitted, in any form or by any means, electronic, mechanical, photocopying, recording, or otherwise, without the prior written permission of Tom Flaim.

I gratefully dedicate this book to Christ Jesus, my Lord and Savior, who loves, empowers, and strengthens me. I pray that in some small way, this book brings Him glory.

There are also many people without whom I cannot imagine what my life would be like. My immediate and extended family, whose love for me and patience with me are both truly incredible. Anyone that has ever uttered a prayer for me during difficult times or shared praises during all the wonderful times of my life.

Lastly, to my earthly father. Once you've read his story here, you'll understand why.

CONTENTS

Introduction 1

1. New Beginnings 7
2. The Father Unknown 21
3. The Rise of Empires 33
4. Just Another Legionnaire 39
5. The Birth of a Freedom Fighter 53
6. Learning to Run 63
7. Death From the Shadows 71
8. A Suitor Comes Calling 85
9. An Entirely Different War 99
10. A Ticket to Munich 111
11. Pietro 121
12. Everyone Sacrifices 135
13. Antonio, the Knifeman 147
14. Meeting Geronimo 157
15. Nowhere to Hide 167
16. From Obscurity to Infamy 181
17. Matteo 189
18. The Ultimate Sacrifice 199
19. The Hunters Are Themselves Hunted 211
20. Clearing the Way 223
21. Robbed of V-Day 231
22. Returning Home 241
23. The Mayor of Genoa 251
24. Treading Water 259
25. Turn the Page 269
26. Go (Mid) West, Young Man 277
27. Red, White, and Blue Collar 2877
28. Freedom at Last 299

Epilogue 3155

Acknowledgements 3166

Introduction

One of the hardest parts of writing this book was coming up with its title. What few words could encapsulate the incredible life you will meet who was my father? Angelo Flaim embodied sacrifice his entire life. This story cannot even scratch the surface of all that he went through during his life for his homeland of Trentino, his adopted home in the United States, and for his family.

Whether it was impacting the Second World War, coming to America, or living an immigrant's life, his story is one of freedom won through extreme and continual sacrifice. He was a part of the Greatest Generation, but with a twist. His unique story was an inspiration to me in my entire life, as well as all that knew him.

You will experience, as this story unfolds, how Angelo found himself repeatedly in dangerous and dire situations yet miraculously survived time after time. By his own words, he should have been dead a dozen times. Within the paradigm of the humble hero, he sacrificed for family, the Allied war effort, and the hope of a new free country of Trentino in Northern Italy. His efforts ultimately saved the lives of innumerable people and became legendary to many.

Revelation!

I'm not sure what it is about fishing that opens people up, but I'm eternally grateful for it. When I was young, roughly between the ages of ten to sixteen, my father and I would regularly go fishing. These were not a couple of hours on an occasional lazy day, mind you. I'm speaking of many full-on weekend trips with just the two of us.

We lived in the Chicago area at the time, and our trips involved driving late into Friday night to a lake somewhere in Wisconsin. It never really mattered where we would go because we honestly seldom caught many fish. We were just grateful to be out together, and since my brother and mother hated fishing, it was always a special time for the two of us.

Something truly magical happened on many of those trips. Since fish rarely actually bite, much time was spent drowning worms and just sharing openly. My father would go off and tell stories of his time in World War II, his experiences immigrating to the United States from Italy, and so on. On occasion, he would really get into it and share insights into his exploits as a saboteur and as the leader of an Italian partisan team fighting both Mussolini's Fascist Italy and Hitler's Third Reich.

As a boy and young man, I was riveted by every word and moved by every tear. These stories of bravery, luck, and superhuman fetes performed by a ragtag family on the run completely captivated me. Like many good fathers, there were many stories told to teach a lesson and such, but the incredible tales of him and his team left me awestruck. Sometimes I would think they're too incredible to believe, but the details provided and collaboration from family and history books ultimately left little doubt.

It wasn't until many decades later at his funeral that I came to realize I was the only person to hold so much of his history. I think that can be because of PTSD or post-traumatic stress disorder. Back then, my dad would just tell me to not discuss what he told me with anyone, and I pretty much kept true to his wishes. I suppose he just needed to tell someone, to just essentially get all the pain and emotion out of his system. And what kid wouldn't cherish a secret bond with his father?

At home, he rarely if ever discussed what we shared on the long summer days in an uncomfortable rowboat. Mom would get the usual message of our generally good time and futile efforts to catch fish. I realized quickly that what happened in the boat, stayed in the boat. To be honest, I learned early that I was the only person to know so much about him. As was borne out when casual conversation returned to those times, even my mother was unaware of the extent of his exploits.

Over time, and without his knowledge, I would write down the stories so that I wouldn't forget them. Then again, without his knowledge, I would research as best I could the facts around his escapades and missions as verification. But it wasn't until the summer of 1979 that I knew the truth of his life's adventure.

At the time, I was a civil engineering intern working on the repaving of the Illinois State Toll Highway. There was a gravel truck delivery person that came several times per day to drop off his load. Part of my job was to log in the delivery, measure it for accurate amounts, and sign off that it was acceptable. Over the summer, I began to get friendly with most of the drivers, but one in particular is pertinent to this book. His first name was Wolfgang, and his last name had way too many consonants to pronounce. I just called him Wolfy. Wolfy was about sixty years of age and enjoyed razzing me on what I did the previous weekend, Bears football prospects in the coming season, or my attempts to find love in all the wrong places. One day, his heavy German accent changed its tone and took an unexpectedly frightening turn.

For some reason, I had printed my name on his order sheet instead of writing it in cursive. After studying it for a while, he asked if I was the son of an Angelo Flaim. I knew enough to lie and told him no, and that my father's name was Bob. As his face took an angered and disappointed look, I asked him why. In a monotone voice that reflected his deep reflection, he said he spent a good amount of time in WWII looking for Angelo Flaim and that he would love to find him now. Fortunately, we were both on working time, and he left to get back to it.

I, however, began to realize the significance of what just transpired. That evening, I went to my parents' home and told my dad exactly what had happened. He calmly thanked me and disappeared into another room. Not another word was said about the incident, but he sat in our living room in a chair by the window just watching the front of our home. That night when I went to bed, he strangely stayed in the chair, just watching out the window. It was impossible for me to determine if he was somehow guarding the house or just in deep introspection.

I didn't have the courage to ask. I knew immediately that my work associate Wolfy was one of the Germans who hunted my father during the war. Seeing as there were no weapons in the house, I think dad was just praying to let this threat pass without further incident. Gratefully, in just a couple of weeks, I returned to school for my final year of college, and nothing more came of it. Except one important thing: I knew my dad's stories were likely true and that one day I would write them down so as to not forget the silent sacrifice of my father. While it's been some forty years since that episode, this book is my humble effort to keep that promise.

After his passing in 1998, it was therapy for me to research even further and dig deeper into his missions. This led me to Italy, specifically Trentino, Germany, Austria, US military and CIA archives, and beyond to piece together the events into the story that follows. The translation of hundreds of relevant documents closed many gaps, and much information gratefully became available at the turn of the twenty-first century when many critical military records became declassified.

This was not an easy or quick matter. Many of his identity documents, which served as wartime passports, had him in multiple locations and different countries on the same date! It was a riddle that I became obsessed with solving. So it is with humble confidence that I lay out the extraordinary true-life story of Angelo Flaim based upon the facts as best as can be verified.

Key Locations

The wartime adventures of Angelo Flaim transpired throughout Northern Italy, Germany, and the USSR (now the Ukraine). The following map displays a geographic reference for the key occurrences.

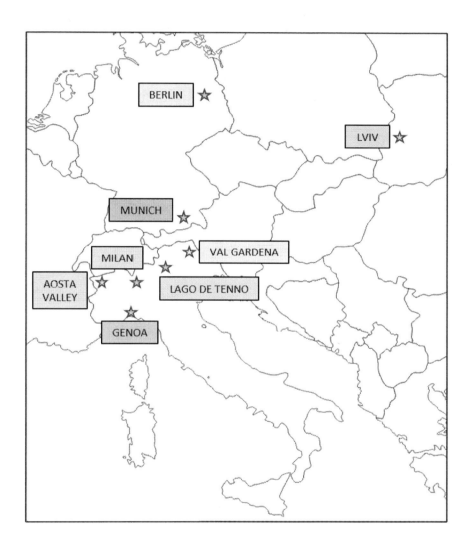

CHAPTER 1

New Beginnings

April 16, 1947
Ligurian Sea (outside of Genoa)

What am I doing? Angelo agonized to himself, hoping that a bolt of inspiration or understanding would suddenly strike him and bring clarity. Looking skyward, no answer would come. No peace, no comforting thought, no reassurance that this new adventure would end successfully. Nothing—not even a break in the sullen sky or the cold rain that made every moment unbearable. Sensing the situation worsening, he summoned all his strength and moved forward with this new personal mission.

How could it be that just a few days ago, he was warm and enjoying the company of family and friends? They'd weathered the storm of war and now laughed and carried on like old friends do. Spending his days dreaming of an independent country of Trentino, he had, at one point, eagerly anticipated taking his place in it.

The County of Tyrol and the Province of Trentino have always been strategic lands, he thought to himself. *Sure, the area was first controlled by Austria and now Italy, but since medieval times, it has maintained autonomy from whatever country claimed it. I've done everything I could to bring freedom to my ancestral home, and now I'll likely never see it again*, he lamented.

Even though it had only been a couple of years since the end of the war and the destruction of much of the country, this was truly a new time and beginning. Sure, he had been through hell, literally, but he had beaten the odds and survived.

No one could venture a guess as to what the world or their beloved homeland would look like. But hope provided an important release and maintained sanity because now he was bound for America! The steering forces of war were to end in the land of opportunity. *Clearly the best place anywhere in the world to make a fresh start*, concluded Angelo.

Even Nini felt it would get better. *And if he thought so, why shouldn't I?* he supposed. He had taken virtually every step and endured every moment of the war with him. They were more than cousins; they were best friends, sharing a bond borne from change, fear, and hope. Long before the war, Nini was everywhere in Angelo's early life. Spending so much time together as youth, people assumed them to be brothers.

Still, even with this cousin, whose relationship and special closeness came from both blood and experience, an unspoken uneasiness never left them. Uncertainty shared with close friends and family is tolerable, even perversely exciting in these uncertain times, but the all-too-recent memories of war and political purge would still make Angelo's heart race.

Private times were an altogether different story. A reservoir of tears hid silently behind his appearance. Fearing even a single outward tear would unleash a torrent, he resolutely held them back. The constant need to release the pressure would often find him mourning uncontrollably. The endless running, constant threats, and being hunted like an animal across Alpine mountain ranges came back to him all too often. Though it had only consumed a few years out of his twenty-four years on earth, it was sometimes hard to remember anything prior. Even so, since everyone was forced to submit to the horrors of this insane war, Angelo derived comfort from just being with people who shared these same happenings.

And yet, this day found him on the forward deck of the *SS Marine Shark*, making his way to America. *How will I make it?* he cried to himself. *I've been alone plenty of times before, but never lonely. It's only the first day of this wretched trip and I already miss everyone back home*, he languished. *Nini, Paldo and Maria, Zio Angelo, and Zia Renata are all I have left, and now I may never see them again. I owe my very life to them, and I'm deserting them.* The same convicting question, "What am I doing?" kept hammering in his mind like the massive waves against the ship's hull.

The vast and endless ocean before him only added to his gloomy attitude, and staring into the never-ending scene, he became lost in a depressing trance.

A few hours after the ship's launch, an approaching stranger asked, "Why so glum? We're headed to America, and this is the best day of my life!"

Angelo didn't even look up. "You don't understand. I left everything, literally the only family and friends I have ever known and the only love I have ever felt."

Disgusted by his depressing attitude and his decision to leave the family that loved him so, the stranger stomped off uttering a single word: "Louse!"

Looking to the floor, he spotted a pad of small papers that had obviously been discarded. Picking it up, he had the idea to document his thoughts. Whether out of boredom or a genuine attempt to document his feelings, he began a crude diary of the trip. A ship's worker was kind enough to "borrow" a pen for him, and he began writing down this trip's experience.

Angelo had never journaled his experiences or kept any notes during the war. Being caught with any information would potentially put his team and their operations at risk. Plus, he didn't need to give the German or Fascist interrogators a reason to be extra thorough. But the emotion of the day left him tired, and any attempt at starting would have to wait for morning.

That night, he fell into a deep sleep. Not the welcome type generated from contentment but instead the capitulating type caused by mental exhaustion. He prayed for a break in the obsessive and destructive visits to his memory, but there was no relief provided. Finally, just after midnight, with the faces of Nini and the men he served with staring at him from the mirror of his consciousness, Angelo collapsed onto the thin hard mattress. The pillow provided was extremely soft and unlike anything he had ever felt. As he lay his head down on the center of it, the sides came up and engulfed his head.

Well, at least it's better than sleeping on the ground. he said with a giant exhale. The end of his first day at sea couldn't have come fast enough.

The next day, Angelo was awakened at 6:10 a.m. by the sounds of a ship at work. The *SS Marine Shark* was a sizable ship, weighing over 12,000 gross tons and 523 feet in length. This first morning at sea found most of its 185-member crew making every sort of noise.

He stepped out from the room where he landed the previous night completely confused by the sight of so much activity. It was just short of sunrise, and already the crew was busily running around like the chickens Angelo would sometimes feed in the morning while growing up. Then, without warning, the big ship let loose its mighty horn. It made a deafening sound Angelo had only heard previously from a distance. Unfortunately, this time, it came from just two decks above and about a hundred feet forward. Following the horn's dreadful blast was an announcement that breakfast was being served on a lower deck.

Breakfast was a terrific surprise! He ate alone that morning but feasted on fruit, pastries, and sweets. Along with rolls and marmalade, it was a perfect Italian breakfast. Espresso coffee with a little milk and sugar rounded off an unexpectedly pleasant start to the day.

Angelo immediately sought to get the lay of the cavernous ship, a testament to his military experience. He had learned years earlier to identify all possible points of ingress and egress in case he needed to make a stand or quick exit. Even though he could not escape a ship at sea, he reasoned, he could at least know how to quickly escape from one part of the vessel to another.

As he made his way from the lower deck, where breakfast was served, to the promenade deck above sea level, he was taken aback by the start of a beautiful sunrise. Having never seen a sunrise at sea, he decided to interrupt his reconnaissance of the ship and take it in. He made his way to the topmost deck and was rewarded with a most serene panorama of light orange against a dark purple sky, draped over a perfectly calm shimmering surface. As the minutes passed, the softer oranges yielded to a brilliant red in front of an azure blue field. Finally, the fiery yellow of the sun quickly consumed the cobalt sky.

The colors were more brilliant than any he had ever seen before, and he stood for a long time enjoying it. The purity of the moment lifted Angelo's spirit. The beauty of that first sunrise at sea seemed to bathe even his nagging memories in a positive light. He stepped away from the protective railing, smiling for the first time in a long time. The memories were still there, but he now reflected with a cautious fondness. He also felt the first tinge of excitement for where he was going and the endless possibilities that would be his.

Angelo could not escape who he was so easily though, and he continued to walk the ship, carefully mapping out its layouts in his mind. He noted passageways, hatches, and bulkhead doors for evasive movement, as well as storage spaces and cargo holds for hiding. Along the way, he started to write down his thoughts. This seemed a good time as any to finally start the chronicle of this adventure.

*****

The next two days brought a routine which suited him just fine. Days and nights passed with little fanfare or excitement, helping Angelo become increasingly content with his choices and decisions. The routine was only occasionally interrupted, like when he saw two small islands in the distance off the coast of Spain. They reminded him of Corsica, a view he experienced many times from the coast of Genoa.

Fortunately, by this point, he was eating so well, his thin muscular frame forged from years of scarcity began accumulating some welcome weight. Always on the thin side from a lack of proper diet and being on the run, he surprised himself at the unforeseen pleasure of a couple excess pounds.

On the third night, Angelo met some new friends and began to feel like his old self. Being a social type of person, he felt much better when in the company of others. While he was far from being at peace, he was at least beginning to feel comfortable in his own skin again.

The next day brought the surprising sight of flying fish! He could not imagine fish literally flying out of the water alongside the ship. He stood by the railing and stared for hours at the sight. The way their pectoral fins pulsed so fast that they actually looked like small birds when out of the water. He enjoyed monitoring the distance each could "fly" and noted that the best stayed out of water for over thirty seconds and went at least two hundred feet. So taken was he by this marvel of nature that he never again approached the edge of the ship without scanning for them. It was also his first glimpse into a future of many new "firsts."

There were other welcome distractions as well. Every day or so, there appeared a ship in the distance to try and identify. While he was born and spent his early years in the mountains, his time in coastal Genoa enabled him to be fairly adept at identifying ships by just their silhouette and sound. Angelo would love to sit on the dock in Genoa and watch the ships come and go. Even though he never dreamed he would have the chance to ever sail the seas in one, his young mind was happy to simply imagine the faraway places they sailed from and represented.

The evenings were spent playing cards. Scopa, tresette, briscola, and others were a small piece of home that he treasured. *I thought my cousins Nini and Pietro were good card players, but there are some really good ones here!* he noted in his journal after a few evenings. Even though others on the ship grew weary of the voyage and monotony of the sea, Angelo regularly found both interesting and familiar diversions.

The fifth day at sea brought a foul temperament that Angelo couldn't shake though. He didn't know why, but he woke up sad and homesick just like the first day. He spent the entire day alone, not eating and giving in to self-destructive depression. By six thirty that evening, he couldn't take another minute and retired to his cabin to hopefully fall asleep. With the rolling sea gently rocking him, a deep sleep finally did come. Still though, his dreams never strayed far from the relatives, friends, and homeland he left behind.

A little after 5:00 a.m., he was abruptly awakened by the mighty vessel lurching violently. This new day was to be different. The gentle roll of the sea had been supplanted by its furious crashing against the ship's steel hull. *For eight hours, we were all really sea sick*, read the entry in Angelo's journal.

Like the other passengers, he tried to eat, but the nausea limited most to just water or an occasional coffee. Toward the evening, he made his way to the top deck and noted that at least three quarters of the passengers were sick. Even if they were not physically sick, most were truly scared by the ferocity of the ocean as it tossed the powerful ship about.

The next day brought little relief. The monstrous seas regularly breached the ship's first deck. Wave upon wave covered the places where Angelo regularly stood to watch his flying fish. Driving the relentless waves was a wind that he estimated to be at least thirty knots. Long before the heavy rains came, the captain ordered everyone to stay below decks. Angelo thought that amusing since the only fools above decks at this point were the poor crew who had to work through the gale.

The next day after the storm, he came upon some ship's hands taking a well-deserved break, and he asked how bad the storm was. Angelo felt a bit naive and embarrassed as the old hands just laughed and said it was nothing.

After another day of rough seas and intermittent rain, the weather broke and all the passengers started feeling better for the first time in a few days. Slowly, like bears emerging from hibernation, the passengers lumbered about. The crew gratefully brought out every available deck chair, and eventually, all the passengers stayed out enjoying the sun and calm sea.

The next day was a copy of the previous and lead into yet another. It had been over a week now, and everyone was tired, bored, and ready to see land.

Pleasant days on deck, however, lead to meeting many new people and interesting conversations. Intrigued by everyone's personal story, Angelo encouraged each to open up. Sharing the experiences that others had over the last half dozen years was very satisfying. Hearing their stories and sharing their suffering seemed to lighten his personal load.

There was the older woman who was going to meet her husband that was stranded in America since before the war. They hadn't seen each other in over a decade, and she was worried about how she had aged and how her husband would react. Another man was seeking riches in "the land with golden streets." A young teenaged woman was going to New York to marry a man she had never met. Her parents feared for her in postwar Italy and were forcing her to become an American through marriage. Two children were making the voyage with their mother after their father had made the same journey a few months prior.

All had the common thread of radical change and new beginnings. Every last person on that ship signed on to a voyage certain their lives would never even remotely be the same. Of course, Angelo could never tell the truth of his past. After all, anyone could have been on the ship. In postwar Italy, he knew better than anyone how many various factions harbored death wishes upon the others. He was determined to keep a keen wit about him and was always wary of speaking too much or too freely.

That's actually the real reason he never took a drink on ship. While others brought various types of liquors on board to enliven the mood and celebrate their personal new beginnings, he wouldn't even touch a traditional premeal aperitif. Amid some mocking about his priestly composure, he stayed vigilant. *I just need to get to America. A little more time and I can finally be free*, he wrote. Still, the razzing by his shipmates became more than irritating.

Nearly every night would bring a loosening of the spirit and tongue. When anyone of war age talked big and loudly, he noted each person, their personalities, and their "viewpoints." Gratefully, most everyone spoke of their anticipated new life in America, and troublesome moments never materialized. Particularly as the trip wore on, people's perspectives increasingly focused on the future instead of the past. It was no different for Angelo, and he now felt strong anticipation for the adventure ahead.

Only three more days till we make it! Angelo began to feel like the ship was going slower with every passing hour. The waiting and boredom were beginning to get to everybody, and tensions flared between new friends where before there were none. Staying increasingly below decks by himself, he silently pleaded, "Lord, *please* speed this ship up!"

That evening, one of the guys that Angelo had been spending time with conspired a grand idea and knocked on the door to Angelo's cabin. Francesco was the one person that really hit it off with Angelo. The two sensed a kindred spirit and would regularly play off each other as is commonly seen among brothers and good friends. While Angelo was of an average build, Francesco resembled more of a fire hydrant. Even though he was short in size, everyone instinctively knew not mess with him. His short stout stature hid a body comprised of nearly all muscle. When he would playfully hit Angelo in the arm or push him, as friends do, Angelo would feel it for some time afterward.

Francesco had heard from one of the crew that there was real Genoa salami, hard Italian bread, fresh figs, chocolate, and an entire round of parmesan cheese stored below for the ship's officers. An entire round of parmesan cheese! Fresh figs!

"We may never see this again once we land in America," Angelo said to Francesco in mock fear. While initially joking, there was a moment when he stopped to consider just how different something as elemental as food could be. *I'll worry about that later, he thought.* This bounty just too good to pass up.

Angelo and Francesco planned out their nighttime raid with military precision. *Memorizing the ship's layout would come in handy after all*, he silently mused. For a few seconds, he felt like he was back in the war conducting another mission. The folly of comparing this break-in with his past exploits caused him to laugh out loud. Anyway, he figured that if caught, there wasn't much they could do. In just two more days, the ship would be docking in New York. He conveniently concluded there wasn't much to lose and a surprise hedonistic reward to be gained.

That night, the two executed their planning. They first went below the common decks to the crew's deck below the waterline. Everyone appeared to be sleeping, except for two men working at writing desks. With the ship cruising along and no trouble in sight, everyone was sleeping soundly. Carefully, and with the quiet step Angelo learned from many silent raids before, they worked their way down to the officer's level. Angelo and Francesco never discussed his either of their lives during the war. But based on the skillful and silent way he maneuvered in the dark, he must have served in some offensive capacity at the front.

Growing up near the Genoa seaport offered Angelo the opportunity to be on large ships before. Knowing that the decks of a ship repeat so that a deck's structural walls are always on top of the structural walls below them, Angelo surmised that the officer's kitchens would be directly below the general use kitchens. Making their way over in near darkness to where he expected to find the kitchen, they were surprised that no one was awake.

The raid was a complete success. Grabbing what they could, they made their way up to a dark area on a common deck and stayed up till daylight, greedily gorging on their illicit feast. The next day, the rest of the group thought it strange that Angelo and Francesco wouldn't eat all day. Thankfully, the permanent smile on their faces didn't give them away.

Tired from being up all night, he retired to his cabin early. In what seemed like mere minutes, the seas kicked up again as if to give all the passengers one more reminder of who was the boss on this voyage. Most people got sick again. Angelo and Francesco bore the brunt of it though after filling to the brim on spicy sausage and chocolate. The miserable night just made the need to get on land all the more crucial.

*****

The last day on ship was a grand party, with everyone dancing and carrying on. Angelo, finally realizing the trip was nearly over, let his guard down and enjoyed some homemade grappa. The uniquely Italian grappa, best compared to a strong brandy, felt like one last shot of home. Knowing he might never again enjoy authentic grappa; Angelo savored every last drop.

The ship's party didn't end with sundown. On the contrary, the party went on all night. The light rain and rolling seas didn't dampen the spirit on the ship one bit. Slowly, the passengers left the party to get a little sleep before the big day. Unfortunately, sleep for most was interrupted regularly as Angelo and a gang of a couple dozen spent the remainder of the night strolling around the ship, singing traditional Italian songs - loudly.

It was that wonderful next morning when, while everyone else was awakening from the night, Angelo spied a student girl on deck. She was beautiful in the morning sun, and he wondered how he could have missed her during the long voyage. Beyond her attractiveness, he was also drawn by her "coloring" her finger nails. Being from the rural mountains and industrial city, he had never seen anyone paint their fingernails. Recognizing this as an opportune opening for a conversation, he approached her with the clumsy line of "Why are you coloring your fingers?"

Diva smiled bashfully but luckily continued the conversation. Within the next three hours, Angelo was hooked. He hadn't realized just how empty his heart was after years of war until he spoke with Diva that first time. Her gentle voice filled him fully with hope and renewed life itself.

It was early, about 7:00 a.m., so he invited Diva down for breakfast and to meet his friends. The two ended up spending the entire day together. Angelo had never met anyone like Diva. She was from a farming town on the border between Tuscany and Umbria. Her family grew tobacco that was used in the production of the famous Toscano brand of cigars, the oldest cigar manufacturer in the world. Yet she had studied in Florence and was conversant on virtually any topic. She had her own wartime horrors, and he needed to determine if she had put them behind and, like himself, was ready for a new life.

The location of her farm was caught between two established German defensive lines, the Trasimene and Gothic Lines. The German commander of Italy, Albert Kesselring, was continually being distracted and operationally hindered by the partisans operating in Central Italy. Leaving no doubt of his intentions, he issued the following orders to punish civilians: "Every act of violence committed by partisans must be punished immediately… Wherever there is evidence of considerable numbers of partisan groups, a proportion of the male population will be shot."

Under the heading "Killing of Hostages," Kesselring ordered: "The population must be informed of this. Should troops be fired at from any village, the village will be burnt down. Perpetrators or the ringleaders will be hanged in public."

The situation was so dangerous for the eighteen-year-old girl that her parents moved her to a cloistered convent in the lower Apennine Mountains, where she lived for nearly two years. Her time of isolation led to a ravenous love of reading, and easily explained her deep, educated demeanor. In the back of his mind, Angelo worried about his unconventional education keeping up with her assumed intellect.

But he refused to let a little self-doubt hinder him, and Angelo spent every second he could with her on this last day of the voyage. After the first awkward half hour talking about Italy and their pasts, they grew comfortable with each other and spoke like old friends. The conversation was dominated by the future, by their dreams, and by their unbridled excitement to start a new life. Of course, there was a sprinkling of politics, family, and friends, but Angelo was taken most by Diva's optimism and charm and, of course, her beauty. After a while, it was obvious to him that while Diva would never forget, she had in fact moved on.

Since both wanted to have more privacy in their talking, they moved the exchange to a deck above the sea line. Angelo boyishly relayed to her about the flying fish he had seen earlier and began looking for them. Diva boldly placed her hand on Angelo's as they both stared out over the expanse. Angelo looked up and caught Diva's profile against the brilliant sun. He couldn't stand it anymore and bent over to kiss her. Gratefully, Diva returned the soft exchange and turned to embrace him. That was it. Both were instantly in love, and Angelo knew he would never want another besides Diva. The rest of their day was spent walking the ship and simply being with each other; but now as a couple.

They were forced to part ways as the late afternoon arrived. The ship was requiring everyone to go to quarters early because at five the next morning, they would be queuing up for their disembarkation and processing on Ellis Island. Unfortunately for Angelo, Diva was an American citizen and wasn't required to go through Ellis Island like he had to. She had, in fact, been born in Chicago in 1926 and had come to Italy a few years later with her father and mother, attempting to escape the Great American Depression.

When the final moment came, he whispered to her, "*Arrivederci*," which literally translates to "till we see each other again." It was a subtle hint to her of the not-so-subtle feelings he had for her. Diva's coy smile reassured Angelo that she, too, felt the unmistakable draw of love.

Like everything else in his life, this didn't make any sense. Falling in love at first sight was as foreign to each of them as one could imagine. Neither had an impetuous bone in their bodies. Yet in his heart, he was hooked and knew there would never be anyone else in his life but her. He agonized briefly over the logistics of how he could make this relationship work. But with every foray into uncertainty, he returned quickly to what he knew for sure; no matter what it would take, they would always be together.

As he went to his cabin for the final night on ship, he couldn't resist one last stroll around the outer deck. This quote from his final journal entry said it all (see photo reference 1.1): "26 April, 1947. The sea was finally clear and calm. The sky was so blue that you could paint it with a brush. The sun was warm, and it was the most perfect day to arrive at my new home."

Angelo was beyond exuberant. He had just met the girl of his dreams and was excited to start a new life full of possibilities in his new homeland. His spirit was front and center, ready to move forward. Yet his unconscious mind still couldn't completely free itself from his past and everything that had led to the radical necessity to come to America.

On his last night shipboard, Angelo replayed his adventure leading to this trip like a tape recorder. He even reminisced about the stories he had been told of the father he never met.

Photo Reference 1.1 –

The final page of the diary Angelo wrote on his journey to America. The original piece of paper is less than five inches wide.

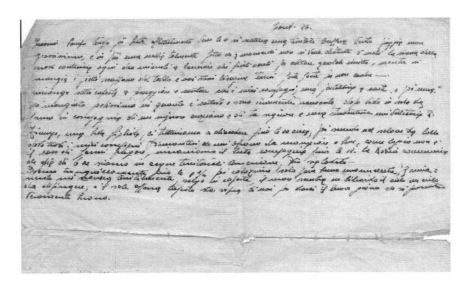

CHAPTER 2

The Father Unknown

July 17, 1923
Lago di Tenno, Italy

The sounds of the First Great War had been officially silenced for nearly a half decade, and yet today brought a pounding heart to Stefano worse than any nightmare. Slave to the memories of a worthless war and its lasting damage to his body tore him apart at the core. The nightmares and constant pain combined with the fear of the future virtually entombed his mind and soul in a relentless and crushing anxiety.

Even on this special day, Stefano obsessed with his dark feelings. Played repeatedly in his mind, he thought, *how could so much have gone wrong, and what will the future bring for this coming child?* Often pitied by others for the damage to his withering body and mental scars, he agonized over how his slice of heaven could have changed so rapidly and how his progeny would fare in the fast-approaching future.

But today was a better day than usual. The anticipation of his first child's birth, filling him with joy and hope, offered an opportunity to revel in the now. Happiness for today and dreams of better times to come helped him temporarily forget the debilitating past. Looking across Lago di Tenno at the modest hotel he had built as a young man before the war, he smiled to himself with satisfaction. He and Erminia had worked hard to recover upon his return from the army hospital that barely saved his life. It was a simple life, but out here at the lower elevations of the Alps in a remote section of Trentino, he at least felt free and safe.

The First Great War shattered Stefano's life in many ways but left a lasting injury to his young body. At one time, he had felt himself lucky to survive the war. After all, his father and every male heir had fallen in various wars since his first known ancestor had perished in the Napoleonic Wars in 1799. With his body now a shell of its former self, Stefano knew he would likely succumb to the same fate.

Nearly every day brought a reliving of those agonizing three days spent in and out of consciousness in a rank trench. Mentally, he felt he was doing pretty well and was grateful for his life, such as it was. The physical damage, however, proved to be another thing altogether. The worst was that Stefano could remember most of it. He clearly remembered the blast of the shell to his right side. After blacking out for a time, he awoke to see his leg severely cut from a large piece of shrapnel that found its mark. He did his best to tie a tourniquet around the wound, but it was high on the thigh and near the groin. Lying in that trench, bleeding profusely and desperately trying to keep his injury away from the contaminated water and mud that was everywhere, he emotionally prepared himself for his demise. He felt it was truly a miracle that after three days in that compromised state, he found himself on a stretcher being medevaced to a makeshift "field hospital" for care.

At some point, an angel had come and stopped the bleeding and dressed the wound. While barely conscious, a person that Stefano assumed to be a medic took a red-hot bayonet and cauterized the wound. This effectively sealed the wound and stopped the bleeding. Fortunately, the medic cleaned the area with saltwater and immediately bandaged it to inhibit infection. Stefano prayed that he would one day have the opportunity to thank the angel that saved his life, but he never even learned his name.

Stefano couldn't say why the doctors didn't amputate. Perhaps they simply had too many higher priority wounded, or perhaps they misdiagnosed the extent of the injury. It didn't matter. As time went on, the initial limb ischemia developed into a gangrenous and infected mess. Without adequate medicines, Stefano never really recovered and lived his remaining days in a general state of painful decline.

Wrestling with his near worthless limbs, he propped himself up against a large boulder. He enjoyed these moments when he could simply bask in the beauty of where he lived. The magnificent mountains presented a unique opportunity for emotional healing and quiet prayers. The tranquil time spent beneath these giant natural fortresses yielded a deep soul and profound philosophies, and Stefano would sometimes be sought by wise people to provide counsel. Daily solitude and tranquility open the mind in a way rarely shared by others. With the warming sun and shear expansiveness of the beauty before him, he could not help but suppress the pain and feel his heart and mood lifted.

Each blade of grass that pushed through the rocky ground brightened the day. The greens here were nearly indescribable, with each type of plant and weed offering its own version of the perfect shade and hue. Together they create a carpet, very much alive and truly woven by the hand of God. Adding to its complexity are the flowers of every imaginable color and pattern. Though tiny and humble in stature, their profound intensity doesn't require competition to catch the eye of the insects that pollinate them. Without any trees, these grasses and flowers constantly flow and ebb like moving water from the refreshing breezes that never depart. Gently swaying fields moved by an unseen breath hypnotized the mind and set it free.

As this carpet of colors reached one of the ever-present mountainsides, it became a wall tapestry with a completely different personality. The sun and shade played a game of hide-and-seek to expose even more varied patterns and colors. The shear vertical walls of the mountains created rising thermal winds that large birds rode like roller coasters. Their silence and contentment were a testament to the humbling quiet and beauty.

But, oh, if these mountains could speak, they would tell the stories of countless wars that ravaged nearly every generation to live here since the Dark Ages. The result of the latest was the division of his beloved Tyrol (see map reference 2.1). With the signing of the Treaty of Saint-Germain just five years earlier, Trentino and the South Tyrol lost their autonomy and were ceded to Italy. "Politicians make fast decisions based on politics, but we all know this won't work," Stefano was known to declare. "We people here in the Tyrol have a proud Austrian and Germanic heritage. How are we to be subservient to those from the South that trace their lineage to the Moors of Africa or the central Italians from Etruscan and Roman heritage?"

On occasion, his hotel would house a person from the traditional Italian regions in Central and Southern Italy, and Stefano knew very well that a divide would always exist until Trentino and the South Tyrol became free and independent.

Stefano's mental wanderings were suddenly shattered by the sound of Erminia crying for him. "Stefano! Stefano, hurry. The baby is coming!" Running up the hill to fetch him, Erminia collapsed about five hundred feet from where Stefano sat. Marshaling all his strength, he arose and haltingly ran to her.

As Stefano approached Erminia, she reached out and embraced him. "*Mi amore*, it's the baby. Help me."

Stefano helped Erminia to be as comfortable as possible, and over the next three hours, Erminia delivered her first child right there on a valley knoll, overlooking their pristine lake (see photo reference 2.1).

Knowing his time left on earth was shrinking and he may not have the opportunity for a second child, Stefano gave a great shout of happiness at the sight of his new son. Healthy and crying, the new child was the greatest blessing Stefano could imagine—a true gift from God, considering his condition. He didn't know how long he would have with this gift, but he vowed to make every moment count.

In honor of the father he had never known, Stefano requested that they name the baby after his father, Angelo. Erminia immediately agreed, and as they rested, they shared prayers of gratitude for this gift and the future of little Angelo.

The warm summer day in the beautiful Dolomite Mountains of the Italian Alps formed a perfect memory. But before the chilly evening arrived, they felt it best to make their way back to their hotel. In these mountains, the night air can take your breath, even in July.

Angelo proved a remarkably healthy baby and moved through infancy without any issue. The same was unfortunately not true for Stefano. Just six months after the birth of Angelo, time caught up with Stefano, and he submitted to his brutal past. Little Angelo would grow to never know his father, just as his father grew to never know his. Looking back as an adult, Angelo understood the legacy of the First Great War, just as it is with every war, is that they continue killing long after an armistice was signed.

Events of the world were also affecting Erminia. Not many around Lago di Tenno recognized the significance of the 1922 coup d'état of Benito Mussolini as prime minister of Italy. Actually, they still looked upon themselves as Trentini and Tyrolians. The political doings of Italy were of secondary importance to Trentino or Tyrolian independence.

However, after the rigged Italian election in 1924 and the growth of Fascism, change was everywhere. Just a year later, all pretenses of elective government were dropped, and Mussolini consolidated his Fascist dictatorship. Declaring himself *Il Duce*, or The Leader, he ruled with an iron fist. Even the remote little paradise of Lago di Tenno eventually became impacted, and Erminia was in trouble.

His MVSN, or Voluntary Militia for National Security as they were officially known, supported Mussolini with a ruthless vigor. Nicknamed the Blackshirts after their black button-down shirts that was their uniform, they were particularly strong in the region just south of Lago di Tenno. They made quick time in taking over many industries under the auspices of the Fascist revolution. Erminia's little hotel on Lago di Tenno was no exception. In 1937, with virtually no compensation and legal recourse, it became the property of the National Fascist Party of Italy (see photo references 2.2 and 2.3).

Erminia begged with them to let her keep the humble hotel. "I built this with my husband, Stefano. He was a brave soldier and lost his life serving in the Italian Army. It is all I have left!" she pleaded.

Unfortunately, this only made things worse. A poor widow with an only child was easy pickings for the government's henchmen. The reality was that the Fascist Blackshirts had just deposed the previous Italian government and despised anybody that served it. Stefano's military service and sacrifice for his country actually hurt her position. With no representation or opportunity to fight the situation, she resigned herself to the desperate reality.

Erminia now felt real fear. She was alone and scared for her life, for her future, and for the future of her son. She also became keenly aware of the political environment that was coming. The Fascists made no illusions about their intentions and openly boasted of their plans. First, they would completely control all of Italy, then move to reassert their land claims in North Africa, the south of France, Albania, Malta, Corsica, and anywhere else where even the slightest reasoning could be defended. When Mussolini invaded Ethiopia in 1935 and then formed an alliance with Hitler and Germany the following year, the writing was plainly written on the wall.

This is no place for me or Angelo, she thought to herself. *I'll go to America and live with extended family. Angelo can stay with my sister's family in Genoa till I return for him.* It took her several years to save the money and arrange her trip to America. Finally in 1940 and nearly broke, she went to America in search of hope and a new, safe life. Angelo, now just sixteen years old, went to live with an aunt and uncle he barely knew and a home he had never even previously seen.

The change of location and essentially losing his mother was critical in his development. He would exchange his life in the mountains for a life in the city. Growing up in the mountains was near idyllic. Even though they had no money, Angelo learned to hunt, trap, and fish to feed the pair. He spent nearly all his time outdoors. The vastness of the great Dolomite Mountains was his backyard. While his young friends spent their time in school, he wanted little to do with it and took every opportunity to avoid it. Given a choice between sitting in a classroom and being out in the open air, the mountains always won. He did officially attend an elementary school but would regularly miss classes because of his responsibilities at home and the ease of skipping out. His primary task was as a shepherd with a flock of sheep. He would gratefully walk for miles upon miles with his flock, all the while daydreaming and thinking deeply. Fortunately, he had a great intellect that enabled him to get passing grades even while missing a significant number of days at school.

Angelo ultimately matured into a strong and vigorous youth and was able to easily run for miles in mountain elevations with low oxygen levels. His bodily strength and stamina, forged from eating nothing but the natural foods they grew or harvested and a lifestyle lived in the elements, yielded peak physical development.

But now living in the city would be very different. Here, schooltime was enforced, and time for play or activities was measured. The city was dirty compared to his pristine mountains. The pace of life was also much faster compared to his time as a shepherd. Everyone did things in groups and with cliques of friends compared to his growth as a lone child in an extremely rural setting. It was indeed a complete change in every way imaginable.

Angelo was left by his mother, on his own, with his aunt and uncle and their unfamiliar surrogate family. Zia Renata and Zio Angelo, living comfortably outside Genoa, loved him as their own. Zio was a leader in the community and had a respectable career as a senior manager in a factory. Zia was the loving homemaker whose cooking prowess was acknowledged by all. While confident in his own capabilities, moving away from everything and everybody he knew initially left Angelo primarily insecure and withdrawn. Over time, he became very close with his extended family of many cousins and even developed close friendships with other boys in the area.

One cousin in particular, Nini, was essentially the same age and like a brother. The two were always together and shared in everything they did and had. Nini was shorter than Angelo but stocky in build. Angelo had no trouble outrunning Nini, but when horseplay was involved, Nini was always the victor. Angelo had never had a best friend, and their closeness would last a lifetime.

As time progressed though, he and his uncle began to noticeably move in different political directions. While his uncle espoused uniformity and led the family with factory-style efficiency, young Angelo was wild and rebellious through his teenage years. They loved each other dearly, but the differences became readily apparent as, over time, discussions of their differing political views consumed nearly every conversation.

This tension grew from the moment Erminia immigrated to America in January of 1940. It was about the same time that Adolf Hitler started his march to world conquest. Mussolini, seeing a unique opportunity to advance his agenda, aligned Italy with Germany less than a year later. While the prospect of another war frightened his uncle, he still appreciated the precision of the German military machine and Italy's alliance. Young Angelo thought very differently.

Erminia eventually settled in Pennsylvania and fell in love with a local shop owner. Seeing a better life for herself, she made the decision to stay with her future second husband, Carmine Poeta. Widowed himself, Carmine was struggling to raise his own children in a Depression-era dirty coal town. Unfortunately, the fates conspired against Angelo joining Erminia in America. Political tensions, Angelo's Italian citizenship, and not being able to speak English while still in his school years made joining his mother impractical. Actually, having spent a few years with his aunt and cousins left him content to stay in Italy.

While not being able to move to America at the time, its lure and reputation did in fact leave a lasting impression on Angelo. With every letter Erminia would write, Angelo gained a deeper understanding and appreciation for the country. America seemed like a wonderful place where anyone could succeed. That fondness for his perception of the "American dream" did, at times, figure heavily in his political maturation. "These Fascists treat people like machines. At least in America, you have a chance to get ahead based on what you put in," he would debate with his friends. The idea of being a cog in a Fascist-controlled factory didn't hold any appeal to him.

But as with everyone that has walked the earth, he would never be in control of the future. He was simply a slave to the rapidly evolving situation like just another speck of dust caught in the changing winds of his times.

Map Reference 2.1 –

This is a map of the historic provinces of the Tyrol, as well as its location within the overall region. North and East Tyrol are now incorporated into Austria. The South Tyrol and Trentino are now part of Italy.

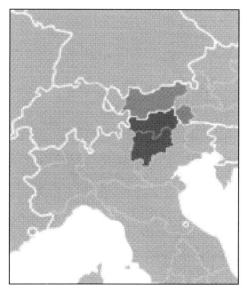

Photo Reference 2.1 –

This is Lago di Tenno, tucked away in the midst of the Dolomite Mountain range. Angelo was born on the grassy area to the lower left in the picture. The small hotel built by Stefano and Erminia, now the Club Hotel Lago di Tenno, is sited further up the hill to the left.

Photo Reference 2.2 –

This is the Club Hotel Lago di Tenno circa 1938. The Fascist government had taken the original humble hotel and expanded it to be larger and contain modern housing amenities. This photo is believed to be from its opening.

Photo Reference 2.3 –

This is the Club Hotel Lago di Tenno in 2018. The popular resort has been expanded many times over the years and now features a wide variety of sporting activities.

CHAPTER 3

The Rise of Empires

June 10, 1940
Genoa, Italy

"Today I am sad, very sad. The adventure begins. May God help Italy!" read the diary of Gian Galeazzo Ciano, foreign minister of Fascist Italy and son-in-law to Benito Mussolini. Angelo was just coming upon his seventeenth birthday as the rumors of imminent war for Italy consumed every conversation.

With Italy's entry into the race for global domination, first aligned with Germany and then Japan, Mussolini sought to recreate the glories of the Roman Empire. The year 1940 was a time when aspiring empires rose and challenged the world, as if playing a ruinous board game without rules. The viscous calculations and planning that played out in this game were, however, like none before. Whereas the world stumbled into the First World War, this affair would be murderously different.

The start of the school year found Angelo in a classroom just outside Genoa with other young men arguing their prospects. "Mussolini will lead us to supreme victory!" shouted one student.

"Il Duce will not fail us," chimed in another. Angelo listened but was cautious to not reveal his true feelings. Had he, he might have told them of his doubt and his resolute desire to not die on *any* battlefield.

Time in school began to resemble military training instead of a place of learning. There were the mandatory marching drills, assemblies where propaganda was broadcast, issuance of identity papers, and other similar preparatory activities. For every minute spent on traditional learning, another was spent on military preparation, and yet another was spent in political debate. While Angelo didn't particularly enjoy military training, it was at least time spent outside. He was accepting of pretty much any excuse to get out of his classes.

As such, Angelo was never a star student. Perhaps he had too much of his father's blood in him for his own good. Or maybe it was his penchant for daydreaming. It could also have been his forays into deep thinking where he would focus on a thought and lose hours. Or possibly it was just his modest mountain education. Growing up in the rural environment provided only a cursory introduction to formal studies. Those that knew him couldn't say, but his consistently average grades did not sit well with his overachieving and highly efficient uncle.

Like most parental figures, his uncle would drone on about the need to do better. Angelo would obediently listen but rarely let the message settle in himself. "Focus!" he would hear repeatedly. But instead, he found virtually anything else to think about. Angelo found it easy to grasp the information, so why should he need to master it? *If I easily get passing grades, why work so hard to do slightly better?* he rationalized to himself.

Because of what was happening around them, many students resigned themselves to live in the military. Cycles of war, ruin, rebuilding, and yet another war faced every generation of this politically and militarily desirable land. Still others couldn't help but be consumed by politics. The "glories" of war can play with the minds of young men. The back and forth of political debate were just a game that get impressionable youth to rally around a flag. The resulting conflicts and horrific consequences came unfortunately too late.

Angelo just wanted to get through it and return to Lago di Tenno and Trentino.

Realities of the day often suspended any traditional form of education. Mussolini had turned Northern Italy into an industrial complex focused on the needs of his ambitions. Angelo shared the sentiment of the silent minority not caught up in the political furor. "We are all going to be stuck on a machine in some factory or another forever," they would lament. "And that's if we are lucky and don't get put in the army!"

Mussolini had a unique view of Fascism and the role of the individual in the state. A person working in a factory for the good of the state was precisely what he thought ideal. Originally a socialist, the political climate leading up to the First World War caused a shift in Mussolini's thinking. In a 1914 speech, he revealed his move from the class system that embodies socialism to the nationalist-focused system of Fascism: "Class cannot destroy the nation. Class reveals itself as a collection of interests—but the nation is a history of sentiments, traditions, language, culture, and race. Class can become an integral part of the nation, but the one cannot eclipse the other."

The transformation from class battle to nationalist fervor resulted in the development of the Fascist movement that he would eventually come to lead. The revolutionary vanguard was now open for any class of person, as long as the nation was put above the individual.

Considering himself Tyrolian and Austrian, and not really Italian, Angelo would have none of it. He was young but very aware. *I'll play along with this as I have to, but I'll always fight for Trentino and freedom.* Smart enough to avoid direct political conflict or arguments, Angelo was content to be a nonplayer in the debates of the day.

His uncle Angelo, however, fell increasingly deeper into nationalist ideology. "The factories are actually doing pretty well under Fascism," he would offhandedly remark. After all, Italy had been crippled from the First World War. Massive debts, high unemployment, a stubborn depression, food shortages, and labor unrest were the issues of the times. If Fascism could continue to make things better, then he was all for it.

*****

Of course, there were plenty of opportunities to be a teenager, and Angelo best exhibited his burgeoning leadership skills while getting in trouble. "Come on, we can miss today's classes. There's a ship coming in from Africa, and I've never seen an African. Let's go and see if we can spot some," he said to Giuseppe and Alfio.

The boys agreed and slipped quietly out the side of the school building before classes started. Using the stealth of teenagers on a mission, they made their way down the side streets and alleys of Genoa to the port area. As the hike was several miles, their young faces, clean clothes, and winded frames sorely stuck out against the hardened dock workers.

Locating the ship while maintaining invisibility took nearly two hours, and Alfio began to complain about going back. As Angelo and Giuseppe properly shamed him into being quiet, they noticed two pretty girls walking about a block away. Mature girls—probably in college—and the three boys hurriedly ran to catch up with them.

With an awkward confidence, Angelo approached first. The girls were indeed in college but were not amused by the boyish advances of three teenagers and politely asked them to leave. Never short on tenacity, Angelo kept up his fruitless attempts for conversation. The girls had just enough and yelled for a police officer to come over. In their boldness, they forgot that the police were all over, always at the ready to thwart any security issues.

With the policeman yelling and running after them, the boys made a hasty exit. Down through alleys, over fences and boxes, around dark areas of the buildings they ran. They found themselves away from the area of the city they knew well and just ran without any real direction or plan to get back.

Surprisingly, the officer continued his chase! *Who is this guy?* Angelo thought as he ran even faster. A block later, they were able to mix in with a crowd of people and give the officer the slip. Unfortunately, shortly thereafter, they were recognized as students that should have been in school and captured. Alfio was not only the youngest, but he also had a very boyish face that ended up giving them away. The great port escapade was to end in failure!

"We're going to get it this time," Angelo whispered to Giuseppe.

"Yeah, thanks!" was his only reply. Brought before the school administrator, they were sent back to their classrooms with nary a reprimand.

Not bad, thought Angelo, assuming they were out of harm's way. Once in the classroom though, the teacher was all too happy to administer their punishment. For the remainder of the school day, about two hours, they were forced to kneel on eaten corncobs in the corner of the room. After just a few minutes, the cobs dug into their knees and inflicted a pain he had never experienced.

Hobbling home that afternoon, he thought to himself, *all that and I never even saw an African! Maybe tomorrow.*

*****

While the general economy and people suffered, the industrial segment, to which Zio Angelo was intrinsically tied, mildly prospered. With the government's strategy to win over the Italian populace through the invasion of Abyssinia (modern-day Ethiopia) and the annexation of Albania, Zio Angelo felt the industrial complex could only improve still. Wartime economies generally prove beneficial to the industrial sector.

At the same time, Adolf Hitler in Germany and Emperor Hirohito in Japan were making their own moves in this vile game of empire building. Alliances driven by necessity and opportunity saw Italy align itself first with Germany and then Japan. Caught in the middle was Russia, and conspicuously absent was the United States.

In 1940, Angelo and the rest of Europe knew another great war was inevitable. He prayed that somehow, he could avoid it. "St. Joseph," he read from one of his prayer cards, "as the father of Jesus and patron saint of the country, watch over me and keep me safe."

Erminia would often write from America and wanted Angelo to come there with her. The United States was stubbornly neutral and most assuredly safer. In 1939, the United States Congress passed a series of acts supporting neutrality, culminating with the Neutrality Law. The law, coupled with the general sentiment to avoid getting embroiled in yet another European conflict, would hopefully mean safety for her son.

During the first week of January 1940, a Gallup poll revealed an astounding 88 percent of Americans wanted to stay out of war in Europe. Though virtually alone in her opinion, Erminia secretly hoped that the United States would intervene. She knew from the First World War the damage that would surely be inflicted on Europe, the homeland she anticipated returning to, her family, and undoubtedly Angelo.

Just eleven months later, Japan would attack Pearl Harbor, and the cry from across the nation was diametrically opposite. The same Gallup organization conducted a poll exactly one year from the earlier poll to not go to war. This time in January of 1941, 97 percent of Americans approved of Congress's declaration of war against Japan. Only 2 percent opposed it.

Unfortunately, any opportunity to get Angelo from Italy to the United States was long gone. Erminia was beside herself with worry but was totally helpless to do anything. Angelo was now old enough for the military, on his own, and about to move from political debate to deadly action.

Again, his prayer cards revealed his angst. "Dear God, please never leave me. Never."

CHAPTER 4

Just Another Legionnaire

January 4, 1943
Genoa, Italy

Angelo was nineteen and a half years of age when there was a pounding on the door. His stomach dropped because for the last few days Mussolini's Blackshirts were going throughout the city and rounding up anyone of fighting age. He didn't need an official document to understand that his time of innocence would be forever gone.

He was being conscripted into the Italian Army. A grand adventure to some, like a proud legionnaire fighting under the command of Benito Mussolini, who saw himself as the reincarnated Julius Caesar. A death sentence in Angelo's mind. On this particularly cold and windy winter day, it felt ironic that it was his turn in the family crucible of fire. Another male Flaim to be cut down too early in life by war. While all his contemporaries were excited and eager to join up and fight for Il Duce, Angelo started conjuring ways to somehow circumvent the inevitable.

Being drafted into military service pleased his Uncle Angelo, and he felt the experience would restrain the wild side of his rambunctious nephew. Young Angelo overheard him tell his aunt that military service would "straighten Angelo up." Familiar expressions like "Just what the boy needs to turn him from a troublemaking kid into a man" infuriated him. Angelo's stubborn respect and love for the family patriarch, a characteristic not uncommon in Italian families, compelled him to hold his tongue yet all the while trying to devise that elusive way out.

Fortunately for Angelo, he had been drafted into the Sixth Alpine Division "Alpi Graie." Quickly his mood softened as he realized the respectability of being in this particular unit of the army. The Alpi Graie Division was primarily light infantry that were specially trained in counter-terrorism, mountain combat and maneuvers. It was a new specialized unit of the Alpini, as they were called, and held in high regard for their mobility and special abilities to operate in difficult mountainous regions (see photo reference 4.1).

Angelo would receive general training to be a gunner in support of artillery. He felt fortunate that the artillery was typically positioned in the rear of any action. Unfortunately, the artillery was also the recipient of enemy barrages that could decimate entire units. Dizzily, his mind went back and forth on the merits of the card he drew. In the end, he knew there was simply no safe place to be in mechanized warfare.

However, his unit of the Alpini was additionally specifically trained in anti-insurgency strategy and tactics. Tito's partisans in Yugoslavia had been a target of the division since 1941 when the Yugoslavs began to inflict mounting casualties to the German war machine. Hitler ordered the Italian Alpini, and specifically the Alpi Graie Division, to study the specialized guerilla and insurgency tactics employed by the partisans. Countering strategies would then be developed and implemented against the partisans for their demise.

With an operational understanding of the enemy, they trained on the best methods to hunt down the partisans, counter their attacks, and eliminate the threat. Many strategies were studied and analyzed. The common theme of them all was the best use of the mountainous terrain, specifically on how to "herd" the partisans into kill zones created naturally from mountain features. When traversing a mountainside, the shear drop-offs and huge boulders typically left only small trails that could be employed to slow and group the men.

Using mortars and light artillery, the division trained on ambushing unsuspecting guerilla groups in these kill zones. The artillery would be used to pin the insurgents down, typically in single file lines through the narrow passes while the infantry would then advance and dispose of the danger.

Other strategies focused on the art of ambush. While there was little cover from bushes and vegetation, the mountains featured seemingly endless opportunities to hide behind boulders and rocky outcroppings. But this assumed that there was time and sufficient intelligence to set up the ambush. The partisans smartly altered their routines when walking from place to place, and foreknowledge of them on a particular path was difficult to predict.

Angelo was proud to wear the *Cappello Alpino*, a traditional hat unique to the Alpini. Made of thick gray felt, the front rim is flattened to protect the face from rain and snow. But the signature feature of the hat was its distinctive black raven's feather situated under the hat band, paying homage to the jet-black bird that thrives in mountain elevations (see photo reference 4.2). It was truly a designation of honor, indicating the uniqueness and specialization of their unit.

Angelo found himself in a familiar environment training with the Alpini. Most of the training received by the regiment happened in the mountain's northwest of Turin. Growing up in much more mountainous areas gave him a physical edge in the specialized warfare they trained on. Being completely at home in the rugged terrain also yielded a confidence in his steps, and he moved about the dangerous slopes without hesitancy or issues. Angelo actually enjoyed the training. It was just like running around and climbing in the Dolomite range of the Alps where he was born and raised. Nimble and adroit on the rocky surfaces, he consistently scored well in his exercises.

Of course, the food was another thing. Military rations of canned mystery meat and unrecognizable foods were no substitute for his aunt's cooking. After a day of climbing and "soldiering" in the high altitudes, he longed for fresh, warm bread and homemade delicacies, polenta to be exact. Being one of the most versatile foods on earth, Angelo cherished polenta made from chestnut meal. His aunt would stir it for several hours and then allow it to cool and solidify into a loaf. Once solidified, Angelo's favorite way to enjoy it was fried up with wild mushrooms and Bolognese sauce. A bay leaf for added flavor and, on special occasions, fresh parmesan cheese baked to a golden brown on top. The thought of it consumed nearly every early evening after a tough day of training.

But like every soldier, he put his **food memories** out of his mind as best he could. Lingering on such remembrances only exacerbated the misery of their dietary restrictions. While there was plenty to eat and Angelo had a voracious appetite, it provided little satisfaction to him. He even considered stealing away for an illicit bite off base. But unfortunately, there would be no cheating away from base for anything good to eat, even if they could, because there was virtually nothing anywhere near the camp.

Being in the heart of winter, there was plenty of snow and it covered all the land in a thick heavy blanket of white. The pureness of the mountain snow, a benefactor from the lack of polluting sources typically found in lower elevations by cities, facilitated an easy access to safe drinking water. The men simply needed to melt the snow to obtain a drink whenever desired.

A good amount of the Alpini education regimen was spent studying winter conditions and their operational opportunities. The main focus was using snow for defensive maneuvers. One particular strategy was to position one's self with the sun at your back. With the sun at the six o'clock position virtually any time during the day, the snow provided maximum glare and hid the person or even muzzle flash from a discharged weapon. Another was the identification of safe snow drifts. Finding those that were formed over boulders and rocky ledges could provide significant cover from pursuing troops.

In addition to utilizing the snow for tactical combat advantages, he also learned valuable survival techniques. While Angelo knew many from living for years in the environment, he appreciated the extended education. He was fascinated by the use of naturally occurring vegetation to soften the extreme weather. While his first instinct was to always find a cave to hide in, he came to appreciate the techniques of surviving out in the open without any shelter. Many of these lessons would come in handy as the war progressed.

Angelo, never shy, relished showing off his abilities on skis. The use of skis during wartime was particularly helpful in traversing large expanses of meadows and valleys, and the cross-country variety of equipment was the standard. It provided troops an agile silent method to approach the enemy, set up ambushes, and facilitate positions that provided optimal vantage points. Skis also helped utilize wooded areas, outmaneuver vehicles near roads, or quickly flee from foot soldiers. The flexibility made available by them was welcomed in most any type of operation when mechanized vehicles were unavailable or ill-advised.

The Alpini always used cross-country skis in their movement, but there could be times when one needed to go downhill to evade pursing troops. Mastering the difficult transition from cross-country to downhill skiing was a rare skill for Angelo. With cross-country skis, only the toe of the boot is attached to the ski, making it easier to propel or "walk" the skis. With downhill skis, however, the entire boot is attached to the ski to provide stability at greater speeds. Skiing in both conditions with only cross-country skis is notoriously difficult and dangerous. Injuring oneself or falling while being pursued could mean the end to even the strongest soldier.

The men regularly wagered on who could do the best or finish first in the many completions set up as learning exercises. Angelo, because of his background, was always sure he would prevail. He didn't, of course, but it helped pass the time and add a sense of enjoyment to the otherwise monotonous training exercises, marching and weapon handling. The little extra money he actually collected was minor compared to the bragging rights with his comrades.

In one particular exercise that saw the men cross-country skiing across a rocky meadow, they were to also aim at targets along a wood line. Very few could master this effectively. One either had to slow to an almost stationary position to fire or fire wildly while skiing quickly and rarely hit anything. The goal of the exercise was to teach the men to find that optimum combination of movement and accuracy. Angelo was challenged by a fellow soldier that also regularly scored well, with the prize being a pack of cigarettes. His rival went first and proceeded to make very good time but missed every shot.

Angelo took a deep breath and began his attempt. Halfway down the course, he hit a target and assumed that he had won the challenge. At the end of the course, he was disappointed to find out that his adversary finished the course with a faster time, and he claimed victory.

The two men argued among themselves over who should be classified as the winner, but the dispute was halted when the commanding officer had everyone remove their gear and return to barracks. Once there, the argument began anew. It was then that Angelo had a bright idea. "Why don't we take the pack of cigarettes, sell it for cash, and split the earnings?" he proposed. As they divvied the winnings, the men laughingly conceded the skill of the other. A few lira in hand can certainly ease tensions.

*****

Training in the Italian Army didn't actually last that long. The years of militarized schooling had most young men in excellent physical shape and remarkably disciplined. Unfortunately, neither of these makes a complete soldier, and the Italian Army was generally characterized as ill-prepared and unready for the war they entered.

With little time for formal operations-level training, the general army was simply not ready for the conditions and situations they would soon experience. Since they were primarily deployed as a frontline buffer for the German troops, their principal purpose was to hold a position in a line and shoot. A significant exception was the intensive operational training of Angelo's Alpi Graie Division for the work of flushing out and eliminating partisan guerillas. This specialized training superseded the regular training received by others. It was this unique training that saw him preparing for Yugoslavia instead of Russia.

The Germans launched seven major offenses against Tito's partisans in Yugoslavia over a three-year period, and the Alpini were heavily utilized until May of 1943. The earlier waves of enlisted men from the Fascist Army of Italy, and specifically Angelo's Alpi Graie Division, had already left for Yugoslavia during the first three offenses by the time Angelo had gotten there.

He arrived in camp just in time for the German Fourth Enemy Offensive or Battle of the Neretva. This was the wave everyone presumed they were in preparation to reinforce. Everyone hoped to be deployed in a mountainous environment for which they had trained. But Hitler was calling the shots, and they would go where he decided, typically wherever the Italians could minimize German casualties and reduce German troop exposure.

As the war effort dragged on, rumors buzzed around the camp like the relentless summer flies that never gave a reprieve. "I heard our division was sent to the lowlands of Yugoslavia to support Hitler's advance. Not even the mountains. We're getting annihilated, and we will be next." Many of the men mocked their regimental motto—*Altius Tendo*—Latin for "reach high." *An alpine division fighting in valleys and along the sea. This is crazy!*

Unfortunately, real, verified information was hard to come by. In addition to little news coming from the Eastern Front, communications in the Italian Expeditionary Corps were not up to the task. The German Army had been preparing for its *blitzkrieg* for decades. Lightning-fast attacks carried out along vast expanses of land requires the latest in electronic communications. Attacking first by air, then artillery, and lastly infantry required precise coordination and communications. Angelo's Alpi Graie Division, for example, had ten times more mules and horses than it did transport vehicles to pull artillery pieces, not exactly high tech by any measure and not even in the same league as the Germans or Allies.

Still, when *all* the rumors reinforce the same ideas, there must be some truth to them. Angelo decided to investigate and find out more. One Sunday, the commanders were all out of the camp, and mostly junior officers were around. While the lunch meal was being served to the men, Angelo snuck off and broke into the commander's offices, attempting to find out what was really happening.

It was the type of foolhardy, impetuous thing to do that showed his youth and naivete. It also displayed a key to his future survival—his daring and confidence. He skillfully picked the simple lock to the outer door and was surprised to find the interior doors all unlocked or open! Making his way through the maze of empty rooms with a stealth honed on the streets of Genoa, he quickly realized he had no idea what he was doing or what he was specifically looking for. He was grateful that the guard at the door was missing, something he couldn't remember ever seeing before.

Realizing this gambit was probably a mistake and his time would be running short, he abruptly made his exit. Unfortunately, the guard at the door that had earlier taken a cigarette break when Angelo entered had now returned. Surprised to see the enlisted man where he clearly didn't belong, he stopped Angelo for questioning.

Normally, being in the command area without proper credentials was cause for detention and discipline. However, the guard determined that Angelo was no real threat and just curious, like all the men. As he let him go, he uttered an ominous warning that chilled Angelo, "Get out of here! I should arrest you, but they're trying to get every man they can to the Eastern Front."

Clearly, the intent was to support Hitler's maddening march to Moscow by sending the division to Yugoslavia like the ones before them. Angelo knew it to be a death sentence and had to get out.

There has to be a way to desert, he reasoned. *I can escape to the mountains and just get lost in the hundreds of caves and natural hiding places everywhere.* But the moment never materialized, and the days continued to march forward with a steadily increasing pace. Day after day, he assessed ways to escape without being caught, but there were too many guards and mechanisms in place to prevent it. And day after day, the anxiety caused by his presumed fate took its toll. The monotonous sound from platoons marching in cadence lingered in his head long into the night after the marching had stopped. He also felt extreme anxiety over his situation, something he had never felt before.

Finally, the word came through that they were to deploy. Commanders began barking their orders to get ready for transport. Each man gathered his rifle, bayonet, helmet, two grenades, and a few other provisions. As they were mustering to leave, verified news ran through the ranks that most of the men in the previous wave had perished. As he sat and waited for the vehicles to move them out, he felt a complete sense of resignation. This proud son of Trentino was going to die in Eastern Europe, for an Italian dictator he despised, after being thrown into battle by a German leader that considered them lambs to be slaughtered. Even at the time, many knew that Hitler thought the Italian troops no match for his armies and cared little to their fate. If someone were to die, better an Italian than a German.

Soon the caravan of vehicles used to usher the men to a nearby train station for immediate deployment arrived. Learning the fate of their predecessors had everyone despondent, and Angelo couldn't hide his emotions. As he resigned himself to his fate, he felt physically sick.

The nondescript Fiat 626 transport truck arrived, and it was now Angelo's turn to load up. As the first person into the vehicle, he shuffled to the front followed by twenty-one other soldiers. Soldiers that were once eager to enter the fray were now disturbingly quiet and contemplative. Angelo hung his head. In a mixture of anger and prayer, he tried to prepare himself for what lies ahead. He tried to think of his family, friends, and everyone back home. He dove deeply into nostalgic memories of Trentino. It seemed like a lifetime ago since being there. *I hate this war. I hate the politicians. I hate everything about this situation. I've got to get away somehow*, he thought to himself. While each made ready in his own way, Angelo eventually developed scenarios for escape that became increasingly far-fetched. The lurching forward of the three-ton workhorse as it began moving saw most jostling clumsily into one other.

Angelo didn't notice or take note of the rain that day—or, for that matter, the two previous afternoons that also experienced heavy spring downpours. Had he, he may have realized that the narrow unpaved road leading from the mountain camp had turned from dirt to mud. The drenching rain also limited the view down or up the steep embankments found on either side of the road.

The heavy truck, loaded with men and weapons, seemed to continuously slide from one water-filled hole to water-filled rut. Its slow and awkward advance had him thinking about jumping out the back and running away. But being the first one in had him all the way to the front of the compartment, directly in back of the cab. He simply reconciled his fate and tried to steady himself as best as possible.

Angelo was completely distracted by the general discomfort of the ride when the truck lost control and the front right tire slid off the side of the road. The driver stopped and exited the vehicle to assess the damage. He made the call and determined that it would require all the men to right the vehicle. Everyone was to leave their weapons on the vehicle, disembark and push the truck back onto the road. As the first man into the vehicle when loading, Angelo was now the last man off. When he jumped off the back tailgate, he instantly saw his chance and impulsively ran down the mountainside.

His fall resembled more of an uncontrolled slide than a careful climb down. Intermixing a few careful steps with sliding, rolling, and falling, he became scratched and bruised from the surrounding foliage and rocks. Angelo assumed he was pretty beaten up by the fall, but his adrenaline temporarily eliminated any pain. Luckily, he had gotten down with only minor cuts and bodily damage, but no broken bones or serious lacerations.

With all the noise from the men trying to right the truck, as well as the sound of thunder and heavy rain blanketing the forest he fell into, it was at least twenty minutes before anyone realized he had jumped. With his heart pounding like never before, he repeatedly reassured himself that he should have plenty of time to make his break for freedom.

He reasoned that he only had to lose them for a short while. The men would likely only divert from their journey to do a quick probe for him before being forced to resume the drive. This was the first time that Angelo used his knowledge of the notoriously dependable trains schedules to his advantage. Trains in most of Europe operated like clockwork, and the truck could absolutely not be late in delivering its payload for transfer to their fate. The train east would not wait for any late transport vehicle.

Thinking the obvious choice would be to run away from the camp that was still only about twenty miles away from their location, Angelo doubled back along the caravan route toward it. As he heard the guards looking for him turn and search in the direction away from camp, he breathed a sigh of relief. Straining, he eventually heard the other trucks in the convoy above him finally begin moving forward again. He wasn't sure how many vehicles there were, but after about twenty, the noise from the road stopped, and he knew he was free. Deserting his comrades didn't sit well with him, but he reasoned it was better than going off to a certain death.

Angelo's gamble paid off. After the war, the fate of the entire Italian Army at the Eastern Front became painfully known. The fighting was horrific. Those lucky few who survived and made it back to Italy complained of poor training, unreliable equipment, and nonexistent leadership. Veterans were hidden from the general public so as to limit the political damage they could sow from interactions with them.

Perhaps the worst criticism from veterans was the lack of military leadership from the Italian officers. When defeat was imminent, German commanders ordered their Italian counterparts to "hold the lines" so the German soldiers could retreat from the bloody and final battles. Italian officers completely capitulated to their German counterparts, leaving all the Italian forces to hold out until overrun.

He would never again see any of the men from his regiment. The Sixth Alpini Regiment that Angelo deserted from fought gallantly and with distinction throughout the Battle of the Neretva. But in May of 1943, during the German Fifth Offensive, the Alpi Graie Division was completely decimated. Also known as Operation Schwarz, Tito was surrounded by a cordon of Italian and Bulgarian troops. After days of brutal combat, he was able to break through, leaving thirteen thousand men dead.

The division that had sent just over four thousand men into battle had only twenty persons surviving after a few short months. All twenty of the survivors deserted and joined up with the Montenegrin partisans fighting the Nazis.

Photo Reference 4.1 –

The only photo of Angelo in his Alpini uniform, taken only two weeks before his desertion. He is on the left in the formation.

Photo Reference 4.2 –

This is Angelo's *Cappello Alpino*.

CHAPTER 5

The Birth of a Freedom Fighter

March 19, 1943
Aosta Valley, Italy

A deserter. A man without honor. The shame of the word sank in as Angelo made his way through the dense forest that first day on the run. His soul was as lost as his body, as he made his way in unfamiliar territory. His training told him to focus on the hike. The wet, thick woods could result in any manner of injury, and the enemy was likely close. But logical thought evaded him completely. *(see photo reference 5.1)*

His family would likely disown him, and even his best friends would surely abandon him. The depth of disgrace would be a stain upon not just himself, but both his family name and future generations as well.

Future generations. The cruel fact of the matter was that his odds of surviving this war made the thought of future generations laughable. Certainly, he would be caught at some point. If by the Fascists, he would be humiliated before the townspeople and then executed for desertion. He knew well the gruesome methods to be employed. Worse would be what could happen to his family. They would spend the rest of the war under suspicion or worse. Zio would likely lose his factory position and be treated as a pariah. If caught by the Nazis, he would be sadistically tortured during interrogations to determine if he knew anything. Once satisfied he had no value, he would be handed over to the Fascists for certain execution. Either way, he had no future and nothing worth looking forward to.

Angelo walked miles the remainder of the day in a trance, staring at the ground as he traipsed through briars, thickets, and wetlands, trudging along in a vaguely southerly direction that he reasoned would ultimately take him home to Genoa. The morning was spent in self-destructive what-if scenarios and internal conversations that never seemed to end.

My situation is hopeless. What will the family think? he obsessed over. Of course, he had no way of knowing at the time, but he was destined to lead great men in daring adventures that would eventually save many lives and help secure victory for the Allies. But on this particular morning, all his mind could summon were dark visions, impossible circumstances, and dwindling hope.

Trying to put aside the emotion of his fall from respectability, Angelo took some time to examine his wounds from the physical fall. Nothing too serious. Still, he was amazed at the amount of bruising and minor cuts across his body. With the adrenaline finally subsiding, he began to feel the pain and stinging. "This will all heal on its own," he said to himself, "but I'm going to need some medical supplies to survive." Satisfied that his body would be all right, he again turned to his dire circumstances.

How could I make this right? he asked the reflecting pool of his mind. *Maybe I can turn myself in and just go to prison for the remainder of the war?* he thought hopefully. But this war was just hitting high gear for the Italians, and the Blackshirts would surely have him executed eventually. Why would they want to keep a deserter around who held no political or military value? Taking up their valuable resources guarding and feeding a worthless deserter just didn't compute.

Maybe I can hide in my uncle's house and sit the war out? That would never work. His uncle Angelo would surely resent him for disgracing his name and failing to live up to his standard as a man. Zia Renata would likely take pity on him and hide him, but it couldn't last for the duration of the war. And even she, who never showed anything but love to Angelo, would surely come to resent him for the danger he brought upon her family. Reprisals against anyone aiding a deserter or partisan were vicious and executed without the benefit of a trial or hearing.

Scenario after scenario played out in his head like the coach of a soccer team down ten to nothing and going into the second half. You know you are going to lose, but you must persevere. Each play fails to dramatically affect anything, but there's an obligation to keep playing. You have to muster any strength and fortitude in your body to keep trying and win the game till the final whistle blows.

At about one in the afternoon that day, the final whistle blew. Stopping for some berries that would make up his lunch, the stark realization hit that there was nothing he could do to correct this decision. What happened had happened, and he couldn't change that. Spitting out a berry that was not quite yet ripe, he said out loud to no one, "Right or wrong, I'm going to have to live with this forever."

Angelo was at the lowest point of his young life. The idea of dishonoring the family name and seeing no future at all for himself nearly drove him to surrender. He was a deserter, plain and simple. He was a shame upon his family—already a dead man walking.

But then something strange happened. A ray of inspiration broke through the cloudy mood in his mind. He literally stood up, faced the now bright sun that finally broke through the clouds, and said out loud: "I am not a deserter! I am not a shame upon my family." His mind raced faster than his heart as he convinced himself that everyone just didn't know it yet. He would do everything he could to free Trentino and the Tyrol from the tyranny of both the Fascists and the Nazis. His voice, now rising to keep pace with his emotion, "If I go down without anybody knowing the truth, at least I will know the truth and die with self-honor."

As he pivoted from self-loathing to self-confidence, despair turned to optimism, and his soul leapt at what could be done and accomplished. He began his hike anew and his stride quickened with that of his heart. Without even realizing it, he was close to running amid the very thick underbrush. He soon paused to pull a thorny vine from his sleeve. As he looked over the scratches on his hands, he even dared conjuring the notion that he could be a hero with the opportunity to play a critical role in defeating the scourge that was raping his homeland.

Unfortunately, the reality was he had little idea of how to do that. But at least now he could envision himself not only surviving but actually making a difference. He may have been lost, but he was no longer wandering. Focused on the positive, he began to think and act as a soldier. A soldier aligned to no government but himself. Free to fight for a return of his homeland to its rightful place on the world stage. He would take his Alpini anti-partisan training and use it to become an effective partisan fighting for Trentino independence.

The next several hours meant more miles filled with a young man's dreams of conquest and glory. His mood lifted significantly with every careful step he took. Visions of heroic actions that would one day be recognized and exalted. His incessant daydreaming was brought back to reality abruptly though, as he rounded a bend and came upon a set of well-used train tracks. He recognized the vicinity and determined them to be the same rail lines that ran near the main camp where he had just come from the night before.

Resting on a large rock and safely out of eye's sight from the camp, he took a break from his hike. It was time to give his illuminations a rest and focus on his next moves. As he concentrated on calming his mind, he took some time to fully survey the area.

The sun filtering through the trees illuminated the natural beauty all around him. He noticed how the flora and fauna here were different than that he knew in Trentino. The trees, landscape, even the rocks were subtly different. He began to miss the fresh air in the mountains, the clear vistas where he could almost see forever, and the comfort of familiarity he longed for. As he plucked a common daisy, he thought, *these areas have a certain beauty, but they can't compete with the vivid purples of alpine crocus, fields of pale blue forget-me-nots, or the pure white edelweiss.*

I need to get back to Trentino - somehow, his subconscious urged him. His family was in Genoa, yet his love, future, and upcoming fight were all in the Tyrol.

But Angelo was on his own now in unfamiliar terrain - totally alone - and he fought hard the undergirding emotion of a man drowning on dryland. He would need many items to survive the daily adventures, cold evenings, and, of course, Fascists, Nazis, and the local population that wouldn't understand his intentions - or the decision of becoming a traitor. He had to assume he would get no help in this personal mission and must ride the war out solo.

The sense of being alone was not only an emotional one but a strategic one. He thought about what he could do that would weaken the Axis war effort. Yet one man does not an army make. Still, he stood there now with a rebel's mentality, where every action supported his singular purpose.

Being a good shot, he schemed initially that he could assassinate key military figures as a sniper. Angelo had been known to be a good rifle hunter, but the idea of taking another life so directly did not sit well. Yes, he hated these people and what they stood for. But in the end, he just couldn't stomach putting another human in his scope and terminating a life. Angelo respected his fellow soldiers that could kill as a part of their job and then return to normalcy after the fact. But that was not him.

His second thought was what he ultimately settled in on: sabotage. He could blow up key locations that would significantly slow down the war effort and yet accomplish success as a lone individual. His efforts could cut supplies from the front, including equipment, personnel, food, fuel, ammunition, and all the elements necessary to equip and move an army. These railroad tracks that lay in front of him were just like all those across Northern Italy, mostly unprotected and ripe for destruction. The number of accessible targets seemed limitless and within reach. A little dynamite, a little courage, and a lot of time could absolutely make a difference.

Sitting there on a rock in the chilly late afternoon, he made a mental list of everything he would need to survive. As he sat, all he had on him was his Alpini uniform, good sturdy boots, and a few personal items. He could definitely use the watch that his uncle had given him upon a graduation from school. It was a well-built, sturdy Swiss-made timepiece that weathered his Alpini training and proved capable of taking abuse. More importantly, he had his Swiss army knife that would surely be valuable at some point in this adventure. Unfortunately, the thing he could use most, the rifle issued to him by the Italian army, was still on the transport vehicle.

Aside from his short list of usable items, he had virtually nothing of value on his body that he could reuse. The weather he could expect in the mountains is notoriously unpredictable, and he knew all too well that his survival from the nighttime cold, rain, and elements would likely be more difficult than from the Nazis or Fascists.

Drawing upon his years in the mountains, Angelo strained to develop a comprehensive list that separated essential items from those of comfort:
- Large hiking backpack to store and keep items dry
- Sharpening stone for his knife
- Thick wool socks
- Needles and heavy thread
- Heavy weight coat, sweaters, and hat
- Lighter and flint as a backup
- A supply of nonperishable foods to be drawn on over time

Once he had the items required for mountain survival covered, he turned his mind's attention to the list of things he would require as an impactful saboteur:
- Hunting rifle with scope
- Pistol for close-quarter exchanges
- Compass
- Field glasses
- Dynamite
- Pencil and paper for planning and communications

At this time of year, the days started getting warmer, but the temperature would fall markedly in the nighttime. By 5:30 p.m., the sun was starting to set and the temperature would soon fall to just barely above freezing. While this day was dry, the previous several days of rain had soaked the ground and, in the shadows where he needed to hunker down, retained its dampness. Lying on damp ground could pull all the warmth from his body and potentially leave him hypothermic. In his youth, he had seen the result of a hiker that had gotten lost in the mountains and died from exposure. The image stayed with him, and he vowed to never to fall victim in that manner.

He longed to make a fire to warm himself, but he dared not give up his position. Taking some boughs of pine tree branches, he made a makeshift bed to lie on. A few more, and he had an acceptable "blanket." Sleeping even a few inches off the ground provided acceptable warmth for this first night on his own. After only a few minutes and with his body's adrenaline completely spent, he fell fast asleep.

Though completely out of character, Angelo slept well into the morning. The later morning light clothed him in welcome heat. He woke up to the sounds and smells of the forest. The fresh morning air filled his lungs; the scent of pine so strong he could literally taste it. Sleeping so late surprised him, given the bright morning sunshine and cacophony of forest sounds emanating from the birds and animals. It was a rare moment of serene beauty that, in the future, he would come back to in his mind many times. His first morning in this new adventure had him saying to the wilderness, "At least I'm still breathing. It's a start."

Now with his mind clear and his future focused, he vowed to execute his plan to make a difference. Well, at least until he was killed by any number of factions eager to do so. Over the next week, he continued his unwavering march back to the outskirts of his adopted hometown, the northern-most part of Genoa. His determined pace and refreshed body enabled him to cover more ground than he thought he could.

Still not entirely certain of his next steps, he found a comfortable place to rest high above the city of Genoa. From there, he spied the busy port city that was an international center of industry and commerce. Despite vestiges of the ongoing war machine, he couldn't help but reminisce fondly about all his friends and relations that were so close, yet so far. Though dirty and dangerous in reality, nostalgia overtook him as he smiled at the city before him and his many memories.

Friends and family, hanging out, getting in trouble together, and just sharing life. He prayed that they all found a way to escape the war in Eastern Europe, as well as cope with the daily struggles at home. Between avoiding the Nazis on their soil, and trying to evade Fascist dangers at their doors, life in Genoa was hellish. While some relished the chance at military glory, he knew of many who didn't, including his cousins. And for just a moment, he could have sworn he smelled his aunt's polenta cooking. Maybe the next morning would bring courage and clarity.

Photo Reference 5.1 –

The Aosta Valley in spring.

CHAPTER 6

Learning to Run

March 29, 1943
Aosta Valley, Italy

The morning broke and welcomed another picture-perfect spring day. Angelo was now in his usual biological routine, meaning he was up with the sun. It's hard to imagine anything more beautiful than this season in the Alps, with lower elevations predominantly thick with deciduous hardwood trees interspersed with pine. The leaves of the hardwoods were just making an appearance; their light green hues contrasted the darker pine and its strong scent after the morning dew.

It was time to execute his plan developed while trekking to this point. *This should be easy*, he thought to himself. Today was a Tuesday, and the town would be in its workday routine. For his uncle, that meant getting to the factory early and developing production plans. His aunt would be at early morning mass, like every day. Their empty house was the perfect opportunity to stock up on all he needed in this new life.

Still wearing his Alpini uniform, Angelo carefully and slowly made his way down to the city's edge and ultimately to the home of his uncle. Knowing of a side window that had a faulty latch made quiet entry easy. Even though he didn't have a lot of time until his aunt returned from church, he couldn't resist the urge to stop and reflect on how much had changed in such a short time. As he gently stroked the length of the kitchen table with his forefinger, he thought of many meals enjoyed there and smiled.

Not all that long ago, he was going through his teens, and home was a place to sleep in between adventures. Now he longed to spend even just one night in his crisply made bed and enjoy just one more home-cooked meal. How he wished that, at the time, he would have savored the simple times instead of taking them for granted the way most youth do. Remembering his aunt's penchant for baking, he instantly thought of her cookies and pastries. He hurriedly looked where his aunt hid some of the goodies she regularly made, but no luck. "None of the good stuff makes it past the weekend," he disgustingly said to an empty jar.

Angelo made his way into his former bedroom and stopped in his tracks. As he passed the mirror, he was taken at by the sight. Still dirty and disheveled from the journey to this point, he looked a mess. His uniform was filthy, and he instinctively brushed the shoulders as if he could somehow be presentable. But most unsettling was his face. His facial hair had grown to about a quarter inch in length, and he had never seen himself with a beard. He didn't like the look. And what of his hair? The army gave everyone a number two crew cut just before departing for the front. The thick, wavy black hair he had sported his entire life was just a memory. "It'll grow back," he gloomily said to himself.

Pushing aside his disturbing reflection and nostalgic thoughts, he silently gathered up what he thought essential and extra clothing. Luckily, most items were common and easy to take. First, he exchanged his uniform for a heavy coat and pants. With each made from wool, he was breaking a sweat within a few minutes. While it was way too warm for the currently beautiful day, they would be essential for the inevitable cold evenings. Changing out of his uniform was like shedding the clothes of childhood; he had a palpable new resolve and growing maturity.

Next was the kitchen where he stuffed his hiking backpack, half full from clothing, with hard salamis and other foods that would keep easily. He wanted to take more clothing and debated with himself over his Alpini uniform. It was another durable set of clothing, but getting caught with it by any faction would be critically dangerous. Ultimately, he decided to leave it behind.

Next came what would become the tools of his trade: his hunting knife and sharpener, lighter, compass, field glasses, hand mirror, and pencil and paper. These were the easy items that were already his. Next, he would need to "procure" items that belonged to his uncle but were necessary for his operations.

Moving into his uncle's bedroom, a place he had actually seldom visited, he pulled a Beretta Pistola Automatica from a dresser drawer and some ammunition. It was an elegant automatic weapon, 9 mm caliber with a seven-round magazine. As he held it, he couldn't remember any time seeing his uncle actually discharging the weapon. Fearing it might be in serious need of a thorough cleaning, he quickly examined it. The short amount of time before his aunt returned enabled only a cursory look, but it luckily revealed itself to be pristine. Angelo laughed to himself. *There's no way Uncle would allow anything to be dirty or out of maintenance.*

The last thing he searched for was his father's old hunting rifle that he had used many times as a boy. The Carcano Modello was a standard issue to most soldiers serving for Italy in the First World War, and it was the only thing Angelo had that belonged to his father. The bolt action, magazine-fed repeating rifle was known for its dependability and durableness. It was such a good rifle, in fact, that Italy continued to produce it well into the Second World War. Its stellar reputation had Italy supplying it to many Axis partners such as Japan and Finland.

At the conclusion of the First World War, the Armistice and Italian government permitted veterans to keep their weapons. Stefano had kept his, and Angelo's mother gave it to him as soon as he was old enough to hold it properly. So expert had Angelo become with the rifle that he regularly went hunting to supply the family their meals. While some thirty years old, the weapon still shot true and felt familiar in Angelo's hands. He immediately felt a connection with the father he never knew and became strengthened and comforted. Because of the shortage of fighting men in the region, he naively assumed that he would rarely encounter more than a few enemy men at a time. He was confident that the six-round internal magazine could easily hold off the scouting parties that the enemy might send his way.

Sensing a pressure to leave quickly, there was little time to write a note of explanation. Besides, how could he explain what he was trying to do or the why of what he had done? Even if he had the time for a lengthy explanation, he knew that nobody was likely to believe it. He settled on leaving his Cappello Alpino with the uniform. Identifying the missing items and seeing the distinctive hat and uniform would surely let the family know he was not at the Eastern Front and instead on the run. Besides, the thick wool hat he exchanged for the Cappo would serve him much better during the future cold nights.

With his essentials taken care of and now sporting civilian clothing, Angelo slipped out of town to begin his new life. While he secretly hoped to run into an old friend, he knew better and did his best to avoid contact with anyone. Since he knew the area well, he located a site to make camp relatively close to the town, approximately ten to fifteen miles northeast.

The recent rains reduced the lowland valley to a swampy marsh. Trudging through the muddy mess that seemed everywhere at this time of the year, he rested frequently but only for a few moments. If he sat too long, the incessant mosquitos would converge and feast on him. Yielding to this unwelcome plague, he had long before given up trying to swat them away. Even covering nearly every inch of exposed skin to provide them the least amount of landing area possible didn't seem to help much. Angelo longed to be back in the mountains where mosquitos could occasionally be found in low areas but rare in comparison. Despite the inconvenience, this area outside the city's grasp was no-man's-land and a perfect place to hide out; yet still close to town where he could continue to pillage for whatever he needed.

*****

The return of his uncle and aunt to their home was not what Angelo had imagined. Coming to the realization that Angelo was safe was a great relief to both his uncle and aunt. The revelation brought tears of gladness that he was all right. Because of his exposure to the Fascist government, confirmed rumors of frequent atrocities and horrendous conditions at the Eastern Front, his uncle was not angry but instead supportive! Likewise, the townspeople were not ready to turn him in but rather were on his side and wanted to help.

On one rainy May morning before sunrise, Angelo was caught sneaking into a local shop to rob it for food. The person that caught him fortunately knew his family and brought him to his uncle's home. Along the way, the person told him about how they were proud of what he was doing, and they wanted to help. "We're just all glad you are okay. Tell us how we can help you!" he said reassuringly.

Angelo spent the rest of the evening catching his uncle and aunt up on his adventures and challenges of staying alive. As he spoke, more cousins and family friends came by and shared their love and support for him. Angelo had become a minor celebrity in his hometown, and he had no idea.

While gorging on homemade breakfast treats and sweets, paradise for this Italian man, he also shared his frustrations at not having the supplies to make a serious dent in the war effort. He had smartly used his time to roam all over this section of Italy, noting railroad locations, enemy troop concentrations, fuel depots, and all the intel he hoped to soon exploit. *Without proper supplies, I can't make the impact I know I can make.*

He begged his uncle to help him get dynamite and serious munitions to do maximum damage. But his uncle had a different plan, one that would enable Angelo to stay in his home and be safe, at least for some time.

Earlier in the winter, the Mussolini government forced his uncle's factory to switch over to full munitions production. He was building heavy bombs that were primarily provided to the Nazis for use in their African campaign. Angelo's uncle hated building bombs for the Germans, often with little or no compensation, and had devised a plan to inflict substantial harm to the Germans and Italians still fighting in Africa.

He suggested that he would forge new identity papers for his nephew and provide him a job at the factory (see photo reference 6.1). With his cousins and others sympathetic to his plan, they would build the bombs but not include key components of the detonators in some of them. He would still deliver the bombs as required, but a percentage would fall harmlessly to the ground. Angelo would still have to "stay low" and out of the city to not draw attention. But he would be seriously impeding enemy bombing damage from the safety and comfort of his home.

Angelo listened to his uncle's plan and agreed immediately. While he longed to make a more direct difference, the opportunity for months of homemade cooking and a warm bed was actually the greater motivation. He knew that his future lay in Trentino, some 275 miles away, but his time on the run so far made this opportunity one he simply couldn't pass up.

With new identification papers secured quickly and surprisingly easily, Angelo, his cousins, and friends became just new factory workers alongside the other men employed there. Factory life was not to Angelo's liking. It was dirty, smelly, and run with military discipline. The heavy work wasn't an issue because he was in the best physical shape of his life, but it certainly took a toll on some of his compatriots. As they worked themselves into the mix of the production lines, their critical omission from the bomb assembly became easier to hide. After a few months, they were estimating that 15 percent of the bombs that left the factory were duds. This wasn't the exciting saboteur life he envisioned, but Angelo was pleased to know that thousands of lives had been spared by him and his family and friends.

Unfortunately, the likelihood of eventually being caught became a threat to the operation. His friend and coconspirator at the factory, Allessio, was stopped by the carabinieri or local police. The officer found an inconsistency in his papers and wanted to take him in for questioning. Luckily, Allessio hid his fear and convinced the officer to instead take him to the factory where Angelo's uncle, the senior manager, would vouch for him.

The carabinieri didn't say a word as he stoically walked Allessio to the factory. While Angelo's uncle was surprised by the visit, he calmly explained where the problem was and that he would correct the situation immediately. With an acceptable answer, the officer left and the incident ended without any consequences. But it also put a serious fear into Angelo's uncle. He quickly determined it was no longer safe to continue their operations at the plant. Plus, the war in Africa had ended that spring, and they were forced to start shipping bombs to many new locations throughout Europe. The new destinations meant new and unfamiliar German officers to deal with. He basically felt it was just best to quit before they got caught. As the head of the family, there was little discussion.

The next day, Angelo and all the men involved, now gratefully acknowledging his leadership, left the city for the mountains. Before leaving, they developed a coded messaging system so that they could let each other know if they were all right or not. Since they initially anticipated staying close to Genoa with their operations, they also worked out a mechanism to be able to come back and get resupplied when necessary.

Unfortunately, their upcoming missions would take them farther and farther east, toward the Brenner Pass between Italy and Austria. This was the area of the Tyrol and Trentino that he longed to return to. It was also the center of railroads and highways supplying the German war effort and, Angelo presumed, the key to ending the war in Italy. The greater distance, however, meant they would never get the opportunity to use their crude messaging system once gone. The team was now on its own, but at least better equipped and prepared for the action to come.

Photo Reference 6.1 –

Angelo's identity papers, cover and inside.

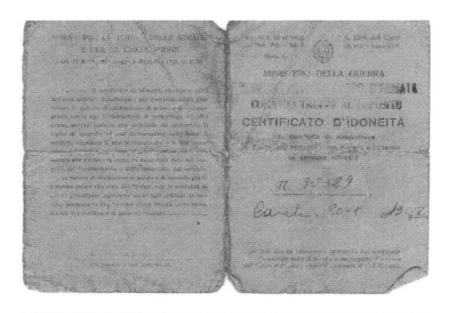

CHAPTER 7

Death From the Shadows

July 13, 1943
Genoa, Italy

Angelo's band of underground guerillas, now numbering ten men, began their march eastward, performing minor acts of sabotage along the way. These were not necessarily carefully planned out operations but more accurately reflected acts of opportunity. Cargo trucks filled with gasoline canisters to refuel advancing German mechanized units were a prime target. When the occasion to cause some damage presented itself, they would engage and immediately retreat.

These were fairly safe and resulted in minor operational inconveniences for the enemy. When they would see a convoy of vehicles, they might take a position high above a critical point and lob a stick or two of dynamite down on the lead vehicle. While it did delay the convoy and occasionally disable a vehicle, more often than not, they would miss the vehicle and blow a hole in the road - still valuable to slowing the enemy down, but they knew they had to become far more effective.

Their biggest scores were boxes of blasting dynamite found at local mining operations. With it, they learned valuable lessons in demolition and created an opportunity to accomplish real results. One such occurrence happened over a bridge spanning a tributary of the Po River. It was an older wooden structure generally used only by locals until the war, and barely two lanes wide.

Being comprised of only two spans and one central pier support, it was a simple structure that they hoped would come down with little effort. Despite its obvious age, their reconnaissance found it to carry a surprising amount of traffic.

Three of the men, led by Angelo's cousin Nini, carefully walked out onto the sturdy structure. As they reached the middle supports, they climbed down onto the supporting pier. Clumsily, they struggled to strap their payload to the pier and not fall into the water. They placed their dynamite toward the top of the center piers and ran long wires back to the detonator on an overlooking hillside. Then they patiently waited for some unsuspecting enemy traffic.

After remaining several hours for the enemy to show, they finally saw a small group of vehicles and men coming toward the bridge. At just the opportune moment, they blew their explosives. Unfortunately, they did not place the dynamite in the correct location. Worse yet, they didn't use nearly enough. The explosion blew out some of the structure and a bit of one bridge lane, but not enough to cause meaningful damage.

It did, however, shake the hornet's nest pretty well. As Angelo's men busily argued about the failure, the German troops crossing the bridge made their way up the river's edge and hillside. The sound of bullets hitting the trees and rocks around them was a rude wake-up call, alerting them to the danger approaching from below. Like a man just fallen in a frozen lake, Angelo jumped up and was suddenly fully alert.

A hasty and coordinated withdrawal was necessary. Angelo had three of the men provide covering fire while the rest retreated to higher ground. Once in a secured position, they provided the cover fire for the three below to also make it up the hill. With all the men making it over the top of the rise, the enemy lost visual contact. Fortunately for the team, they broke off the engagement and returned to their vehicles. Had the Germans continued their pursuit, they would have seen Angelo's team running like mad across the fields and woods, arguing with each other the entire time.

The proximity to imminent danger bothered some of the men more than others. But being young, battle often becomes an opiate. To be so close to death while still alive was an exhilarating adrenaline rush that would fuel many a coming mission. Later that night, they regrouped and made some valuable decisions. They were never going to be able to steal enough dynamite to take down any bridge of meaningful size, so they needed to be more strategic. They decided to blow the bridge where it's connected to the road. This would have the result of blowing the first section of bridge, plus a section of roadway leading to it and part of the embankment. Repairs would be easier to accomplish, but it would take multiple teams of men with different skills and varied mechanical resources to facilitate them. As such, the overall repair would likely take nearly as long. Maximum impact with less ordnances.

Operationally, they would utilize Fulvio, the team sharpshooter, in a primarily support role. Like most of the men, he was older than Angelo and in his early thirties. He had the surprising background of a bartender. "Our best shot is always around liquor!" one of the men said jokingly. His bubbling personality manifested his years of serving drinks for tips. He was also tall and slender, with a pencil-thin mustache that was all the rage.

But Fulvio's marksmanship was never questioned. He had won many local competitions prior to the war and possessed that rare ability to make himself completely still. His routine was always the same. He would get his target in sight and first steady his body. Then, almost ritualistically, he would take a deep breath, exhale, wait a few seconds, and take a second deep breath. While holding his breath, he would squeeze off the round. Whatever was in his sights generally fell immediately. Fulvio would now take a position high over the operation site to provide cover during the planned retreat.

They would also plan their operations with the end, or retreat, first. Everyone agreed that excellence in the escape was far more important than offensive planning. Knowing exactly where each team member was going to be once the engagement began minimized the need for midbattle communication and enabled extremely fluid and efficient team movement.

A few days later, the group would split up to recon a greater sweep of land. If they were going to be more strategic in their choice of missions, they needed better intel from a larger geographic area. Angelo took Nini, Pietro, Gianni, and Daniello and went south to explore a train track that seemed a good target. One of Angelo's best friends, Ricco, led Fulvio, Vincenzo, Mario, and Silvio to scout the northwest. Angelo's team determined the tracks were not used enough or by valuable enough transports to risk an attack. They proceeded to make their way back to their shelter and wait for Ricco's team to return.

When an hour had passed after the expected time of return, Angelo readied his team to search for them. As soon as they headed out, Ricco appeared through the dark woods. His face broadcast the pain in his heart. Taking him back to the safety of the cave they were in, he told them of the ill-fated excursion (*see photo reference 7.1*). They had found a German rifle team camped out by a small broken-down farm building. Seeing the opportunity to commandeer weapons and other essentials, Ricco's team engaged the three men they saw. He was unfortunately unaware of four other men sleeping in the building. When they quickly emerged from the protection of the building, the larger force soon dominated the firefight.

Amid the onslaught of rifle fire, Vincenzo and Silvio both fell at almost the same time. Ricco and Mario both smartly threw the two hand grenades they had into the German position, quelling the relentless fire for a few brief moments - time enough to disappear into the thick woods.

The remaining team immediately agreed to avenge the death of these two brothers. They quickly made their way back through the black woods and surrounded the broken-down building. After seeing the site for himself, Angelo had the men pull back about a quarter mile to fully plan this attack. While emotions had everyone just wanting to go in with guns blazing, Angelo and Nini didn't want to risk losing anyone else. They had enough men to completely surround the broken-down structure. The previous battle meant the Germans knew underground were in the area, and they would be expecting them. But everyone was confident that their now eight men could overrun the seven Germans. Ultimately though, the need to retaliate for the lost brothers left them no choice.

The team carefully considered the mission and potential concerns. Ingress would be easy because there was plenty of cover. Aside from the main structure, there were also smaller rock walls throughout the area that offered ample protection. Egress was another story. If they failed to finish off all of the enemy contingent, the remaining men would likely alert other nearby units. The team wanted to be sure it avoided facing a much larger and better-prepared enemy force.

Angelo knelt on the ground and drew the site out in the sandy loam using a stick and some pebbles. The crude image provided little value, except as a focusing point for everyone as emotions were running high. He told the men to spread out in a large perimeter and evenly surround the building. On command, everyone would slowly move in at the same time and take positions behind the small rock walls and fallen trees. On a second command, everyone would open up and secure the objective in a withering cross fire. They determined egress would be in the opposite direction of their camp. If something went wrong, they didn't want to be followed to the camp. The idea was to exit the opposite side, break into several groups of two men, and then backtrack to camp via different paths.

The men said a quick prayer and fanned out in a very loose perimeter. Angelo then gave a bird whistle to close the perimeter. When everyone was in their position and as close as safely possible, he fired a round toward the building to start the battle.

Gianni focused immediately on a guard that was the farthest from the building. After taking him out with a single shot, he smartly grabbed his two grenades. Drinking deeply from the well of rage, the men showed no mercy. The team opened up with relentless rifle fire. Gianni used his two grenades to further the chaos around the building. Within ten minutes, the German six-man rifle team was completely eliminated. Fearing that a larger contingent of German troops must be near, four men carried the bodies of their brothers out while the rest of Angelo's team greedily gathered all the food, weapons, ammunition, and grenades they could carry.

Before moving out at the break of day, the men used the last of the night's cover to hastily dig two shallow graves for their fallen comrades. Surprisingly, no one felt better. The revenge that they hoped would cleanse their souls did nothing for their spirits. Their cherished brothers-in-arms were still dead. The rage displayed in battle had ultimately subsided, but left behind in its place intense sorrow, pain and personal loss.

The demise of these loved teammates formed the soil from which the seeds of generational hatred nurture. Like a weed, it sprouts and grows quickly. But also like the weed, it doesn't die easily. It only gets stepped down upon and angrily suppressed. Unfortunately, over time the hate supplants normality and becomes the new usual.

The first deaths to the team hit everyone harder than they imagined. Of course, they assumed it would happen to all of them at some point, as nobody had illusions of surviving this mess. But when it actually did happen, everyone searched themselves deeply. All the men regularly "talked big" in naive bravado and acted like they didn't give a damn. In reality, each man gave a big damn.

The next day, after putting many miles between themselves and the firefight location, the men found an excellent cutout from the mountain to call camp. The Alps, Dolomites, and even the Apennines, to some extent, are full of these openings in the mountainside. Not exactly deep like a cave, but deep enough to provide shelter from the elements and the scouring eyes of passing patrols. This was an opportune moment for everyone to rest and examine the weapons absconded from the German unit.

Ricco grabbed the German rifle and studied it carefully. The standard bolt-action Karabiner 98K "8mm Mauser" was the basic infantry rifle issued to German soldiers. Being used by nearly all troops, it made replacement ammunition readily available. With a range of eight hundred meters, five-round magazine, and shorter stock, it was both lighter and more efficient than the Italian equivalent.

Nini told the team that they needed to secure as many of these as possible in their coming raids. Angelo reinforced the point. "We will be operating behind enemy lines, and we need to understand and use their equipment all the time." Within a few months, it became the standard used by the entire team.

However, the item that most caught the attention of the men was the German *Stielhandgranate* (German for stick hand grenade). This was a very unique design and very different from the hand grenades used by the Allied forces and other Axis forces. Its stick handle was specifically designed for mobility and to be housed under one's belt, easy to carry and easier to deploy.

The functional design was also radically different than those Angelo and his men had been trained on. The Italian military used the *Bomba a Mano*, a roundish design similar to what the Americans and British used. However, the design difference of the German model yielded a significant tactical difference.

The Italian hand grenades were like the American version: an offensive, antipersonnel fragmentation weapon that scattered shrapnel upon explosion. They were lethal within a radius of up to fifteen meters and generally able to be thrown twenty-five meters. The German model was a defensive weapon, lacking significant shrapnel and used primarily to slow an enemy unit down so that the men could overtake a position. The clever design enabled the user to throw it an additional five meters, similar to throwing an axe versus a ball. It also tended to stay where one threw it. Round grenades could roll significantly before exploding and often would miss their mark. The German stick model would be perfect to cover Angelo's men when trying to escape after an operation. Simple dynamite would suffice for their offensive needs.

The run-and-gun strategy employed by Angelo was actually like a tricky dance the team played with the enemy. They had to keep on the run, then stealthily attack and flee. They didn't want to stay in any one area too long for fear of raising an overtly visible and significant profile.

The men all recognized that the team needed to train on all three aspects of their missions: target approach, mission execution, and escape. The men each took turns developing likely scenarios and then trained on all three aspects. Angelo wanted to enforce a sense of methodology in their operations. Tactics needed to be second nature if they wanted to act like a team. In this way, when situations warranted an automatic tactical response, they would all have the best opportunity to survive.

They weren't being hunted at this point, and they did everything possible to avoid that frightening prospect. A lone mosquito buzzing around one's head is an annoyance. But many incessant mosquitoes require attention until eliminated. When the results of Angelo's team went from annoyance to significant damage and operational exposure, the Germans were sure to put special teams into play and eradicate the pest.

Worse yet would be getting captured and interrogated. The sure torture endured by the individual would force them to give up information on the team and their hiding locations. Staying on the run and moving their camp every few nights ensured nobody would be forced to put the team in jeopardy. Their plan was to move in a generally easterly direction toward Tyrolian territory. They hoped that the locals who would be sympathetic to their cause and support them with materiel, information and housing options. "Because it's the only way to get to Germany from Italy, the war has to eventually go through Tyrol," Angelo reasoned.

*****

The summer of 1943 saw the official end of Benito Mussolini and his Fascist Italy. The country was essentially up for grabs once they put Mussolini in jail in late July. It wasn't until six weeks later that Hitler would rescue him and reinstate him as a puppet leader of the Salò Republic, located just north of Genoa and very close to where Angelo's family was. The Republic extended from northern Italy to just south of Rome. While it officially declared Rome as its capital, Mussolini had his offices and functioned out of the small town of Salò on Lake Garda.

This move provided Hitler with an ally to hold off the Americans and the Allied Forces marching up from Sicily. It became apparent that the might of the German war machine was turning its attention away from their defeat in Russia and toward defending their homeland. Northern Italy soon became one of the most important theaters of the conflict, a literal gateway to end the war. Angelo's team and future operations would be right at the heart of it.

Most Italians rejoiced at the demise of their delusional tyrant, but a surprising number stayed faithful to the ideals of nationalism and fascism. This resulted in many groups of Italians fighting each other as well as the Allies and Germans.

At this time in the war, when there was no clear leader in Italy, Italian land endured occupation from Germany, the United States, Britain, and others. Confusing the matter even more were the dozens of splinter partisan groups, loyal fascists, and anarchists. While most of these groups followed some form of fascism, communism, or socialism, one could still find themselves fighting liberalists, social democrats, and even remaining monarchists mostly in Southern Italy. Identifying sides became nearly impossible and resulted in not trusting anyone for fear they may be aligned with an enemy.

Operationally, their near-constant movement made it impossible to connect with any locals who could assist them in a myriad of ways. Without a stable base of operations, they had to steal everything they needed from not just fallen German soldiers but also local farmers and shopkeepers as well.

The men became hungry and thirsty. Most had some experience in survival techniques and knew how to manage from the land, but it became clear to Angelo that they were going to need local support for stable sheltering and supply requirements. Even covering just the basics of life was taking a significant amount of time and was extremely distracting to the missions at hand.

As summer continued though, the weather persisted with its regularly occurring rainfall, living up to the Alps' notorious reputation for summer rain. While the wet weather made living conditions difficult, it certainly aided in their operations and nondetectable movement.

One early afternoon while going through the mountains after a typical rainfall with his sharpshooter, Fulvio, Angelo descended down a ravine into dense, thick fog. Fulvio had earned a solid reputation with the team for his marksmanship. Still, while valuable to the team, it was unfortunately the wrong skill set to have when venturing through heavy fog.

Summertime fog in mountain valleys can be very thick, particularly after a rainfall. Daytime heating of mountain lakes and wet areas causes water vapor which then gets lifted over tall peaks, resulting in fog that settles heavily in the valleys. On this day, they were walking down a path in a wide valley, lush with heavy vegetation. It was one of those quiet moments where one would never guess there was a war going on around them. The men walked carefully but couldn't help be taken by the beauty of walking through a cloud in the mountain valley. They spoke freely and dreamed aloud of home, girls, and victory. As late afternoon settled in, the fog became so thick they could not see more than several feet in front of them.

For safety's sake, they began walking in silence and watching the ground in front of each step. Carefully continuing down the path, they heard another set of footsteps coming from a path opposite them, and then within a minute, a third set of footsteps were coming from the position to his left on an intersecting path. At this particular junction, the three different paths converged, with the center being comprised of several huge boulders the size of a bedroom. Angelo could feel the wind and birds still themselves, as if all nature could sense a coming battle storm.

Nobody dared speak. Nobody peered out. Nobody moved. Angelo knew about the "fog of war" from his Alpini training, but this was ridiculous. The three entities were all hiding behind boulders a mere thirty to forty feet from each other. Fearing the others were the enemy, each stayed quietly in place. During the standoff, Angelo thought he made out Italian whispers, but his gut told him even if they were Italian voices, they were not likely friendlies. Actually, given the minimal amount of Italian insurgency at this time, it seemed entirely likely that the others were indeed Fascists, Germans, or an enemy of some type.

On occasion, one of the persons involved would try to climb a boulder to see over and determine who was actually there. Each time, Angelo or Fulvio made a similar noise pretending to be climbing the rock and dissuading the other from coming over the top. As time dragged and the fog thinned, every type of strategy conceivable for dealing with this situation was discussed in hushed tones.

It was indeed tricky because the last thing anyone wanted to do was accidentally kill a friendly force. And unfortunately, any type of grenade usage could backfire by rolling back off the boulder and explode close to themselves. Plus, if you take out two from one contingent, there were still the two from the other contingent that you might then be exposed to. So, everyone seemed content to sit it out as the passing of time would lead to the fog thickening again and an opportunity to escape. A dangerous proposition, and Angelo was feeling vulnerable.

If one of the two contingents were Nazi soldiers, reinforcements would surely come looking for them. While a possibility, Angelo was sure he never heard the squawk of a radio transmission. If they were Fascists, others would most certainly come looking for them as this was their territory.

With the evening approaching and his stomach growling, Angelo decided to make a break for it. The late summer sun still set fairly late in the evening, and it would be another three or more hours till complete darkness set in. While any meaningful cover from the fog had dissipated, Angelo decided to get out before anyone else showed up and tipped the scales to one party's advantage. He gathered all his courage, quietly stepped backward as far as he could in absolute silence, and ran down the path with Fulvio away from the others. It wasn't elegant or pretty. Angelo prayed the surprise of their exit would catch the others off guard and not positioned to do anything. The noise from his escape made determining the disposition of the other forces impossible. He could only assume they eventually took the opportunity to run as well.

The next day, he learned from local townspeople that one set of persons were two Fascists from a neighboring region and the others were two Fascists from the local area. The great "Italian Standoff," as it would come to be known, became the talk of the *ristorantes* and *birrerias*, quickly attaining legendary status in the area. With the excitement of the situation waned, the men in the team laughed and joked for some time that nobody could figure a way to diffuse the situation.

"Sometimes there is no viable military option and you just need to run," he said to the group as if turning the happening into a teaching moment. The men listened and thought for a few seconds before degrading into extended mocking laughter.

Photo Reference 7.1 –

The entrances to some of the caves used by Angelo and the team for shelter.

CHAPTER 8

A Suitor Comes Calling

August 19, 1943
Mountain foothills, northeast of Milan, Italy

As the summer progressed, the team was starting to get its feet under them. Regularly succeeding in random acts of sabotage on significant targets actually had them making an impact. They continued to employ the guerilla tactic of strike and disappear, trying to make it impossible to be followed.

They relied heavily on the black woods to extend the protection of the night. The woods in the higher elevations have a peculiar trait of being black, even during the day. Nearly all logging operations happen at lower elevations closer to cities and rivers because it is easier to transport the logs. But here, the woods were far older and the canopy lush and thick. The lack of sunlight on the forest floor not only made it very dark but also kept scrub and brush to a minimum. The terrain had little to impede movement—a perfect habitat for escaping after an operation.

As the men continued their march eastward, they continued exploiting the woods and mountain foothills to hide their movements and provide daily refuge. Avoiding muddy valleys and wetlands was paramount. Not only could they be tracked, but trudging through mud would also sap their dwindling energy even more.

Their goal for a final destination was agreed to be Val Gardena, which is located in the South Tyrol close to its historic border with Trentino, but at a low enough elevation to help survive the coming winter weather.

They kept on the move, first through the Bergamo region and then past Brescia. The steady, exhausting pace was difficult, and they had little to eat. Resorting to eating grubs, worms, berries, and whatever protein they could find, each man did what he could to conserve energy. Gratefully, as they reached higher elevations, they were greeted by ripening fruit trees like apples, cherry, and persimmon. Each night they would hike in silence. Each day they would day camp and get necessary rest. The physical demands were wearing on everybody.

Finally, the men hit the major obstacle of Lago di Garda. It is an extremely formidable lake, the largest in Italy, and some thirty miles long. They had no choice but to proceed either north or south to get around it. Going south would take them many days longer and expose them to heavily fortified industrial locations. To go north would mean very difficult steep climbing and virtually no towns to garner vital support. If their energy was depleted before, the northern choice could end them.

The team took a day of rest and discussed their options. Tired from this, their latest test, they vigorously argued the pros and cons of each choice. Angelo was impressed at their passion, given their sorry state. The clinching argument was made by Angelo that the northern trek would have them close to Lago di Tenno, where he was born and spent his early youth. He hoped he still had some memories that could aid their cause or that the local people would recognize his name and support him.

But many of the men had never experienced the Dolomite Mountains. Angelo felt it home, but to the majority, it was an unknown. They would need to traverse two ranges and the imposing Monte Baldo, standing over seven thousand feet in elevation. Even in late summer, the nights would be colder than some had ever experienced in Genoa by the sea. So, already weakened by walking across much of northern Italy, the men turned north and ventured into the imposing mountains (see photo reference 8.1).

Their choice necessitated them hiking up and down the shear slopes that make up the western side of the massive lake. The hike was grueling and dangerous, with many natural obstacles to overcome.

"At least we'll never see any Germans or Fascists up here!" Marco said to try and bring positivity in their dangerous reality. Marco always had a way of seeing the positive despite the truth. Angelo, knowing what was coming, smiled and just nodded his agreement. But to himself, he thought, *Germans are the least of our problems, making it safely up and over these mountains is the real test.*

The men proceeded at a quick pace initially but were soon tired from the reduced oxygen common at high elevations. Still, by following goat trails, they discovered several mountain passes that afforded them the chance to avoid hiking the summit. At one point, Angelo looked back at the team and saw them spread out in a single file that stretched nearly a quarter mile. "Let's take a break and rest for a while," he said.

The men were spent. Some clearly could handle this environment better than others. Angelo called Nini over, "Hey, watch out for the stragglers. They are falling behind, and we need to stick together." Angelo reinforced the need to stick together and move like a team. Exhausted, the men continued on. They were nearing the northernmost point of the great lake just before the town of Riva del Garda when Gianni stepped off a boulder the wrong way and twisted his ankle. While not serious, he would require a week or two to recover fully.

The men established field quarters deep in the wild woods just west of the town. These were the same rough quarters they had endured during this entire arduous journey, utilizing the materials found in the forest like tree branches and limbs. While the men worked on securing their shelter and getting food from the nearby river, Angelo and Nini discussed going into town to scope it out. They decided on just them two, enabling the remainder of the team to take a day off and rest. Gianni certainly needed a couple of days completely off his ankle to heal properly.

Angelo hoped that him finding receptive friends would work out. On the northern edge of the town was a restaurant with a bar. That day, while getting a cup of coffee there and trying to find help, he met a waitress who was also from the Tenno region and remembered their family with the little hotel. Angelo was ecstatic. She immediately connected him with others sympathetic to partisans like himself. They were given shelter in farm homes, and the men could finally rest with a modicum of comfort and safety. With an actual bed to lie on, Gianni would get time off his ankle and recover much more quickly.

The waitress further introduced Angelo to an elder in the region who was very interested in the team and their intentions. Angelo spent an entire evening laying out his plans to hinder the German war effort through sabotage and develop an independent Trentino again. The man commended the entire team for their sacrifice. This was the first time Angelo had heard anyone say thank you. They had given up their lives and had been on the run a long time. It was pleasing to finally hear someone say thank you.

At the end of the evening, the man told Angelo he needed to meet a person in the Veneto region just east of the Trentino region. Unlike Trentino, they had a formal garrison of partisans loyal to the partisans' Committee of National Liberation for Northern Italy (CLNAI) in Milan. It was highly organized and boasted some ten thousand men by the end of the war. Angelo listened to the older man and agreed to meet with one of their leaders.

The several days it took to arrange the safe meeting location was welcome time off to all the men. Angelo spent it reconnecting with the places he remembered from his youth. While not extending his travel too far for safety's sake, he did venture to places where he remembered visiting with his mother. Leaving the rest of the men behind, this was his time to reconnect with the purpose of their mission. The autumn was settling in and his heart soared at being at least close to his home and birthplace.

The small town selected for the meeting was about four hours away on the eastern coast of the lake and seemed like an ideal out-of-sight location. "The restaurant will work great, close and easier to defend if anything goes wrong," he said to Nini.

His cousin agreed. "There's only one way in and a back door. Easy to defend and plenty of cover if something does go wrong."

However, several in the team had significant concerns. Nobody knew this person or anyone from the region. Deep in thought, Pietro rubbed his pronounced chin. He and Mario urged extreme caution, but knew they had to go.

The team was beginning to develop its culture, with Nini, Pietro, Ricco, and Mario always promoting a more controlled and safe approach. Fulvio, Gianni, Antonio, and Daniello were just the opposite. Always looking for a fight and eager to kill Germans and Fascists at any opportunity. Angelo became grateful for the team personality. While there were always disagreements on how to proceed and the Italian culture of passionately debating virtually anything, he knew that his decisions would be influenced by every perspective, ultimately leading to optimum decision-making.

As always, Angelo weighed the opinions of everyone. After talking privately with Nini, they decided that four other men would also go with them for a potential defensive stand. Pietro and Daniello would sit at a table close to the bar, which all restaurants on the beach feature. Their primary concern would be the bartender who could possess a hidden weapon and the back door. Pietro was given the bartender to cover while Daniello kept his eyes on the hallway to the back door and listened intently for any sounds coming from the back room. Mario and Ricco would take a table by the main entrance and provide protection if the place was raided during the meeting (*see photo reference 8.2*). Because they were dressed to walk the streets openly, none of the men carried anything except a handgun tucked in their belt.

With their assignments in hand, everyone relaxed and enjoyed the rare comforts of their hosts. After another hour talking with the team in a more casual tone and setting, they decided to add Fulvio and his trusty rifle to the expedition. While there was only one road in and out, and there should be plenty of warning to any approaching trouble, Fulvio would scout the woods behind the building and alert the team inside of any potential danger.

On September 12, Angelo, Nini, and the five support men left for their meeting at the restaurant in Navene. They purposely arrived over an hour early to watch for any suspicious activity around the quiet restaurant. When everybody was content that nothing seemed out of the ordinary, Angelo and Nini cautiously stepped into the restaurant at 10:00 a.m. sharp. There was only one table that was occupied by two men already sitting there. Angelo assumed it must be their contact and made his way over to them. Scanning the premises as he cautiously walked, he felt it odd that the man chose a table in a far corner of the restaurant. Angelo would have preferred a quiet table in the back and close to an exit.

As he approached the table, he observed that one of the men sat with his hands under the table, clearly in protective mode. The other stood up immediately to greet Angelo and Nini. "Which one of you is in charge of this conversation?" he said abruptly.

Angelo stepped forward to shake his hand and said unemotionally, "I am. I'm Angelo, and this is Nini." As they shook hands, Angelo joined everyone else in quickly studying the faces of the others. After a quick moment, everyone sat down.

As they spoke, Pietro and Daniello entered and sat by the bar. A moment later, Mario and Ricco came in and sat by the door. The man in charge looked toward the men sitting by the door, then glanced to the bar to see the other two. Without making eye contact, he smiled coyly to himself. His large round face exuded confidence but revealed little else.

He then raised his hand and waved for the waitress. "Four coffees, black!" he ordered with an assured tone.

Just the act of ordering coffee for the four implied his leadership and imposing character. While waiting for the waitress to arrive with their drinks, nobody said a word. Even though it only took a few minutes for the waitress to assemble things and make her way over to their table, it seemed an eternity to Angelo. The unsettling situation was only heightened by the second man, who never took his eyes off Angelo's men at the bar and by the entrance. Angelo took advantage of the brief interlude to assess the situation and players, and instinctively run through potential scenarios that might need to be played out.

Finally, the man looked up from his coffee cup and sharply said, "I am Antonio Roasio, but you can call me Paolo." As he said his name, he took a sip of coffee and looked up over the rim of his diminutive espresso cup to see if there was any reaction from Angelo or Nini.

Angelo and Nini had no idea who this individual was and provided no reaction. A bit surprised, the man then said proudly, "I am the CLNAI regional brigade commander for Veneto and Emilia."

With that announcement, he started asking Angelo all sorts of questions about their past missions, operational protocols, enemy targets, and others. "Oh, and you can have your men stand down."

Angelo feigned a confused look.

"Look," Paolo said, "you have the man by your side with a pistol aimed at me under the table, you have two men by the bar covering the bartender, and you have two more men at the door protecting you from anyone coming in." Then he laughed and said, "Don't worry, we are on your side."

Angelo relaxed and had Pietro and Daniello join the conversation. However, he maintained the two-man presence at the door, still not entirely comfortable that trouble couldn't surface quickly outside. Angelo and Nini endeavored to learn what the relationship could mean for them, the resources they could gain from a relationship, and the politics of independence for Trentino or the Tyrol.

The discussion lasted well into the afternoon. While Angelo answered all his questions appropriately, Paolo remained stoic. The imposing figure was a hard-core Communist, trained at the university in Moscow. Angelo was being grilled by someone that obviously knew his business, thinking it actually felt more like an interrogation than a conversation. With every answer provided, another question followed almost immediately. At some point deep into the process, he asked himself, *who is this guy, and how does he know so much about sabotage and guerilla warfare?*

After several hours of a one-sided conversation, Paolo became hungry and suggested they get some food. Angelo and the men, always ready to eat, heartily agreed. Everyone ordered the traditional sandwich of the region: prosciutto and valcasotto cheese, drizzled with balsamic vinegar on fresh baked baguette. The traditional simple sandwich was served warm with the strong cheese melted. Along with more coffee and a glass of water, it was the go-to for most of the locals. During lunch, the men spoke more personally about family and the devastation and suffering caused by the war.

With lunch over, the "conversation" renewed and became a lecture on the glories of communism. Paolo spoke passionately about the people's right to equality and the dispersion of wealth among everyone in a society. "Why should a few have all the wealth of a country when it's the workers that make them the money?" he asked rhetorically. And then he continued without a break to breathe, "Fascism is all about the state having the power, and capitalism reserves power for the privileged. But communism uniquely puts the power into the hands of the working class."

Angelo, never a political type, found himself intrigued by the diatribe. After what he experienced working in his uncle's factory, he couldn't really argue against the man. At the end of a particularly long rant, Paolo finished with a statement that really made Angelo's head spin. "If you think Carl Marx was the first Communist, you would be wrong. It was Jesus Christ!" he declared with a wry chuckle. The thought made Angelo sit back in his chair and audibly gasp. Paolo, recognizing he scored a major point, sat back to let the moment really sink in with Angelo.

It's true, thought Angelo to himself. Although he tried to remain distant from Paolo and the conversation, he had to confess to himself that this blowhard made some good points. For quite some time, Angelo's mind drifted as he tried to get his head around the idea of his personal savior as a Communist. Even though he tried to convince himself otherwise, when comparing the three monetary systems that control the world, communism could indeed be thought to reflect the teachings of Christ the most.

Then suddenly, Paolo broke into Angelo's thoughts and blurted out, "I think you should join the Garibaldis and organize a brigade in Trentino. We have no one in that region, and you would be perfect."

Angelo was surprised and grateful but remained professional and non-emotional. Nini smiled with pride at the recognition for his cousin. This was clearly a major moment for him personally and all the men he led on the team. Although understandably difficult, Angelo pushed aside his ego and regained his focus. It was now his turn to ask some hard questions.

All of Angelo's questions revolved around three basic questions: what resources could the Garibaldis bring to the table that he didn't already have, what level of independence would he experience, and how would this move help reinstate an independent Trentino?

The Garibaldis were the predominant partisan force in Northern Italy, and by the end of the war, they fielded over fifty thousand men in all. Approximately half of all Italian partisans belonged to this one group. Their greatest resources would be in coordinated attacks and greater access to Allied drops of arms and cash. But nearly all their forces were centered in the two major cities of Genoa and Milan. They had little to no representation in the eastern half of Italy except for Paolo's men. Worse yet, Paolo had his hands full on the Yugoslav border, and virtually all his resources were tied up there.

This made little sense to Angelo, who thought the most critical region in Italy was the Tyrol. Clearly, all German troops and weapons had to pass through the Brenner Pass and travel the length of the Tyrol. Even though all rail and truck activity passed through it, there was virtually no underground activity to speak of. Angelo understood why they were looking for him to change that. Unfortunately, it seemed that he would be providing a lot and receiving little in return.

On the question of operational independence and mission selections, Paolo provided a quick and direct response. There would be very little. Angelo would be a commander in a new partisan army with orders coming from their headquarters in Milan. Over the past six months, the Garibaldis had woven together a patchwork of partisan units under the flag of Communism. With little time and many commanders having their own aspirations and designs, infighting was rampant.

At the moment, there was some semblance of independent thought, but that was sure to quickly slip away. The notion of being in an army, even as a regional commander in one of only ten regions, simply didn't set well with the entrepreneurially minded Angelo. He and the men had gotten used to determining their own moves and operations, and the thought of taking orders from a leader on the other side of Italy was not appealing.

Plus, the Garibaldis spent a lot of time organizing and very little time executing. Angelo determined he would be spending more time recruiting partisans than carrying out operations. Much later, during the last month of the war, the general uprising called by the organization surely aided isn the rout of the remaining Nazi troops. But for now, the German war machine was still firmly in charge, and Angelo was not impressed by the Garibaldis lack of engagements.

Paolo understood Angelo's drive for the reinstatement of Trentino. The First World War resulted in the dismantling of the region, and much of that war was fought in the area now controlled by Paolo. This point of agreement bonded the two men who could not have been more different. By the end of the day, Angelo promised to consider the offer and get back to the commander within a week. It would be a team decision, and they needed some time to thoroughly discuss it.

It was dark outside when Angelo finally said goodbye to Paolo. Their daylong meeting had covered so much that they lost track of the time. As they were leaving, Paolo vowed his assistance to the team no matter what but gave one last shot for his cause: "Freedom lies in a Communist Italy controlled by the worker. You should be a part of our new future."

Angelo and his team began their walk back to Riva. Along the way, they all took turns going over what they heard and what they should do. Fulvio, who had spent the entire day patrolling the woods behind the restaurant, began complaining about not having anything to eat all day. The men took the opportunity to properly shame him. While everyone was laughing, Ricco remarked that it was odd how they spent the entire day in the restaurant and not a single patron came in. Mario, who had worked the door with Ricco, quietly agreed.

While everyone else had moved on in their conversation, Angelo continued his thoughts to himself. *Could Paolo have actually had the people of the little town stay away from the restaurant because of the meeting? Just how much power does he have here?*

Even in the dark, Angelo could see the enthusiasm in the men, except for Nini. At some point along the walk, Angelo and Nini had created some separation from the other men, and they spoke freely.

"We have no idea when this war is going to end or if we will make it. I want to spend my time left making a difference and not sitting around playing army," Nini said. Angelo listened intently, and they each played the devil's advocate to each other's points. "They have a name. We will likely have little trouble finding people that will house and feed us if we are a Garibaldi Brigade," he offered.

Angelo rebutted, "Yes, but they may insist on an operation we determine to be too dangerous or not a high enough value. I don't want to lose men merely to satisfy the orders of someone in Milan." This back-and-forth continued for much of the walk back.

By the next day, Gianni's ankle had improved, and he was able to walk extended distances. However, the hike to Val Gardena would entail some difficult climbing, and Angelo wanted him completely healed. Angelo decided to wait another week in Riva. They had safe and comfortable accommodations, Gianni could use a little extra recovery time, and Angelo wanted quiet time in peace to pray about the difficult decision they had to reach.

"Actually" - he chuckled to Nini - "there's no reason to walk to Val Gardena if we decide to become Garibaldis. We would just have to walk right back here again!"

The men spent their time discussing their options, often in heated and spirited ways. But Angelo was surprised that nobody had set views on either option, whether to stay independent or to join the Garibaldis. The discussions were mostly rational points and counterpoints given to help flush out the answer. Angelo hoped that by the end of the week, a clear choice would surface.

Photo Reference 8.1 –

Photo of the west coast of Lago di Garda. Note the vehicle on the road at the bottom for scale. It was this formidable mountain range that Angelo had to traverse to make it to Val Gardena.

Photo Reference 8.2 –

Photo of the restaurant meeting location. The original restaurant has been added onto many times since the war.

This is inside the restaurant. The area to the right held the bar and back door. Paolo would regularly meet with partisans at the far table. Mussolini enjoyed the view from the table closest in the picture. An elderly person that lived her entire life at the property said laughingly that when "Mr. Mussolini" came down the road, the partisans would run like rats out the back and into the woods.

CHAPTER 9

An Entirely Different War

October 7, 1943
Riva del Garda, Italy

By the end of the week, Angelo notified Paolo of the team's decision. In initial conversations, it seemed like a great fit. Their small band of men would get recognition, they would be better positioned for a postwar life, and they would have the benefit of relationships and local support for the remainder of the war.

However, as the week went on, the ramifications of being under the thumb of a central authority didn't sit well. The men had already been through so much. They were operating as a machine now, with each knowing how the others would react to virtually any situation. Merging with a larger organization would jeopardize all their sacrificial gains from this arduous journey, from fighting together under extreme duress and from loving each other as brothers-in-arms.

And then there was the thought of taking orders. Angelo and the men enjoyed making their own decisions and choosing targets themselves. But even greater than that, they had become seasoned warriors forged by battle, certainly, unconventionally, and willing to do most anything. The natural arrogance that comes from achieving unique accomplishments against significant odds doesn't lend itself well to taking orders in a military hierarchy. Additionally, the Garibaldis were consolidating power in the western and far eastern sides of the country, with little to no concern for the central and Tyrolian regions. They could see no way to get past the differences in overarching goals and operational requirements.

As the team recalled the mounting sacrifices they had made over time, the more entrenched they became in their loyalties. For once, everyone seemed in general agreement on the decision. They were adamant about not becoming political and bending to the directives of any authority.

"We will stay independent and fight for Trentino and each other!" Nini declared, as if to put an exclamation point to the conversation and the decision made. Immediately, Gianni and the rest of the team chimed in, and there was complete agreement.

Angelo never forgot the friendship that started with Paolo though, and in the years to come, he would be remembered fondly. But Angelo and his men were simply not cut out for politics. They had come too far and wanted to be significant in this conflict, not merely a part of it. The team was finally rested, fed, strong, and focused again. It was time to get to Val Gardena and plan the next phase of their own personal wartime contribution.

As they continued their hike up the mountains to what they hoped would be a new base of operations, the cold nights of autumn stung Angelo back into reality. The team enjoyed great morale at this point, but Angelo worried about how long it would last. He knew they still needed to find local support or they would likely never survive an Alpine winter in the elements. The entire team just finished enjoying the huge difference between having local support and fending for themselves in the wild.

The team's condition led Angelo to postulate as to the enemy's condition as well. The Nazi's African campaign failed because, in large part, of the determined Allied pressure. Now the Russian campaign was also faltering. Hitler had only three fronts left to defend: the north Atlantic that exposed the Western Front, the Slavic areas which were the key to the Eastern Front, and the Tyrol that led to Italy.

Angelo surmised based on observation, local intel, and radio reports that German troops were routinely being rotated in and out of Italy from their African and Russian campaigns. In both theaters of war, the men were fighting at very low elevations where the air was easy to breathe and the topography was mostly flat and easy to traverse.

Chasing Angelo's team in the extremely thin mountain air and mountainous terrain would be a significant challenge. Regularly conducting missions at elevations between five thousand and nine thousand feet put the enemy at a significant handicap. The advantage the team had in this new terrain cannot be overstated. When using roads, they would be easy to track and vulnerable in any season. But the rocky elevations now posed a significant challenge to the enemy tracking them when there was no snow. The rocks and boulders they encountered everywhere couldn't capture footprints like the mud and dirt of the lower elevations. By using the many animal trails and narrow mountain passes as escape routes, the team felt comfortable in its ability to escape capture or extended firefights.

"The terrain will force the *Tedeschi* [Italian for German] to break off chases quickly," Mario reasoned.

And with the advantage of being in the lead during a chase, they could stop and set up defensive ambushes for the men pursuing them either on foot or with motorcycles. Angelo's men discussed and flushed out modifications to their exit strategies that fully exploited the conditions they anticipated in the Tyrol.

Nearly all the men had the feeling of "being home" in the mountains. Coupled with the restful setting of the previous two weeks, the mood of the team lifted noticeably. None could explain it, but at least temporarily there was a general feeling of security and happiness that could only manifest itself amid the mountainous beauty.

They made plans to engage the enemy near the most difficult terrain possible. Once the mission was executed, they would literally run for the hills instead of the woods for cover. As they arrived in Val Gardena, they prayed for a mild winter and felt prepared for a lengthy offensive that would take them to spring (see photo references 9.1 and 9.2).

But the deaths of Vincenzo and Silvio just a few short months earlier continued to haunt Angelo in quiet or private moments. In his mind, he could still see them playing like friends do when young. He lingered on Vincenzo and the special times getting in trouble together as teenagers or doing schoolwork. He had always wanted a serious or steady girlfriend but would now never have that opportunity. Silvio, in particular, was difficult to shake, with his baby face and youthful appearance regularly coming back to haunt Angelo's sleep. He laughed silently as he remembered teasing him about his inability to grow even a mustache on his face. While actually a little older than Angelo, his boyish looks made sure he was always treated as a rookie.

Angelo often struggled to chase away the constant feeling he was responsible for the two being gone. He found it surprising to see how some of the men, Daniello and Fulvio in particular, could continue looking forward to the next engagement. It seemed they felt nothing and lived to kill. In some ways, he was impressed and grateful for their ability to move on and not be troubled. But he always had reservations about the hearts of men that could be hardened to such a degree.

Nini could see Angelo's burden in the quiet moments. Sitting beside him alone under a perfect moonlit night, he quietly said, "It's okay, cousin, I miss them as well. The innocent feel guilt, and the guilty feel nothing. We are who we are."

Angelo simply acknowledged that stinging truth with a shrug and forced smile. Apparently, it continued to taunt some of the others as well. One evening while sitting around the camp fire for warmth, Ricco approached Angelo. He sat for a few moments in silence, seemingly composing himself. Then slowly and with a dejected sullen look about him, he pushed his wavy black hair from his blemished forehead and stood up. Reaching into his pocket, he produced a picture of himself that he gave to Angelo. Speaking in a meek, timid voice, he said it would be a remembrance of him after his death.

Instead of graciously accepting the intended gift from his brother-in-arms, Angelo scolded him for talking like that. "*Sta Zitto!*" he said aggressively.

Ricco had never had his friend tell him to shut up in that tone before. Ricco immediately jumped to his feet, looked down at Angelo in anger, and began arguing. Angelo was in no mood to fight however, and he ordered Ricco to sit down and again shut up. After the short exchange, the two separated to mull over their thoughts.

A condition found in virtually all young men is their confidence in being indestructible. There was a keen and ever-present awareness of death all around them, but it was the fate of others, not their healthy, strong bodies and clever, shrewd minds. As confident young men, death was assumed, but always to others and not one's self. On the other hand, as soldiers living behind enemy lines for years facing daily danger, they felt certain a bullet somewhere had their name on it. The dichotomy was maddening when it hit home.

Two nights later, Ricco would be killed in action trying to steal some food, boots, and of course the most valuable commodity, ammunition. The mission should have been an easy one. Ricco, Pietro, and Gianni had spied a small German outpost that must have sent its patrols into the woods. This left only a few men behind, and they were just milling around a trash barrel with a fire going. The impromptu mission was to raid the outpost, eliminate the enemy, pilfer their goods, and run before they could be caught.

Making only a cursory plan, Ricco made sure everyone was in favor of the mission. With no objections, they lay in wait and scrutinized the site to ensure there weren't any additional Germans out of view. After thirty minutes, everyone was satisfied, and they decided to go. Everything went well, and the team caught the few Germans completely off guard. The men then took everything they could easily grab and began to run. Ricco, however, really needed new boots as his were literally falling apart.

His decision to lag behind and steal one of the dead soldiers' boots would be his downfall. In the few minutes it took to undo and remove the boots, a nearby German patrol heard the firefight, returned, and decisively ended his life.

Knowing that this patrol would surely radio other enemy patrols in the nearby woods, they were certain more troops would soon arrive. Each wanted to fight and retrieve Ricco's body, but the growing number of enemy soldiers that they anticipated would quickly overrun the two of them. Instead, they decided to double time it out of the sparse woods and return to camp via a goat trail that went up and over the mountain. The circuitous path would add significant time to their return but ensure the safety of the remaining team waiting for them.

Upon their late return, Pietro conveyed the story of what happened. Angelo was brought to the saddest point in his life. He took out the picture Ricco had given him. Now staring earnestly at the image of his fallen friend, he turned the picture over. Written on the reverse side in Ricco's hand was a note to his dear friend:

> *Let the beast sleep, my true friend, and for me, I fear the furnace of hell will follow. Sleep is an unreasonable ideal for my life. Only Christ the Judge will be able to say no to my shame and make me his property. Good luck to you.*
> *Ricco*

Angelo went off on his own and wept uncontrollably. The depth of his sadness was like nothing he had ever experienced. Speaking to the air, Angelo sought Ricco's forgiveness. "I'm sorry, dear friend. I'm sorry I yelled at you. I'm sorry I wasn't there to defend you. I'm sorry. I'm just sorry." In a daze, Angelo grabbed his rifle and inspected it. He stroked the barrel and thought about how much death he had witnessed.

The men all took time in silence to remember their fallen comrade. The decision was made to quickly move from their present position as the Germans could be counted on to search diligently for the guerillas that took out their men.

Angelo's quiet time was ended by Mario. "Hey, come on. We're all hurting, but we need to get out of here."

Again on the move, Angelo now found himself second-guessing everything. He felt constant pressure, and he and the men were in a continual state of anxiety. He couldn't shake the reality of their situation even for a few precious moments. Mountain-based guerilla warfare was taking its toll, and its realities never left his mind. It was significantly different than fighting in the lowlands. Every turn, every random boulder strewn across a field, every animal trail they followed, and the entire terrain that surrounded them could hold the enemy. Additionally, they were far behind enemy lines and truly on their own. The emotional cost of being "on" all the time was aging him faster than nature intended.

He knew it was only a matter of time till they would run out of area to operate in, and everyone would perish. Not only were the potential areas of operations limited, but evasive movement could be easily tracked in the deep snow that blanketed the region. That would gratefully change when summer returned, but for now, mission extraction would be their greatest challenge.

*****

Angelo was grateful that the remaining seven men in the team had significant experience surviving in the mountains on nothing but their wits and skill. The men subsisted primarily on wild vegetables, fruits, nuts, plants, and mushrooms, and supplemented these by hunting game and snaring smaller animals. Depending on the season, they could find vegetables like carrots, turnips, parsnips, radishes, and beets. Fruit trees could be found offering apple, pear, and plum. Nut-bearing trees like walnuts, chestnuts, and pecans were also plentiful, as were plants like dandelions and lilies and hundreds of mushroom varieties. The men knew what to look for based on the season and took great advantage of the oft-available delicacies. The longer they went without raiding local farms and stores, the easier it would be to garner support.

The one thing Angelo kept relying on was his belief in an independent Trentino or Tyrol after the war was over. He hoped that since they were now in the southern area of Trentino, he would be able to find some sympathetic locals. He didn't know anyone here, but he placed his faith in the idea that, like him, nobody wanted to be under the control of Italy.

The decision was made to hunker down and expand his team with local individuals who they determined loyal to the historic County of Tyrol. Angelo thought to himself, *surely these people must hate the occupation and the Germans. They must want to help us bring change.*

But they still had the issue of being caught if they conducted too many operations in a limited area. Towns and potential targets for sabotage were far fewer in the rural landscape of the mountains than the great valleys and industrial areas they had come from. Complicating matters, with enemy traffic increasing daily in the region, they would surely be discovered at some point and eliminated.

It was at this time that Angelo had his most daring and reckless idea yet. Everyone recognized that they had to do operations as far away from their home base as possible. But they couldn't drive on the roads even if they stole a vehicle or take trains for fear of likely being caught. He determined the best solution to the problem was to get German-issued identity papers that would enable them to take trains to far off regions, conduct their missions, and then safely return.

Addressing the team, he said, "Brothers, we need to become fake Germans." The rejection of the team was expected and understood. Angelo then laid out his plan and reasoning. It took a bit, but eventually, all the men reluctantly agreed.

Angelo imagined that the forged papers should be for a position that would be questioned as little as possible. Ideally, officer's level papers. Because of the continuing political chaos experienced in Northern Italy at the time, Italian and Alpini officers loyal to Mussolini and Hitler were regularly in the company of German officers and, importantly, able to move with impunity nearly everywhere.

The men debated extensively which branch of the military they should get the papers made for. Within the German army, there were many levels that could serve their needs and provide the desired safety. The SS in particular seemed a good fit. The only drawback to this branch of the army was the need to speak fairly effective German since the SS were responsible for large numbers of men and would be required to speak often.

Ultimately, they decided the best type of German officer to impersonate would be the Gestapo. The terror tactics used by the organization and their Nazi fanaticism were intentionally well known to intimidate everyone. The organization was feared not only by the enemy and civilians but by the German rank and file as well. Few wanted to speak to them, and they were known to work independently.

"Everyone is afraid of them, and nobody questions their orders," Angelo reasoned with the team. Even better, they were classified as "police" and wore civilian clothing. It would be the perfect cover to enable free movement by train or vehicle into and out of virtually anywhere.

It was a highly dangerous plan. To be caught would mean certain death. Even if the enemy never caught them, the audacity of the play would surely lead to an all-out manhunt for them. Angelo once again took out his prayer card for Saint Jude, the Roman Catholic patron saint of lost causes. *Saint Jude, intercede for us in this effort because everything is against us. Have Christ himself put a protective hedge around us as we execute this mission.*

Taking a break from their normal operations, everyone took part in the planning for this unique mission. Reconnaissance moved from identifying targets of opportunity to observing train logistics. Even vehicular and troop movements were studied and analyzed for consistencies which could be exploited. Actually, the move from offensive operations to planning was a welcome change for all the men. Despite their strength, they had become exhausted both physically and emotionally.

Having learned the importance of planning versus improvising, Angelo exercised even more strategic thinking for this gambit than any other mission thus far. He knew the key to success lay in extensive preparation, counterintuitive moves, and faith that their mission was somehow ordained by God himself.

Every minute detail was considered: the train schedules, the number of guards at the station by time of day, points of ingress and egress from train platforms, military versus civilian transport, train maintenance schedules, the length of time the train was stationary or moving at speeds that still enabled jumping on or off, and so on. Angelo wrote out every step and procedure, and then everyone practiced their part. They repeatedly practiced the military doctrine to "train as you fight, and fight as you train."

Even though this mission would employ only a two-person team, everyone participated to ensure nothing was overlooked. The men role-played reactions and responses to potential threats. This practice developed natural responses to likely interactions with German guards and soldiers. When challenged, the men would need to be able to respond with authority and in character.

The mission to obtain German Gestapo agents' papers was finally settled after weeks of comprehensive planning. Their intel had revealed that the nearest location of an official German printing press was in Munich, well into the heart of German territory. They were convinced the Germans would not have as many guards milling around as they were used to seeing in frontline areas. Angelo tried half-heartedly to convince the men that it was less dangerous than what they had been doing all along, but everyone knew the extraordinary risk.

Angelo and his cousin Mario would take a late afternoon Munich bound train from Bolzano. They determined this train normally contained many Italians returning home from working in the local industries. Hopefully, they would fit in and not raise suspicions.

The night would be spent in hiding, with the following day used to locate the authorized German printing companies. Once they had the papers, they would use them to ride back to Val Gardena in secured comfort.

After all was said and done and despite extensive planning and analysis, the scheme was fraught with uncertainty and jeopardy. Mario turned to Angelo and said in a deadpan voice, "I hate this war." With that, the men all retired and tried to get some last-minute sleep.

Photo Reference 9.1 –

The valley and town of Val Gardena with the imposing Dolomite mountains around it. The men had their headquarters in a barn up the slope to the left and around on the north face (not visible in photo).

Photo Reference 9.2 –

Angelo and Diva in 1997 drinking from the natural spring in Val Gardena (10,500 feet in elevation), which was the primary source of fresh water for the team during the war.

CHAPTER 10

A Ticket to Munich

November 26, 1943
Ponte Gardena train station, Italy

At 6:04 p.m., the harrowing mission began. The civilian transport train was packed with primarily Italian workers returning home from work. Mario made light of how their team was always starting their work at the time when most others were coming home. His gallows humor fell on silent ears as Angelo intently searched the crowd covertly for potential trouble. Angelo felt surprisingly comfortable among the large crowd of workers. He felt at ease as he temporarily melded into the throng, similar to the way small fish will find safety from predators by swimming with others in a bait ball.

The screeching brakes jostled the passengers as the mighty locomotive finally came to a stop at the station. Angelo and Mario took their place in line to board the second car from the front and completely blended right in. Each carried a single nondescript piece of light baggage. The small weathered bags contained a single dark gray overcoat and some dried salami and nuts for each of them. In addition, both men carried concealed sidearms and sound suppressors tucked in their clothing.

The two deftly moved about the train car to avoid roaming guards, all the while praying for their success. In case they were discovered, the original plan was to exit through a small emergency escape hatch that could be found in the floor of every railway car.

Unfortunately, they had to quickly abandon that escape idea. The Germans smartly had guards secure the hatches, with some literally standing over them. With their initial idea for quick egress infeasible, they began looking for other means of escape should trouble ensue.

As people made their way home, the rail cars became increasingly less crowded. As such, the men were more visible now, and they fought the nervous body language that would certainly give them away. Angelo had the nervous habit of bouncing his leg, specifically his right leg, while seated. Whenever he became nervous, his leg would start shaking, and his foot continued the motion by tapping the floor. His go-to method for avoiding this unconscious disclosure was to stand instead of sit. This was going to be a long trip, and the five-hour train ride began to disturbingly resemble a suicide mission.

Luckily, the men didn't draw any unwelcome attention. It's impossible to overstate the chaotic nature of the Northern Italian region at that time. If civilian workers were in good and appropriate clothing and didn't give any cause for alarm, they were typically not bothered. The Germans routinely used Italian citizens for work. Dressed like everyone else and placing one's self in the middle of a group of workers returning from a day's labor served as camouflage and provided a modicum of safety.

The men eventually passed the many hours of travel time safely by standing and occasionally sitting openly with the other workers or by intermittently hiding in various toilet facilities and storage areas. Moving around regularly was key to not raising suspicions. Angelo was so exhausted from the stress of the trip that he couldn't imagine how he would make it through the next day and the ride back. It would be another long twenty-four hours.

At 10:50 p.m., the train started slowing. After a few minutes, the conductor blew a sharp whistle and announced the train would be pulling into the Munich station in five minutes. Angelo and Mario made their way to the junction of two connected cars and looked out at the pouring rain and muddy embankment. Angelo stood in the doorway blocking the window as Mario put a sound suppressor on his pistol.

Thankfully, they didn't have to wait long for the train to go around a long curve and slow significantly. The men quickly opened the door to the car and exited onto the coupling mechanism. The train jostled violently as they braced themselves against the cars. Within seconds, Mario fired two shots to the left side of the train, striking some farming equipment. The pistol's suppressor didn't give their position away, but the bullet hitting the equipment made an unusual and unexpected noise. The surprising sound made every guard look to that side of the train for a brief moment, and he and Angelo jumped off the right side and rolled down the embankment.

Swiftly gaining their composure, the two scrambled hastily to the safety of the woods only a short distance from the tracks. It was the evening of November 27, specifically chosen by the men because it was a perfect new moon. Its weak level of lighting created the darkest of nights and the best opportunity to not be seen. Fairly confident they were not observed jumping, the men felt confident they wouldn't be chased. Once certain that indeed no Germans were following, they quietly looked for a rock outcropping that could shield some of the bone-chilling rain. After finding some suitable cover, they stayed a few hours and welcomed the eventual stoppage of rain and the chance to assess their situation.

Soaked from the rain and covered in mud from the fall, they exchanged their wet outer clothing for the dry, heavy coats in their briefcases. Even with the warm coat, neither man could stop shivering from the near-freezing temperature, wind, and fear. Once morning had broken, the pendulous clouds lifted and yielded a broken sky that was gratefully clear of any rain or snow. The men made their way back toward the tracks that they then followed on into the city.

Angelo and Mario hiked approximately ten feet inside the wood line parallel to the tracks to avoid detection. At least the dense forest would provide some cover for a firefight in case they ran into guards. The rising sun was unusually warm this fall morning, and they were grateful for the measure of comfort. The bright daylight quickly burned away any remaining clouds and provided welcome visibility in unfamiliar, hostile terrain.

Their painfully slow, cautious walk into the city, intermittently halted by any unfamiliar or unusual sound, consumed the entire morning. It was midday when they found themselves at the edge of the city, and they cleaned the mud off their shoes and tried to make themselves look presentable. In minutes, they were surrounded by German citizens and soldiers busily walking the narrow streets of the bustling commercial city.

Now in the city, they faced the most difficult part of the mission: finding a printer with the proper plates to make their forged papers. They started by going into the first printer they saw, a small but surprisingly busy shop. Angelo introduced the pair as Italian officers in need of government authorized printing services. Speaking very little German and only understanding the most basic words, they became aware that this printer was a typical commercial printer without access to Nazi identification paper stock or plates. Disappointed, they asked where they might find an authorized printer. The shopkeeper expressed his understanding and directed them to a shop deeper into the city.

In the completely alien city, they only understood the basics of the directions given. It took a surprisingly long time trying to find the next printer, particularly because they couldn't ask for directions. After more time than they planned, they finally found the shop and were again shocked to see the level of business conducted. Even the general street traffic was surprising: a woman walking her infant in a stroller, three men arguing loudly with each other, dozens of vehicles coming and going, and an old woman hunched over and leaning on a cane trying to cross the street.

As they stood outside for a half hour surveying the busy situation, they counted eight patrons leaving and entering the store. When there was finally a lull in the business, they went inside and told the printer the same story they had given before.

But this time, the printer was clearly suspicious. He questioned the pair and said he rarely saw any Italians this far into the city and away from the transportation hub. Angelo feigned like he couldn't fully understand and repeatedly asked where he could find a printer that could make their documents. The printer was becoming increasingly aggressive in his questions and manner. As the printer became more and more impatient with the conversation, his tone and demeanor reflected the common German business acumen of brusqueness. All three men began looking and acting defensively, and openly displaying the product of the increasingly tense atmosphere.

But then a stroke of luck. Two attractive women entered the store. Angelo saw an opportunity to lighten the mood with the printer and took it. With a broad smile on his face, Angelo nodded at the women and winked his eye at the printer. Without any words, the printer got the message that Angelo appreciated feminine beauty and the printer smiled back, clearly confirming that he, too, appreciated the women. After that bit of very shallow bonding, the printer wanted to get rid of the men that clearly would not make him any money and to focus on the women that likely would. He dismissingly told them that there was another printer only a few blocks away that would be able to make their documents. The men thanked the printer and quickly exited the shop. With the exchange resolved, they proceeded to find this third printer.

Even though it was only a few blocks, the men managed to get lost. A dangerous-looking situation involving civilians being questioned by German soldiers had developed on a corner they needed to cross. Without an adequate knowledge of the street layout, they detoured several blocks to safely avoid it. Every block, every building, every person they passed posed a potential threat. This mere inconvenience of a few extra blocks managed to effectively intensify the already stressful mission.

Mario said to Angelo, "I'm seeing more Germans today than I ever want to see in my life again! Let's find this printer and get out of here." Angelo replied with a disgusted nod of his head.

They finally made it to the location of the nondescript print shop with a small sign that simply read "Druckdienste" (printing services). Crossing the narrow cobblestone street, Mario was taken by the street's condition. "This street and the buildings look like they haven't seen any war. They are in perfect condition."

Distracted, Angelo momentarily took notice and agreed. A split second later, he told Mario to focus as they approached the printer's building with extreme caution. It didn't take long to observe that the few patrons at this location were of a government and military nature. With the day wearing on, they hid in an alley by the shop until after the 5:00 p.m. closing time.

Several employees left at or just after the close of business. Mario walked past the storefront and observed that the only person left in the building was a single older man, likely the owner. As the shopkeeper was leaving and closing the door behind him, Angelo and Mario approached him and said they had business to conduct. As the man turned to tell them he was closed, he saw Mario's pistol trained on his heart.

Angelo calmly nodded to go back into the shop, and the man complied without question. As they entered, Angelo instructed the printer to not turn on the lights but to instead go farther into the shop and a back room. There they could do their business and not be observed from the street. The man and Mario caught each other's eyes, and Mario implied their desperation without saying a word. The printer locked the door behind him and slowly started walking.

Leading his guests slowly down the hallway, they passed two small unoccupied offices and a large unkempt supply room. Finally, they entered a very large open back room that held four sizeable machines. The room was already lit dimly from outside lights coming through the many skylights in the roof, but Angelo instructed the man to turn the lights on. Angelo was certain the printer was using these few moments to discern a way out of the situation, and he wanted enough light to see every move the printer made. He was sure someone in this business would have firearms planted in the building, and he told Mario to search the desks and workplace for any weapons.

Once safely in this production room at the very back of the business, Angelo made his demands known. He would need two sets of documents for him and Pietro that identified them as Gestapo *kriminalrat*. The officer's grade and position were important. The kriminalrat had the equivalent of a major with less than three years' service in Department D of the Gestapo. This was the specific organization charged with administration of occupied territories. In addition, they would require three more sets of papers at the level of *kriminalinspektor*, a lower-level rank that served under the kriminalrat. Angelo then produced small photos of all the men for the identity papers. Luckily, the size of photograph for German papers was the same as those for Italian papers and fit the space provided perfectly.

In another stroke of good fortune, the printer had experience working with Italian government and military officials and spoke a cursory level of Italian. Between his limited Italian and Mario's limited German, they were able to adequately communicate. The printer used this modest competency to repeatedly explain in a panicked voice that he could not do the work. At first, he claimed he didn't have the proper equipment. Next, he pled that he had to go home to a sick wife. Lastly, he simply fell on the floor and begged the men not to shoot him.

Angelo realized they would run out of nighttime if they didn't get started on the documents right away. He needed to motivate this person to get started immediately. They needed to be on the return train during the busy morning rush to provide the best chance at making it.

As he looked around the shop, he saw a picture of two older boys on a table. In a disarming voice, he asked the man, "Are these your children?" The shopkeeper nodded yes and said that they were about the same age as Angelo and Mario. Both were currently serving in the German military, and he hadn't seen them in a long time. Angelo surmised that since there was no picture of a wife, and his boys were off fighting, that the man was likely alone. He could work all night on the documents, and there would be no one getting nervous or suspicious if he didn't return home. Angelo posed that deduction to the man, and instantly his demeanor and body language indicated that Angelo was right. Mario again trained his weapon on the man, and Angelo made it clear that they could kill him right now and nobody would be the wiser till the following morning. The man reluctantly acquiesced and finally began working on the documents.

While the man worked and Mario guarded the door, Angelo tried desperately to put the man at ease. He repeatedly told him he would not be killed or harmed if he just made the documents as requested.

Awkwardly, he labored to find something to say that would connect with the printer and ease his guard. Finally, he asked about his children and what had happened to his wife. Angelo soon felt pity for the man as he told him that his boys had been sent to Russia, but he didn't know if they were alive or dead. Angelo could easily guess the sons' fate based on what had happened to his Italian brothers-in-arms who went to the Eastern Front. It was an unspoken secret that everyone kept locked up in their internal prisons. The trip to the Eastern Front was punched with a one-way ticket.

He went on to say that his wife had left him because of the stress of likely losing their sons and because of the extreme hours he worked to satisfy the demands of the Reich. This man was living a nightmare just like his family and friends in Italy. Ultimately, they weren't that different at all, and everyone caught up in this war suffered tremendously. Most importantly, the tension eventually eased, and the unburdened man worked at an acceptable pace.

Around 5:00 a.m., the printer informed the men that he had finished his work. The papers seemed perfect. Importantly, the photos of the individuals were secured to the paper with a special glue and looked absolutely authentic. Angelo hurriedly gathered his contraband as it was time to leave. Mario left his post by the door and quietly returned to the men.

Without any words, Angelo aimed his silenced pistol at the heart of the printer and told him to turn around. With a surprised and terrified look, the man slowly turned and faced the table. His face cringed as he closed his eyes in anticipation of the bullet that would end his life. He braced himself on the chair by his side and gave one last glance at the picture of his boys. With tears welling up behind his despondent eyes, he readied himself and waited for the shot.

But after adjusting his aim, Angelo placed a single shot in the upper back by the shoulder of the printer. The poor man fell forward over the chair and landed on the floor with an acute cry of pain. Angelo's carefully positioned projectile wouldn't do any long-term damage, but would provide a life-saving excuse. Angelo and Mario helped the wounded man off the floor and told him it would be all right. Sitting him in the now up-righted chair, they relayed their journey.

"We called on two other printers, and they asked a lot of questions," Mario relayed. It was almost certain the Nazis would be showing up asking questions. They then fed the man his cover story.

He was to say that he did have two Italian-speaking men come in and demand papers. He initially refused but then led them to the production area with the idea to escape through a back door. He distracted the men by implying he heard someone knocking on the front door. One of the men went to the front door to investigate, and the other followed him to the entrance of the production room. When both were looking away toward the front of the facility, he ran for the back door and was shot in the back. The hardest part would be that he had to wait in the room, bleeding and in excruciating pain, until his workers found him when they came in for work in about an hour.

The man thanked Angelo and Mario for sparing his life. They had the printer lay on the ground in the position like he had fallen from a shot. Then, papers in hand, the men left the shop. Before proceeding, they made their way to a side alley where they each stopped to scope the surrounding area. Comfortable that their way back was initially clear, they stood out of the shadows and nervously smiled at each other. They were halfway through this impossible mission.

Mario had found a map of the city in the printer's office and was able to determine exactly where they were. They plotted a route back to the train station and hoped for an uneventful ride home. They both knew the papers would likely get tested the hard way at some point on the trip back. The early morning hour saw the streets full of people walking and vehicles of all types that, gratefully, were primarily civilians.

With an air about them that implied they belonged there and self-assured in their newly printed identity papers, the men made their way back to the train station.

Even though they felt confident they could get through any security checks with their disguise and papers, there was no point in "poking the beast."

"Let's stay low and at least make it to the train without being stopped," Mario suggested.

Angelo agreed, and they kept to alleys and streets that provided some cover, generally following the path Mario had determined the safest and fastest. As they walked, Angelo thought about Mario and how he felt completely comfortable and safe with his distant cousin. *At the start of this, I barely knew him and took him on at the advice of Zio Angelo. Now I would place my life in his hands. Zio would be so proud to see him in action.*

Mimicking their success from the previous night, they boarded an early morning train when it was at its busiest and had no issues getting back. It took them all day to get back to their base of operations in Val Gardena. Tired and spent, but finally safe.

CHAPTER 11

Pietro

November 29, 1943
Val Gardena, Italy

Everything changed with the addition of the forged identity papers. They could now travel to distant targets and be even more daring in their sabotage of critical infrastructure, weaponry, and troops. But it also meant they could winter in one area and develop local relationships who would provide critical security and supplies.

Angelo stood with his first cousin outside their temporary quarters overlooking the beautiful mountains before them. The men quietly stood, rubbing their hands together for warmth, simply enjoying the quiet. Eventually, Pietro turned to Angelo when he noticed the first snowflake of the day waft down near him. "The snow will start getting heavy, and we can't go down the mountain any further." Angelo concurred, but thought about the significance of the weather coming relative to the German and Fascist situation.

Being in the heart of Trentino and the South Tyrol in winter could only mean positive things, even though the Germans were becoming increasingly invested in the area. The southern border of Germany was her best hope to hold back the Allies, and she kept it reinforced with a steady stream of supplies. Even if the Allies could break through the mountains of Central Italy, they would still have to contend with the Dolomites and Alps, which have historically repelled conquerors for millennia.

This natural defense was a mixed bag militarily. On the one hand, it enabled Hitler to move critical troops north to shore up the Western Front in anticipation of an Allied invasion, which would later be D-Day. The mountainous border likewise freed up troops to resist the Russians rapidly approaching from the east. On the other hand, though, because of the steep mountains, troop movement and supply chains in winter were restricted to major roads. Few could, or even knew how, to use the rugged terrain to a military advantage. Angelo's men concluded that they could reduce significant German encounters by just staying off major roads. Coupled with a secure home base and the new ease of travel, they were entering a new level of capability and capacity.

The men wasted no time in visiting locals and getting to know the population. They assured the farmers and townsfolk that they would protect them from German and Fascist atrocities. At that time, there were two Italian governments fighting over these lands: the fascists that remained loyal to Mussolini and the Salò government in Northern Italy, recognized by the Axis governments, and the newly reconstituted monarchy of King Victor Emmanuel III in the South, recognized by the Allied governments.

From this point till the end of the war, many brigades of partisans, ultimately comprising over one hundred thousand men, would be forced to choose allegiances. Options included: one of the two formal governments, different factions of their ideologies, the Americans, British, or Communists coming from Russia. Too often though, they would viciously fight each other for local power and positioning. The in-fighting had Angelo increasingly grateful he turned down Paolo and the Garibaldi partisans.

In early December, Angelo's team connected with another group of partisans comprised of six men and three women that all came from the Val Gardena area. Their local knowledge and relationships with townspeople could ensure quality intel and additional capabilities. Angelo's team had already developed a reputation in the region, and their ability to navigate the terrain and wartime combatants to make it to Val Gardena put them in a leadership position.

Even though this new local group had some experience, Angelo's team had its history of success and fighting experience. Most importantly, Paolo had recommended they work under Angelo since they wouldn't work in his region. The new group yielded to Angelo's command, and the team accepted the new members. Their total force grew to sixteen combatants.

One of the women, actually a seventeen-year-old girl named Alessia, was particularly adept at communications. Her diminutive size and young age enabled her to pass through checkpoints with relative ease, all the while gleaning information about troop numbers and locations. The other two women were more mature and in their late thirties or so. While both were beyond courageous and willing to go on any mission with the men, Lucia in particular was an excellent shot. While many partisan groups diminished the role of women, typically used only to supply clothing, food, and information, Angelo's brigade welcomed them as true equals in all action. Each carried a rifle and participated in all enemy encounters.

One of the six new men, Rosario, was especially creative with explosives. He was much older than anyone else on the team, easily in his forties, complete with a middle-age potbelly and painful "sermons" that everyone respectfully listened to half-heartedly. He did, however, have a good level of experience, and he despised the Germans. "I was a child during the last war, and our family has never really recovered from that nightmare. All I want is to blow up as many Germans as possible."

Angelo anticipated leadership issues with Rosario because of the age difference. However, Rosario put that to rest almost immediately by declaring, "I'm honored to serve under you, Angelo. I know we will have great success!" Angelo genuinely appreciated the gesture but knew there was much he could learn from this motivated warrior. Along with Nini, Rosario would always be included in strategic planning moving forward.

Rosario's craft was well established, and he had been responsible for blowing up multiple bridges and convoys. His special skill was to dynamite an area far above a road or bridge outlet. He would specifically seek out a stretch of railroad or paved road that had a very steep embankment or cliff on the opposite side. When a particularly long or slow-moving convoy would pass, he would detonate his ordinance from thirty to fifty feet above the victim vehicles. The resulting rockslide would both fall onto the vehicles and damage the road under them. Lacking anywhere to go, the vehicles would end up either crushed, buried, or blocked.

The addition of these welcome and critical resources afforded new opportunities, and the team moved into high gear. Angelo did his best to immediately profile the new persons by whether they were "thinkers or doers." This quick assessment tool helped him understand the operational fit of the new assets. His hope was that he could identify and develop a few thinkers who could conduct operational planning and lead smaller teams. Rosario was a good start. The rest would be doers who had special skill sets to fill mission capability gaps. With increased resources and excellent new local intel now available, the scope of operations increased.

One such operation was to eliminate a critical rail spur that led from a fuel and munitions depot. It had Angelo, his cousin Pietro, and one of the new younger men named Marco taking out the train system. Pietro was not just a close cousin, but the life of any party. His face seemed to always carry a broad, infectious smile. The team all thought him more of a salesperson than soldier. Beyond a gifted combatant and survivalist, he and Nini were Angelo's closest confidants. Angelo would rely on Pietro's opinion for everything from operational planning to his postwar dreams. The two were simply best friends.

It was now December 10 and time to move on the mission. Angelo didn't know it, but the day would be remembered and grieved for the rest of his life.

Using their Gestapo disguises and papers, they easily made the trip into Vipiteno. The industrial area south of the Brenner Pass was essential to the German movements. It was a major railroad hub, heavily guarded by German troops stationed at the nearby Sprechenstein Castle. Major and repeated bombing raids had been attempted to destroy the railroads and the castle, but none had succeeded. The men cautiously walked the areas allowed for civilians and made mental notes of many crucial factors.

With their intel secured, the men boarded a the train for the trip back to Val Gardena. They assumed their usual traveling protocol with Pietro in the lead car and Angelo and Marco in the second car but still within viewing distance of each other. Angelo always required the men to stay within sight of each other unless absolutely unavoidable. But sometimes fate can hinge on the smallest occurrence, often changing minute by minute.

The train had just leveled off after struggling up a three-mile grade when two German guards entered at the forward car. "*Ausweispapiere!* [identity papers]," barked the first soldier to the entire car of passengers.

They immediately came upon Pietro seated in the first row of seats. Pietro promptly complied and looked straight ahead with an air of superiority and arrogance. Reviewing them carefully, the guard, believing him to be a Gestapo officer, didn't say a word. The soldier handed his papers back and slowly continued through the two cars until they came to Angelo. Marco was sitting in quiet observation across the aisle from Angelo and had not yet been approached. Angelo, acting lazily and with the authority of a Gestapo agent, complied when the guard wanted to see his papers. The guard uncomfortably proceeded to study them for a long time, with the second guard never taking his eyes off Angelo or his finger off the trigger of his automatic weapon. After several minutes of hushed discussion between the two guards, one stayed with Angelo and the other returned to the front car to reinvestigate Pietro's papers.

Marco understood a little German and could make out that the one guard thought the papers were a duplicate of ones he saw earlier, and he wanted to look at Pietro's papers again. Mario tapped his bag to get Angelo's attention and silently signaled that there was serious trouble. While the first guard returned to Pietro in the front car, the second guard stayed with Angelo to watch him. The guard then properly split his attention between watching to see what was happening in the front car and ensuring his partner had backup, and watching Angelo. The young guard, maybe nineteen years old, looked the perfect Hitler youth with blond hair, blue eyes, and muscular tone. From their body language, this young soldier was clearly the subordinate of the other.

To mentally lull the young guard watching him, Angelo shrugged his shoulders, closed his eyes, and appeared to try and get comfortable to fall asleep. His hope was the soldier would let his guard down, spend more time watching what was going on in the front car, and give them an opportunity to act if something went wrong. All three men then silently watched as the first guard approached Pietro and began questioning him. Pietro couldn't answer in German, and all the other passengers practiced good sense by not getting involved to translate. After a few minutes, the guard trained his Luger pistol at Pietro's chest, shouted an order, and motioned with his pistol to get up. Pietro stood up and put his hands in the air; he was under arrest.

Immediately, Marco drew his weapon and shot the guard watching Angelo. Both men made a dash for the train doors, overpowered several people, and jumped from the slow-moving train. Regaining their composure after a clumsy roll down the embankment, the two lay in the drainage swell at its bottom and paused to take stock of themselves. Angelo was unhurt, but Marco was in significant pain and had what appeared to be a separated shoulder. As normal, the men quickly ran into the woods to hide while they watched their comrade continue on in custody.

All of this happened within close proximity to the station and the train was still very close to the Sprechenstein Castle. Angelo assumed the engineer would observe protocol following an incident on a train by immediately breaking to a full stop. As he did, the unmistakable screeching noise of a train as it applied its brakes confirmed his expectations. It slowly came to a stop about a half mile from where Angelo and Marco had landed and directly opposite the Sprechenstein Castle.

Angelo was certain Pietro would be taken to the castle for questioning and processing. Marco, understanding the woods would be crawling with soldiers looking for them, wanted to do the proper thing and immediately leave. Angelo insisted that they needed to stay and see if they could rescue his cousin.

It was nearly dark and Marco's assessment was unfortunately correct. It was indeed too dangerous, and his shoulder needed medical attention. Yet because of his respect for Angelo and his understanding of the situation, he followed the orders of his leader. The men moved silently through the ever-darkening woods toward the base of the hilltop upon which the castle rested (*see photo reference 11.1, 11.2*).

As anticipated, a contingent of guards exited the train to search for the men. They gathered for a moment beside the train car the two had just jumped from to determine their move. Angelo and Marco hid silently behind a thicket of brush by a small log pile and watched. The moment lasted forever. If they came their way, they would be easily overpowered and would have no chance for escape. Marco bit down on his cap to stifle the painful scream he wanted to let out.

Luckily, and as expected by Angelo, they chose to look for the men along the tracks leading back to the city. Both men had hoped they would follow the logical choice. Angelo looked at Marco and smiled. "Who in their right mind would run toward the enemy base and all the soldiers stationed there?"

Marco shook his head, and they proceeded forward. But first, he attempted one more time to get Angelo to abandon a rescue effort. Angelo didn't even respond and simply moved forward.

The two climbed the small mountaintop and got unsettlingly close to the castle. All castles were built on hills or mountaintops to provide strategic advantage during medieval warring, and Sprechenstein was no exception. The stately structure, dating from the thirteenth century, once housed great noble families. But now it was home to a significant contingent of German forces. The elegant castle, however, refused to surrender her dignity even while housing a brood of vipers.

Studying the outside structure, they could see only a few lights, likely powered by generators. The normal power supply to the castle had been blown in air raids long ago. The only exception were the spotlights mounted on the top of the walls that illuminated the exterior. While there was plenty of natural cover from the spotlights, Angelo worried there may be dogs inside the castle. Being less than one hundred feet from the castle walls, the trained animals could potentially pick up their scent and give up their position.

On two occasions, they heard rustling sounds in the distance back by the tracks. Certainly, German soldiers, but likely some train guards because they didn't hear any dogs. Any patrols that would have originated from the castle would certainly utilize guard dogs.

Angelo had a tremendous fear of German guard dogs. The thought of them chasing, catching, and repeatedly biting him was his most dire fear. These animals were trained to literally rip a victim apart. The Nazi's assumption was if the dogs are chasing you, then you likely need to die or suffer. The sound of their barking alone brought chills to his body. Worse yet, he had heard stories of the Germans letting the dogs inflict damage to the victim even after the person was captured, supposedly to reinforce the dog's training. Perhaps there was some truth in that, but Angelo was certain it was more the sadistic men controlling the dogs. Either way, he wasn't about to get caught running from the dogs under any circumstance.

The men moved up behind some brush and sat within ear's distance of the castle walls. Angelo nervously bit his nails and racked his brain for ideas to rescue his cousin. Mario minded to his tender shoulder and kept nagging Angelo to get out as there was no hope. Ideas flooded Angelo's consciousness, only to be shot down quickly for one reason or another. After about thirty minutes, they could hear noises and yelling from inside the walls. After a mere five more minutes, they simultaneously saw the lights flickering and heard Pietro screaming. After fifteen minutes, the same thing happened again. Angelo was riddled with anger and fear at the same time. They were electrocuting his cousin to gain information, and he couldn't imagine anything he could do about it. With him only carrying a sidearm and Marco nursing a separated shoulder, there just wasn't much of anything they could do.

Nazi electrocution methods were crude but highly effective. The first utilized an electroshock type gun. It was applied directly to the heart area or head and could result in quick death. The second used electrodes placed on strategic parts of the body that send electric currents through it. This type was the most common used in torture because its duration and strength could easily be adjusted. It also resulted in the most pain. The electrical resistance generated caused deep and debilitating burns.

They sat there for what seemed like days listening to the torture and trying to find some way to rescue him or at least cause a distraction. They could hear Pietro wailing in pain and agony, first crying out for his mother and then later Jesus. There was nothing they could do, and worse yet, they knew Pietro would ultimately say something under the horrific torture. Angelo felt like his soul was dying by a thousand cuts. Every time Pietro would cry out in absolute pain, Angelo wanted to also let out a scream, hoping that a primal release would ease his pain and anguish.

The repeated cycles of electrocution, flickering lights, and screams continued for two hours. Several times during their torture, Angelo could actually hear men laughing inside. Laughing, as if they were in a bar watching a couple of drunks in a fistfight instead of a man barely clinging to life. Pietro was in unspeakable pain, with his body slowly dying, and these animals thought it was amusing.

"I swear we'll get Pietro out, and we are going to kill every one of these bastards!" Angelo whispered to Marco. But Marco wanted nothing to do with it. He, too, loved Pietro, but he knew they had to get out while they could. Finally, after a short while, the lights flickered once again, but there was no more screaming. For a short period of time, there were no sounds at all. Angelo's opportunity for rescue, however implausible or impossible, had now passed. The silence was almost worse than the screams of pain. Angelo's cousin had perished, and Angelo was forever changed.

With any chance of hope now lost, the morning came rushing upon them. Angelo's lips quivered in anger as he gave the order to leave, even though his heart sought revenge. Silently, they started to make their way back to the train tracks. As they walked, his mind wrestled with the conflicting thoughts of hatred and desire to kill every German he could and fond memories of all the two cousins had shared since childhood.

Initially, anger won. Marco tried to console Angelo, but he would have none of it. After a while though, he moved beyond the anger to his love for Pietro. He couldn't imagine what he was going to tell his aunt and uncle when the war was over. How could he even conceive delivering such terrible news? The thoughts were incapacitating, and they walked for miles without saying a word. Eventually, Marco needed to stop walking because his shoulder was in so much pain. Angelo snapped out of his numbness and finally paid attention to Marco and his situation. He needed immediate attention to have the shoulder set properly.

Angelo, without any idea of what he was doing, told Marco to place his cap in his mouth between his teeth. This was going to be painful, and they needed to silence his scream. Angelo took one more look at the shoulder hanging limply and told Marco to lean against a large boulder and to take a deep breath. Then with little fanfare and no notice, Angelo shoved the shoulder back into place. Marco nearly bit through the wool cap in pain, but it was done.

Angelo let Marco sit for a while to recover his strength. Shortly though, the men were forced to continue their journey. Fortunately, they soon came upon a junction in the road and hitchhiked back. It was late morning, and they hoped to find an Italian farmer or worker who would have pity on them. They knew they only had one chance. If they stumbled on a German or Fascist, they would be turned in. But they had to try or Marco would have become too great of a liability in their escape.

Luckily, the man they flagged down was indeed an Italian worker who had just finished an extended shift in the nearby industrial area. Realizing the pain Marco was in, he gave the men a ride all the way back to Ponte Gardena, the intersecting town where the road to Val Gardena exited the autostrada. There, they were able to take the uneventful forty-five-minute train ride back to their base.

Exhausted, Marco collapsed into a sound sleep within a few minutes of the train's departure. Angelo stayed on guard and silently thought. His mind drifted to better times as they rode past the southern Dolomite Mountains and mighty Mount Perez, standing at nearly nine thousand feet in elevation and already completely covered in deep snow. The dry light snow caught in the morning sun's bright light resembled diamonds briefly falling from heaven. He thought of Pietro and his life in the same way: beautiful but fleeting.

Angelo spent the time on the train dreaming of every conceivable way to get back at the Germans. Still, he found himself surprised that even though surrounded by pain, inhumanity, and death, God's handiwork couldn't be restrained. So beautiful yet strangely hollow after the loss of Pietro.

As he rode in silence, Angelo's mind knelt at the foot of the invisible cross that his heart saw perfectly. The world and the war were temporarily silenced as he prayed once again for survival and the elimination of the pestilence from their lands. At one point, he thought of his enemy as unfortunates caught up in a war they didn't ask for, just like him. But this experience changed him. "*Animale tutti*," he said to himself; all of them animals in need of slaughter.

The train lurched heavily as it shifted and changed tracks, bringing him back to his frightening operational realities. How much intel did Pietro give up before he perished? Their names? Home base? Support network? It was almost too much to bear. Pietro would be strong, but who could fully resist while being tortured as he was?

Certainly, from the identity papers, they knew where the team had been. They also likely knew the extent of the damage Pietro and the team had done and perhaps even his name. But the real issue was how much the guard from the train could remember of Angelo. Could he recognize him or make him out in a crowd? Could he provide enough information for a sketch?

As the men reunited with the team, alarm bells went off in every member. Angelo expected a mass desertion, and he honestly wouldn't blame anyone. How could he? The new part of the team had only been involved with Angelo's team a short time, and the result of Pietro's torture would likely be catastrophic. For all they knew, the Germans were on their way that minute to execute every one of them.

Angelo gave a speech offering anyone the chance to leave with no hard feelings. They were now compromised, and separating into different cells in other regions was likely best. One of the newer men and a woman did fall out and leave, and Angelo never knew what happened to them after that. But, surprisingly, the rest of the team stayed. Indeed, they vowed to become even more brazen in their attacks to avenge the life of Pietro whom everybody loved like a brother. As he looked into the faces of the members still there, he was humbled by their devotion, courage, and determination.

Unfortunately, their boldness didn't last. In the ensuing weeks, they still carried out reconnaissance and planning, but everyone also assumed an extremely defensive posture, waiting for the inevitable door to be knocked down and a spray of bullets to take them out. Still, as a new day followed the night, the winter snows came and buried the land. In this part of the world, that means movement was nearly impossible. There would be no more faraway raids until the weather supported an appropriate exfil. Angelo's strategic planning had not changed: start with how to get out first and then determine how to conduct the operation.

Photo Reference 11.1 -

The site of Pietro's torture and electrocution, Sprechenstein Castle in the South Tyrol, as seen from the valley and tracks below. Angelo and Marco hiked up the slope and hid beneath the trees along the left wall where they could easily hear the torture from inside.

Photo Reference 11.2 -

The location of Pietro's torture. This is inside the walls of the Sprechenstein Castle. The cut-out areas of the walls housed machine gunners looking out onto the woods where Angelo hid. The specific location of the torture was in between the two machine guns close to the wall.

CHAPTER 12

Everyone Sacrifices

December 25, 1943
Val Gardena, Italy

Christmas. It hadn't even been a month since losing Pietro, and the emotional wound that cut deeply into Angelo had barely scarred over. Even the rest of the team felt dejected and disheartened. Anger had surrendered to gloom. Angelo looked around the room at his men and tried hard to remember their faces from better times.

Gianni was once again winning virtually every hand of cards played. While one might think it wouldn't matter because they shared everything and were only playing for pride, the men inevitably accused him of cheating. After undeserved accusations that sometimes became heated, he was regularly forced to take guard duty during the worst weather. Gianni didn't mind. It was a badge of honor that he had to sit outside in the cold and snow because he was the superior card player.

Lucia and Alessia were sitting off to the side talking and darning the holes in everyone's clothing. It was an unspoken law that the men not approach the women in any personal or romantic way. Even though both would have turned a head or two before the war, nothing happened. Staying alive meant staying professional, and the relations between the men and women in the team were always businesslike. It didn't really matter now because everyone was clearly drained emotionally and just treading water.

The war had taken its ugly toll on the townspeople as well. There were no Christmas celebrations. Food was in short supply. Medicines were not to be found anywhere. Even firewood was regularly stolen by marauding gangs and families alike. People were just hanging on and surviving.

Unfortunately, it was about to get much worse.

But for now as the normally merry day pressed on, Angelo's Christmas memories brought moments of quiet happiness. As the special day progressed, the entire team felt their spirits lighten and laughter could be heard coming from the dilapidated barn that was the base camp. By evening, sitting around a crackling fire, the team decided to do something unorthodox. They went into the town to thank the families that were supporting them. Knowing that the German troops in and around the town would be gathering together in their own celebrations, they surmised that there would be few, if any, troops on guard. This region was still solidly under German control, so there was no need to maintain extensive defenses. Quietly and in small groups of two, they visited many homes and wished blessings upon those helping to keep them alive. It wasn't much, but most of the people gratefully entertained them in their homes for a while with all they had to share - prayers and conversation. It wasn't as nice as the previous Christmas spent with family in Genoa, but it did make everyone feel better.

By New Year, they got tired of self-pity and boredom, and there was a new desire to get back into action. Nothing was going to bring Petro back, but they could avenge his torture and death by resuming operations. They wanted to continue making a difference. They were rested, spiritually invigorated, and loaded with regional intel. Undertaking missions far from their base was unfeasible as the weather caused increased enemy exposure, but everyone wanted to get back in the game. Back to the art of sabotage at which they had become very capable.

They wasted no time identifying their first target; a small fuel and ammunition dump on the other side of the valley that served the local army regulars. Blowing it up would reduce the enemy's ability to refuel the supply caravans which regularly brought critical sustaining supplies farther south in Italy toward the Gothic Line.

Lucia began to gather in-depth intel by innocently walking past the depot every day for a week to determine the body of force protecting it. Because there were trucks coming and going all the time, the number of men guarding the supplies varied significantly at different times of the day. It seemed that in the early hours of the morning they would encounter the least amount of resistance. Antonio was one of the team's newer men from this valley and had significant local knowledge, so Angelo had him lead a four-man team.

Antonio was a big man. His appetite was always the largest on the team, and he took significant ribbing over how he would always be the one to eat the last scrap of anything edible. He would smile, and his quiet demeanor would never retaliate in any way. The men felt that fortunate as he could take any of them in a fight with just one arm and his trusty knife.

At dusk, the men began their hike to the depot. As they made their way on a trail through the woods, they were surprised by a rifle company of German regulars. With the cover of the night, they were able to retreat and make it back to the base without incident. The men guessed that the Germans smartly reinforced the surrounding woods to impede any longer-range attacks against the depot via mortars and the like.

The team elected to pass on the depot and find an easier target. Another of the local men knew of a rail line that was a spur from the main line through the Brenner Pass. Antonio again led two local men and went off on the five-mile hike to recon the area and assess its target viability. Three days later, the three returned and delivered their intelligence report. They determined that there wasn't any large-scale German force in the remote area. Although it was possible to run into patrolling guards, it was as good as a target as they could expect.

The tunnel they targeted had only one rail line going through it, but it seemed to carry a lot of traffic based on the condition of the rails and surrounding vegetation. Learning from the past, they started playing it safer. They would blow the entrance while there were no trains in the vicinity. While it wouldn't damage any trains or cargo, it would render the tracks inoperable for weeks, and they were less likely to run into any enemy force.

The plan was to wait for a day when it appeared that snow would likely come. From growing up in the mountains, most of the men could not only tell you *if* snow was coming but also specifically *when* the storm would happen as well. They planned to place and set off the charges, then escape through the woods where the new falling snow would hide their tracks. Once through the woods, skis would be utilized in the large valley that they needed to cross. The team discussed all the ways the operation could fail, as well as its risks, rewards, and entry and exit strategies.

For several hours, the exchanges progressed as they diligently worked toward a go- or no-go decision. After hours of discussion and countering opinions, there was a consensus that the operation had a high potential reward with manageable risk. Besides, the team was itching to deliver on an operation of significance. Ultimately, everyone agreed it seemed a valuable opportunity and deemed the mission a go.

Three days later, all the conditions seemed perfect for a major snowfall that evening. The men gathered their weapons, explosives, and other tools of the trade; carried their skis on their backs; and began the five-mile hike. Leaving base camp at midmorning, they would be at the site by midafternoon with time to set the charges above the entry to the tunnel. Detonating the payload by late afternoon would have them back by evening, just as the snow would begin falling to cover their tracks. With high hopes, Angelo led the team of six men and Lucia.

Everything went according to plan, and they reached a hidden rally point some five hundred feet from the tunnel entrance by about three in the afternoon. Pausing, they carefully assembled the satchel charges and dynamite bundles, then wired the remote detonation plunger assembly. A few newer men's hands shook from either the cold or nervousness. After about another thirty minutes, they began carefully walking around the tunnel entrance to place the ordinates over the entryway. Three men climbed the mountain that formed the tunnel's side and roof while the other three men kept guard watching for trouble. Lucia positioned herself behind a fallen tree some two hundred feet from the men to provide an optimum line of sight.

In a stroke of bad luck, two German soldiers emerged from the entrance to have a cigarette just as the men were approaching the placement location for the bombs. They were unarmed and appeared to have been working inside the tunnel, probably repairing damaged track. Matteo, Daniello, and Mario above them had no idea the soldiers were below them and began moving rocks and earth to place the bombs. Hearing the commotion above them, the soldiers stopped to see what was going on. Quickly realizing the danger above them, they turned to run back into the tunnel.

Lucia, the sharpshooter, didn't hesitate. Her initial bullet struck the first soldier, and he dropped immediately. Unfortunately, the second dove back into the protection of the tunnel and escaped her second shot. Her third shot eliminated the downed soldier as he began crawling back toward the safety of the tunnel.

Hearing the commotion below and shots fired, the men dropped their satchels and dynamite and ran off to the side of the mountain. Just as they made it to the tunnel base, a host of German soldiers emerged from the tunnel entrance firing at will. Angelo, Antonio, Benino, and Lucia provided covering fire as best as possible, but Daniello and Mario fell as they ran for cover.

Matteo managed to make it to the rally point, and the entire team exercised a coordinated retreat, with two men supplying suppressive fire to hold the Germans in place while the rest of the team climbed up to a safe position. Once in place behind the protection of some boulders, they provided covering fire for the two men still below. This proceeded for about an hour, with the Germans continuing their pursuit uphill. Angelo wasn't sure of exactly how many men were chasing them, but it was surely more than a dozen.

Having good local terrain knowledge, they proceeded ahead of the Germans and stopped at a shallow cave to rest and regroup. The men started to argue about what went wrong and if they could find a way to retrieve the bodies of their lost friends.

Angelo, after reloading his weapon and checking the status of everyone, determined they needed to keep going and leave immediately. It was fortuitous that they only lost ten minutes because as soon as they proceeded again, the Germans had caught up to them and the chase began anew.

Because it was now getting dark, the logical approach would have been to find a railroad track, road, or other trail to follow. But Angelo assumed that the German team had radioed for backup and the roads and trails would be covered by fresh troops that had driven ahead in an ambush attempt. Instead, Angelo led the team through the darkening woods, away from any landmarks and eventually toward a large open valley.

The men walked through creeks and climbed up and then down two mountain tops. Exhausted and close to life-threatening hypothermia, they persisted in their desperate escape. After about an hour, the snow came. It was the heavy-wet type, and the dangerous snowfall became steadier as the night progressed. Reaching the valley, they rested for five minutes, donned their skis, and continued their withdrawal.

Normally, the snow would have aided their getaway. Had they made their escape before the snow fell, as planned, it would have served to cover any tracks they left behind. But now, with the wet snow already down while still retreating, any trailing troops could easily follow their movements. Angelo could only pray that they had put adequate space between themselves and the Germans. He hoped the enemy had been thrown off by walking through creeks and wet areas a painfully long time, and by being on skis for a good part of the distance.

Completely exhausted, the team reached the old barn, their makeshift base of operations. Most of the men immediately collapsed into a deep sleep. They didn't even ready their weapons for the possibility of being followed. Nini and those that didn't participate in the operation were stunned. Grasping that the team had nothing left, Nini instructed those not involved in the operation to inspect and make ready the weapons and arms allocations of their comrades. "Let's get these guys ready in case we need to act fast." He then instructed Gianni and Allessio to guard duty.

Despite his condition, Angelo insisted on taking part in the first watch shift. As they went out to take position, Nini came over to join him and began asking questions about the operation. Angelo appreciated his concern but told him he needed to be alone. Nini knew his cousin well enough not to argue and went to check the status of the other two on guard duty. Even though Angelo was completely exhausted, his mind ran wild as the gravity of this blown operation took control. The obvious initial concern was that the Germans could surprise them at any moment if they were indeed able to follow them. Angelo and everyone else knew they would be no match for the large force, but he felt fairly confident they made it to the barn without being followed.

No, the greater concern for him was the explosives left behind. The satchel coverings were made by a local woman who, during peace time, made purses. The dynamite came courtesy of a local mine theft, which the enemy might be able to trace. Even the plunger was made using local materials.

It took about four days for Angelo's fears to become reality. The operation wasn't exposed, but the German SS and Gestapo came to town intent on finding this local partisan gang of saboteurs. The Germans proceeded to systematically harass and torture the town's inhabitants for information.

Unfortunately, the team had been identified by the German war machine for elimination. A gang as sophisticated and advanced in operational methods as theirs had to be hunted down and destroyed. The nuisance had officially become a pest.

Life for the local population during the German occupation had been more difficult than one can imagine, but now it became overtly dangerous. Random individuals or those suspected of supporting Angelo's "terrorist organization" would be arrested, held, and questioned at random. Any sign of guilt or weakness would signal the Germans to ratchet up their sadistic actions. The threat of torture would often times be enough to turn individuals. When it didn't, a few were often taken captive and made "examples" of.

This general destruction of the people continued for several days. During this time, the team had to bear the pain of knowing what others were suffering on their behalf. The local people all remained quiet until the mother of Benino gave in and confessed what she knew. She begged forgiveness for her son, explaining that her husband had been killed in Russia fighting with the Germans. It was to no avail. That morning the SS took her and her daughter to the front of the village's butcher shop and hung them with meat hooks through their backs. It was a slow and painful way to die, with two insidious purposes: one, to instill terror on anyone witnessing or hearing about the spectacle and two, to draw the intended quarry in. Benino's mother only clung to life for a little over an hour, but his sister wouldn't yield her last breath for another eight hours.

Nobody was allowed to assist the victims or remove the bodies after death until the Germans got who they wanted. Friends weren't even given permission to clean the puddles of blood under each body. The intent of the gruesome undertaking was to force the man they were looking for to make a rash or emotional move. That day, Benino and Lucia did just that. They vowed to stay and exact revenge on the Germans for their atrocity. Angelo vigorously fought to make them realize the folly of their plans. He urged them to instead follow him away from town to fight another day. But unimaginable anger and the need to avenge two wrongful murders trumped anything Angelo could say, and they tearfully parted ways.

As Angelo could no longer rely on the townspeople to keep them alive and provide intel, they agreed to leave immediately. Determining who he could and could not trust would now become a daily exercise. Those who would gain from turning him in were literally everywhere, and it would take resources to forge new relationships where he would feel safe.

With it now mid-February, the dead of winter, Angelo had to lead his remaining team out into the wilderness mountains. His plan was to proceed directly west, back along the base of Mount Perez to the Barbian area. It was similar to the area of Val Gardena and still a solidly Trentini region, a place where they could hopefully replicate the support they had at Val Gardena.

The team set out and walked about three days when they realized the futility of their quest. The terrain in the middle of winter was essentially impossible to navigate, particularly with little food and no shelter. Reluctantly, the decision was made to return to the Val Gardena area. As the team made their way back, they simply couldn't avoid the frequent German troop movements in and around the town. Fortunately, the continuing snow and wind enabled them to move discreetly and avoid direct contact.

The team decided to settle in at the very small town of Uletta, comprised of about five farm houses and a dozen barn structures (*see photo reference 12.1*). Uletta was only a short hike up a manageable mountain slope from Val Gardena and at the base of the Geisler Mountains. From its hilltop location, it provided an unobstructed view down the farmed hillsides. There wasn't a great deal of cover, but it did offer plenty of notice should anyone come looking. In addition, the west side of town was a very short sprint to the dense forest leading up to rugged terrain, providing an ideal opportunity for escape.

Fortunately, Alessia had known one of the farmers since she was a child, so getting a barn close to the woods where they could stay was easily accomplished. Gratefully, it was a barn filled with firewood and not attractive to roaming bands of soldiers looking for food or contraband. The scattered stacks of firewood also made great cover should they get into a firefight.

To further their safety, the team dug a large hole under the floor of the barn sizeable enough to fit several men. The excavation was difficult, but if they couldn't escape to the woods, they could at least go underground and hopefully avoid detection. If they had to use the pit, the idea was to cover the opening with loosely fitted floorboards that could let air in and then pile stacks of wood over removeable boards. Angelo dreaded the idea of being locked underground with no light and in complete silence. "Please, Lord, keep me from having to use this coffin," he prayed as he dug.

The farmer knew all about the murders in Val Gardena and was willing to make any sacrifice to avenge the deaths of his extended neighbors. This was fortunate because the plan hinged on him. If the Germans approached and they couldn't make it safely to the woods, he would be relied on to secure them. That night, as the men sat and ate with their new host, they learned the fate of the teammates who stayed behind.

The morning after the hanging, while the bodies were still on the hooks, Benino and Lucia entered town to do as much damage as possible. They proceeded to blow up the small hotel used by the Germans as a makeshift headquarters, killing several of the enemy. Unfortunately, the bulk of the Germans were waiting in other village buildings. When the explosion went off, they descended on the two unfortunates and quickly eliminated the threat. The next day, thinking that they had killed the underground unit causing them so much trouble, the entire contingent abruptly left the village. As the town had no significant military value, they executed a complete pullout and didn't bother to leave any troops behind.

*****

As the winter turned to spring, the men continued conducting relatively minor operations, trying not to raise any suspicions. In addition, they were careful to mend fences with the people of Val Gardena. The team still needed their intel and resources. Given the horrible winter and the team's recent and significant losses, they also needed to regain their emotional strength. As Angelo would later say, "If one's heart is not in the fight, then the fight won't last long."

Photo Reference 12.1 –

This is Uletta. The barn that was used as the headquarters for the men is near the trees to the center right.

CHAPTER 13

Antonio, the Knifeman

May 12, 1944
Uletta, northeast of Val Gardena, Italy

Rumors of an Allied invasion on the European mainland finally reached the remote outpost where Angelo and his team were still holed up. The Allied advance up the spine of Italy had come to a brutal stalemate throughout the winter and spring of the year. The team believed that opening the Northern and Western Fronts would likely relieve some German troop presence in Tyrolian territory and Northern Italy. A welcome and hopeful development to be sure.

In addition to the anticipated Allied invasion, the Russians were making steady progress into Eastern Europe. Though they had initially been overpowered by Germany to within just miles of Moscow, the Russians now had significant success along their Southern Front closest to Italy; they had actually fought back and reclaimed all of the Ukraine, Romania, Bulgaria, and much of Hungary (*see map reference 13.1*).

The Russian communist model didn't necessarily appeal to most Italians, but they did send messages of support to the various partisan groups. They urged the people of the Tyrol to rise up and one day take their homeland back the way the Russians had done. The key to a new Tyrol was for a revolutionary uprising of the people against both the German occupation and Italian monarchy.

Assuming that Russia would likely control huge amounts of land after the war, and having had enough of fascism and monarchist leaders, many of the partisan forces declared allegiance to communist principles. Angelo's team never fully committed to the Russian influence on partisan organization,s but was supportive of others. "The Americans and will go back across the ocean, and the British the sea, but the Russians will remain on European soil. Call it anything you want, if it gets us a free and independent Trentino, I'm for it!" Angelo would later recall.

The result became dozens of partisan brigades fighting very loosely alongside each other against Germany and the Fascists, the common enemy. Perhaps not surprisingly, most were aligned with the Communists. While Angelo was encouraged by potential Russian support of a new Tyrol, and he was sympathetic to the Communists, his particular partisan brigade would retain strict independence. They knew who they were, their principles, and the reasons for sacrificing their lives. They were fighting for Trentino and Tyrol, not for Russia and communism, not for Italy and nationalism, and not for America and democracy.

Amid the bitter cold of the winter and the snowmelt of the spring, the team continued its reconnaissance and planning work. But the eventual warming of the weather made the team itchy to reengage and get back into action. The devastating wounds from earlier events had healed over satisfactorily, and they were once again ready to be an organized military unit.

After some minor engagements ambushing patrols and generally being belligerent pests, they decided it was time for a strategic operation. The selected target was a railroad station and yard where many trains sat ready for the Germans to ship personnel and equipment to the Italian front in the center of the country. The Americans had seen early successes in southern Italy, but were now paying dearly for every inch of Italian soil. While slow by every measure, the push from the south by the Americans kept steadily edging its way north from Central Italy, particularly after the fall of Monte Cassino.

Their mark was an offshoot of the main rail yard in Trento. The small switching center was located about thirty miles north of the main terminal and holding yard in Zambana. As such, it was significantly less guarded than its more strategic counterpart to the south. Allied bombing ran routinely, targeting the main yard in Trento, but this smaller yard remained unscathed. Importantly, this adjunct yard was still on the critical north-south line that carried indispensable German train traffic.

Getting to Zambana would require the team to once again use their forged papers and ride the rails, as the distance was about sixty miles from Val Gardena. They would first ride from Val Gardena to the Waidbruk-Lajen train terminal in Ponte Gardena. They would then take the train south and connect in Bolzano. After this connection, it was a direct ride to Zambana.

Unfortunately, the nature of the mission limited the team size to just three men, something Angelo tried to avoid. A strategic retreat required at least four men, ideally five or more. The team now numbered ten and maintained plenty of strength if they wanted to risk more men. But the mission was more of a burglary than a street fight. The goal was to get in and out unnoticed and to avoid enemy contact at all costs. Given the value of the mission and its goals, they settled on going in with a three-man team. Angelo picked Nini and Antonio, his two most experienced soldiers, to join him on this dangerous mission.

The weather was a picture-perfect spring day when they started their journey south. To avoid suspicion, they traveled past their destination and exited the train at the northernmost station for Trento. Once disembarked, they made their way by foot to the switching station at Zambana, a little less than three hours via some back trails.

Part of their disguise was that each member would carry a briefcase containing some papers, spare clothing, dried foods, and common personal items. They would try and appear to be Gestapo agents on a short trip if something went wrong and they were questioned. However, the *valise* of one of the men would carry the explosives and detonation equipment. Spare clothing was worn under their outer clothing to provide extra dry layers should they need to escape on foot.

The exit strategy for this mission first had the men hitchhiking and walking the back roads in a circuitous route. Then they would get a ride from a local farmer, hike through the alternating farms and rugged terrain a while, obtain another ride from a different person, and repeat several times. It was a well-established method to throw off anyone potentially chasing them.

The operation began well enough. As expected, they found a significant number of guards in areas which housed rail cars containing strategic cargo. However, there were two areas close to the fence and relatively unguarded. The men carefully left their reconnaissance point and stomach-crawled to the security fencing surrounding the yard. Angelo and Nini kept guard while Antonio cut a sizeable hole in the fencing. Using only his knife, Antonio silently neutralized a guard between the fence and target rail cars. As they drew nearer to the target, two more guards were dispatched to their fate via Antonio's efficient knifework.

They then quickly hid their payload in the undercarriage of random train cars parked in strategic locations on the line. The contents of the cars were less important than disabling the tracks. Stopping for just seconds, they hurriedly scanned the area for probing eyes. Maintaining their clandestine invisibility, they set their timers for thirty minutes and swiftly exited through the hole in the fence.

The men were free of the fence for only a few minutes when they heard the whistle of a guard discovering one of his fallen comrades. Angelo gambled that even though the Germans knew something was up, they wouldn't have enough time to find the bombs. Having purposely placed the bombs in cars away from the fallen soldiers, they would be the last places searched. If they discovered the cut fence, again, it would only draw them to look for explosives in the wrong area first. Either way, the Germans wouldn't discover anything until it was too late.

The three men made their way as far as they could with the thirty-minute lead time they had. At zero hour plus twenty minutes from their exit, they began looking to hitch a ride. Because there weren't many privately owned vehicles in operation at this time in the war, giving hitchhikers a ride was considered a courteous and normal thing to do.

It only took a few minutes for a welcomed ride to come along. They quickly climbed into the vehicle, with Angelo in front and Nini and Antonio cramming themselves in the back between piles of cargo. Minutes later, the explosions from the railyard could be heard in the distance. The driver instinctively braked and immediately looked at Angelo in the passenger seat beside him with a look of dread. After a few seconds of tense silence, he started driving again. The vehicle continued without a word spoken between the two.

After about twenty minutes, Nini asked the driver to stop and let them out. It was time to switch vehicles and move in another direction. Angelo thanked the man, and the three made their way through the woods to a different road. Hopefully another willing vehicle would appear shortly. But then misfortune struck. The roads were now teeming with German troops looking for the saboteurs. Since it was late in the evening at this point, the men elected to forego securing vehicles and began walking back. They would need to exploit as much of the night's darkness as possible to safely complete their journey. Not wanting to risk any additional rides, the assumption was that they would be walking the entire distance.

As morning broke, they decided to stop their hike back to camp and take a much-needed rest. As they sat at the base of a rocky ledge, gathering their thoughts and breath, they were surprised by enemy troop movement just fifty yards from them.

The ledge extended outward on the hillside and rested on a collection of large boulders, seemingly placed there to support it. Each man ducked for cover, crawling deep under the ledge or behind the boulders. The team was completely hidden from view in short order. As they maintained complete silence, they watched the contingent of German soldiers walk directly past their position without incident. The cadence of the German troops echoed in the mountains as their boot heels struck the rocks.

Regrouping after the close call, the men crawled out from their concealments. They began brushing themselves clean from the dirt, discussing the close call just experienced. Unfortunately, they didn't see the second contingent of soldiers following behind the first. The enemy force, numbering about two dozen, opened fire on the men and pinned them to their positions. A short firefight ensued, with the Germans moving steadily on their obscured spot. The first group that had passed them immediately circled back to join the fight. Fortunately, for the team, the leading soldiers were still a fair distance from them. Two of the German forward men threw grenades in the direction of the team, falling well short of their position behind the boulders. Taking advantage of the resulting cover from smoke and debris, Angelo's team ran in full retreat.

Exploiting the momentary chaos and without planning, they ran in different directions. Nini and Angelo went up over the hilltop while Antonio went along a path away from the enemy. At the top of the hill, Nini and Angelo continued running but in opposite directions. No goodbyes, no silent glances, just a full-out sprint through the heavy woods and rocky outcroppings.

Angelo ran until he couldn't take another step. It was now midday, and he was lost, exhausted, and hungry. He rested by the side of a local trail that had some track marks, praying that some sort of transportation would come by soon.

That prayer would soon be answered by a farmer pulling a hay cart. After the initial surprise of the farmer, he looked at Angelo and straight up asked him if he was the saboteur that blew up the train yard. Angelo didn't flinch. Looking the man directly in the eyes, he said yes, and he was trying to make it to safety. Without any hesitation, the farmer thanked Angelo for his work and told him to bury himself under the hay in the cart. Angelo sat on the rear of the broken-down cart and worried it wouldn't even hold his weight. He made a small hole in the hay and started working his way into it. Between the animals pulling the cart unevenly, the dirt road riddled with holes and ruts, and wagon wheels that could barely be considered round, the rickety cart had Angelo jostling uncontrollably.

Within five minutes of lying in the hay, Angelo began sneezing. At first it was just an occasional sneeze, but within minutes, it was regular and uncontrollable. The dust from the hay was irritating Angelo's grass allergies, and he simply couldn't restrain his sneezing. The farmer became extremely nervous at the muffled noise coming from his hay pile in the cart.

After about only ten minutes, the farmer told Angelo to jump off. Not only was the sneezing going to eventually give them away, but they were coming onto a road which had a military checkpoint and many German and Fascist units on it. Angelo immediately thanked the man, apologized for his endangering sneezes, jumped off, and ran into the woods. The farmer continued, and a few minutes later, he was indeed stopped and the soldiers thoroughly searched the hay in the cart. Had he stayed on the cart, both men would have surely been executed.

Angelo was on foot again but closer to home and relative safety. While walking, he prayed for Nini and Antonio, hopeful they would all make it back safely.

The walk back was treacherous. The Germans had obviously made it a priority to find and eliminate the team. There would be no ride, and he would need to walk the gauntlet of potential capture all the way back to their base.

After two more days, Angelo had made it far enough to recognize the unique Rosengarten group of mountain peaks. Because of its position to the sun and structure, the cluster often produced a rose or pinkish tone that furnished its name. The huge mastiff was like a beacon that could be seen from great distances (*see photo reference 13.2*). Another three days of walking and he would be near Val Gardena. Walking at night and resting a good part of the day, he cautiously hiked toward the familiar landmark. By dawn's slow awakening, every step was a labor and his hunger was affecting his stamina. The decision to stop along a picturesque lake for the day was an easy one.

Exhausted, he allowed himself a few moments to take in the bright morning sun over the pristine Alpine lake, sparkling like snow in the summer. The encompassing quiet was only broken by the occasional songbird. Then utilizing the heavy pine boughs that were all around, he made a bed and camouflaged sleeping quarters. Not a comfortable setting to most, but heavenly to the exhausted man.

The lodging was one he had made hundreds of times in the past, even as a boy playing not that far from this very location. He started with several sturdy branches which would be positioned between two trees facing the wind. Pine boughs and leafy branches were then placed over the side facing the wind, with the reverse side left open.

The design not only broke the wind and provided shelter in case of rain but also the open side could enable a quick exit in the unlikely event he would hear someone coming through the woods. With his completed shelter, he proceeded to secure a dinner of fresh fish.

The small lake was shallow enough to wade in a fair distance. Reaching for one of his German stick grenades, he readied himself by dropping everything and freeing his hands completely. He then carefully unscrewed the base of the device to detonate it. A few seconds after throwing the grenade into the lake close to shore, it exploded several feet below the surface. The blast created a large splash of water but very little noise.

Within minutes, fish began succumbing to the underwater concussion and popped to the surface. Angelo greedily grabbed the biggest he saw. Taking his knife and flint, he hurriedly made a small fire. The pine cones and pine kindling that were all around enabled the fire to catch quickly. While waiting for the modest fire to become hot enough, he crudely gutted the fish, threw them in the fire, waited for them to cook thoroughly, and then enjoyed his feast.

The rest of the morning and early afternoon were spent sleeping. Angelo groggily said to himself when he finally awoke, "If I can get to the mountain foothills, there shouldn't be any more interference." But just getting to the mountain would be perilous. He sat back and emotionally prepared himself for the next leg.

Map Reference 13.1 –

This map shows the progress of the Russian counter offenses and territory reclaimed and gained, specifically at the end of the spring in 1944. Of note is the proximity to Angelo's location to the westward push of the Soviet Union (purple color).

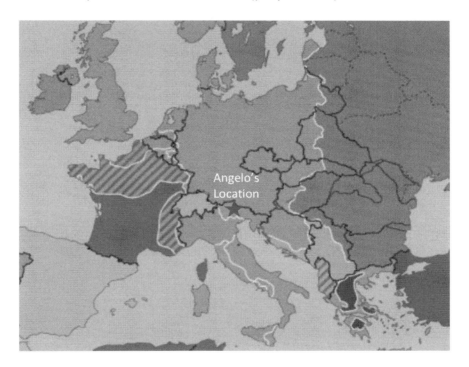

Map Reference 13.2 –

The view of the Rosengarten Mastiff from the trail Angelo hiked in his escape.

CHAPTER 14

Meeting Geronimo

May 19, 1944
Mountains southwest of Uletta, Italy

Standing to stretch and regain his bearings, Angelo once again viewed the beautiful lake, now close to sunset. Setting his goal to reach the Rosengarten mountains, he began his hike with a deep sigh of resignation. The next segment of the journey required crossing the valley farmlands where cover was nearly impossible to find. Crossing meant virtually complete exposure. Walking the tree line would be less dangerous but would also result in a longer route that had him hiking the terrain interface between farmlands and woodlands. It would add possibly a day or two to the walk, but it was far safer than crossing the open land.

Angelo continued hiking the woods in the darkness and debated with himself over which path to take when he eventually made it to the valley. In the beginning while he was refreshed, he felt confident in taking the longer way around the great valley for safety's sake. Later though, as the night wore on and his strength waned, his consideration would swing to crossing the open valley and taking the risk. When he finally reached the valley at sunrise, he simply decided on staying put and regaining his strength.

The next night, after a day to rest, he made his choice and began his big swing around the farmland, changing direction from generally north to southeast. The plan worked, and he felt grateful that the enemy mechanized units rolling south from the opposite side of the valley were too far away to see him. Hugging the woodlands around the valley floor, he felt comfortably out of sight. As he made his way toward the fairly wide river which dug the valley floor thousands of years ago, he approached the bridge cautiously and scanned for German troops. It was now in the dead of the night and quiet reigned.

The bridge was sited about one-half mile from the relative safety of the tree line on the other side. As he started to cross the sizable structure, he was nervously aware of his exposure. His walk quickened and soon became a dash for the cover offered by the woods. Only one hundred feet from crossing the bridge, he heard vehicles approaching from the road hidden by a hillside. He had to make an immediate decision: run for the woods or double back and hide under the bridge.

Intuitively, he knew there was no way to make it all the way to the woods in time, so he hurriedly ran back to the bridge and crawled underneath. He found a small opening underneath where the structure met the dirt, well above the river's edge. Having likely been formed by a swollen river eroding the shore during the heavy spring rains, it was just barely deep enough for him to scrunch himself into. Using his knife, he expanded the hole out as best he could. Scraping and pushing the dirt outward, he carefully stopped every so often to listen for movement above or anything approaching the bridge.

In the deep darkness, he felt confident that any probing eyes couldn't see him in this makeshift den. Lying in the dark hole, wet and cold, he felt as if he had just been through the full force of a hurricane and was being rewarded with a few moments of peace in the great storm's eye. Of course, he had no way of knowing that this moment of peace would stretch into hours.

The vehicle movement on the bridge above seemed never ending, and the men marching in unison echoed under the bridge like a drumbeat. *Why such heavy movement of troops and vehicles so late at night?* he wondered to himself. He assumed they must have been quickly trying to get to a coming battle or to reinforce an ongoing battle. Either way, they were gratefully not taking time to search for a lone partisan like him, and they weren't stopping for any breaks.

That didn't mean he hadn't any close calls. Every so often, a soldier would walk down to the river's edge to urinate or check for saboteurs' activity. The nearly black environment, coupled with Angelo's wearing a long dark-gray overcoat, provided excellent cover and he remained unnoticed. Even with the early morning light, his position was still very dark and only mildly affected by the growing illumination. Still, he prayed for a break in the enemy movement.

While he waited for that break, he couldn't help worry about not only his own situation but also about the disposition of Nini and Antonio. Both men were excellent at hiding and covering their movements, but it was hard to imagine they would all make it. *This hole is a tailor-made gift, but could the others have been so lucky?* he thought to himself. With this many troops on the move, they were sure to have their own enemy engagements. The most dangerous times for Angelo were the quiet ones like these. He couldn't help himself agonizing about the team and their safety.

The several hours spent in the hole was miserable. Trying to stay near motionless became harder and harder as the time wore on. The location was cursed with a small amount of water that kept seeping in the hole from the high-water table next to the river, and some animal had defecated in the area recently. Combined with the cold, damp nature of the raw ground, he couldn't wait for an opportunity to run.

That opportunity finally came at about nine in the morning. With no traffic in the area for over half an hour, he climbed his way out, using the structure for temporary cover. Seeing it was clear, he took a few seconds to stretch his cramped muscles. With his legs again functional, he sprinted across the open farmland to the woods.

Angelo's assessment of the remainder of the hike was correct, and he crossed over the rocky ridges uneventfully. Unfortunately, while trying to stave off dehydration from hiding earlier under the bridge, he drank water directly from the river. Lacking the opportunity to boil it first, he rolled the dice that he wouldn't get sick. About twenty hours later, giardia and amoeba from the untreated water had him retching violently and battling diarrhea. In his sickened state, he replayed delusional memories of home and family. After brief moments of enjoyment, he fought with himself in an attempt for focus. His march to safety had to be his sole priority. On his knees from vomiting, and with his head pounding he prayed, "Please, Lord, just get me back, and Nini and Antonio too."

Tired, sore, hungry, and dehydrated, he finally limped into the barn. His eyes immediately fell upon his cousin Nini. Hugging him deeply and thanking God privately, he instantly felt better. Nini asked him if he was all right. Angelo simply said it was a rough hike back and immediately asked about Antonio. Rosario delivered the sad news that he had been shot the day after they split from each other. Nobody knew the circumstances, but the bullets in his back inferred he was shot while running away. Angelo dropped his head in quiet remembrance and dejectedly shook his head.

Antonio hadn't been with the team long, but he had quickly been welcomed into the brotherhood. He was older, and Angelo hadn't even bothered to ask his age. Nini estimated he was in his mid-forties but that was just a guess. Antonio had the ability to simply meld into the background. As they remembered their fallen brother, nobody in the group could recall very many personal details about the man.

Raising his wine bottle toward the heavens, Nini said loudly, "One hell of a knifeman. To Antonio!"

All the men grabbed a cup of whatever was available and solemnly toasted their fallen friend.

As Angelo settled his cup, he realized there was a stranger in the back of the barn. The man stepped forward from out of a corner and identified himself as Geronimo, working under Colonel John Riepe with the American Office of Special Services (OSS). "I'm sorry about your friend being lost."

Nini simply replied with a subdued "*Grazzi*." Angelo just nodded.

Operating out of the northernmost Secret Intelligence (SI) branch field office in Merano, Italy, Geronimo was tasked with developing field agents in Angelo's region. This was not a public or recognizable office of the American government. Located at the base of the Ötztal Alps and on the other side of a large Dolomite mountain range, Merano was in the center of the South Tyrol and the belly of the beast. While only forty miles away, it was extremely difficult getting there.

Geronimo praised Angelo and his team on all they were doing to help the war effort. He repeatedly attested to the difference their operations were making and also seemed to know a great deal about the missions the team had already completed. Angelo felt comfortable with Geronimo and found him to be genuine. Most importantly, he assured the team that the United States wanted to help.

He also confirmed the rumors that a coming invasion on the European mainland were true. Germany was being squeezed, and an important component of Allied victory was for the Americans to work their way north, through Italy, ultimately past the Alps and into Germany. Once the English Channel was crossed and troops were landed in France, the Alps represented the only remaining geographic obstacle to Allied victory.

If Angelo had been near exhaustion, there was little sign of it now. His flesh was fatigued but his spirits soared. He eagerly soaked in all the intelligence Geronimo provided. Geronimo wondered why this team had resisted working with others in the area and maintained an independent force. Angelo told him their motivations in no uncertain words: he would be proud to help the Americans, but they were fighting for their own independent country. Perhaps it was the exhaustion or maybe the fresh loss of Antonio, but Angelo laid it out plainly.

As he spoke, he heard the words coming out and worried he would offend their guest. This agent could supply them with all they could ever want from intelligence to supplies. But was he jeopardizing this resource by not falling in line? He immediately toned down the delivery. Firm in their position, but not to the point of belligerent. Still, the body language of the agent implied an easy-going, almost casual nature. His tall, thin frame and nondescript face weren't the least intimidating. He resembled a boy scout leader more than a special agent for the organization that would become the CIA only a few years after the war.

Angelo's concerns were quickly allayed as Geronimo said their small nimble team would be better suited for certain assignments than a larger organized partisan garrison. Most importantly, he was looking for men that were unaffiliated with the CLN. The OSS was looking for intelligence agents, and being apolitical was considered a positive trait. He even lamented at how he was having difficulty finding partisan groups that weren't affiliated with any political factions.

Geronimo stated plainly, "I have no issue with your team's motivations, as long as we have a mutual enemy."

The men spoke well into the night. Conversations covered a broad spectrum of topics, although never mission specific or militarily sensitive. Angelo found himself drawn to the agent and felt a friendship and trust developing. He was grateful to see that the rest of the men, in particular Nini and Rosario, also felt at ease and comfortable with the agent.

The next day, Geronimo simply disappeared into the woods. He told the men before exiting that he would be back in touch when the Americans had a permanent presence in Northern Europe - that is, after D-Day. He also told them to think about the items they needed to be most effective in their operations. He would need to get approvals for the new team, but he was certain it would be no problem.

For the next few weeks, the men planned on a wish list of items they could use to better enable their operational success. It was almost a feeling of Christmas coming to children. Don't get in any trouble till a special day, and then all sorts of goodies would magically appear.

Their excited anticipation was suddenly interrupted one late afternoon by the sudden knock and rushed opening of the barn door. Matteo, who had been on guard duty, suddenly ran in and said he spotted a patrol of Germans approaching the farmhouse. Angelo was alone in the barn, as the rest of the team was out hunting and checking traps set in the woods.

Angelo and Matteo quickly gathered all incriminating evidence and realized they couldn't get it all out of the barn in time. They opened the floor hatch and threw everything into the hole that they had previously dug for such an emergency. With everything safely deposited in the hole, they went to the door expecting to escape to the woods and the support of the team. But as Matteo turned the doorknob, the farmer was also turning it from the other side. He rushed in and said there was no time to make it to the woods. His wife was stalling the soldiers at the house; they had to get down into the hole. Immediately, the men cleared the floor again to expose the opening. Angelo and Matteo climbed down inside as the farmer replaced the floorboards. In the blackness, Angelo couldn't even see Matteo lying mere feet from him. Dust from the floor rained down on them as the farmer covered the opening with stacks of wood.

Please, Lord, don't let me sneeze! Angelo pled silently.

Minutes seemed like hours without any movement above. Then, suddenly the door was bashed open, and the two heard the unmistakable sound of German boots above. In silence, they each prayed for their lives. Step-by-step, the soldiers above came closer to the trapdoor that was the only thing separating them from death. Soon, they could hear someone above searching behind a woodpile. After what seemed an eternity, they finally heard the soldiers leave the barn.

Both men silently thanked God for their narrow escape and expected the farmer to come back soon to let them out. Unfortunately, the farmer did not return. With no reference to sunlight in the blackness of the hole, the men had no idea how long they were there. Each wanted to say something, but they both knew better and stayed in complete silence. Their only form of communication was an occasional tap by one of them to make sure the other was all right.

Time dragged on, and neither the farmer nor the rest of the team returned. The men had no way of knowing how long they had been there, but it was long enough that Matteo urinated in his pants. After even more time, the stale air in the hole became engulfed by the stench. Through it all, the men stayed motionless and silent.

While Angelo and Matteo lay silently and motionless under the floor of the barn, Nini and the rest of the men had their own close call. Unable to find the band of partisans in the village, the Germans proceeded to send patrols into the surrounding woods. Nini could hear the troops quietly walking about. Spread out along a loose line at the edge of a gulley, the men hid under fallen forest debris that was strewn about. Each man readied his weapon as they listened for any sign of the enemy approaching.

After a while, Gianni, hiding with Franco under the extended root ball of a huge fallen tree, heard the unmistakable crack of a branch being stepped on. They trembled as the footsteps came ever closer. When it was clear the men above were near and coming toward them, Gianni also readied two grenades. With the rest of the team spread along the gulley, they at least had an opportunity to defend themselves against the oncoming German patrol.

Knowing he was the farthest away from the barn, Gianni guessed that the men he heard coming were the lead elements of the patrol. If that were so, Gianni could engage the lead person the rest of the team would have clear shots at the following line of soldiers.

German patrols were typically comprised of nine men, with the squad leader in the forward position and the machine gunners directly behind him. For the team to have a chance, Gianni would have to neutralize the machine gunners and squad leader with grenades and rely on his hidden teammates to take out the remaining riflemen with their weapons.

Luckily, he heard the steps begin to walk away from them. Gianni smiled broadly to Franco lying next to him. Apparently, instead of going into the gulley where the men would have been exposed, the Germans chose to walk along the ridge above and get a better view of the area. The team stayed in their positions for another hour to ensure the danger had indeed passed, and each gave a prayer of thanks for surviving the extremely close call.

For Angelo, hunger ultimately set in, and he would have given anything for a drink of water. Every muscle in his body atrophied or cramped up, causing excruciating pain that he could not alleviate. In his mind, Angelo tried to determine how long they had been captive but couldn't. Soon, rational thoughts were replaced by hallucinations. Over time, he visited with his mother, Pietro, many friends, and finally the father he had never met. It was in this near-psychotic state that he was surprised by the removal of the floorboards above. In his altered condition, he hadn't even heard the men above moving the piles of wood or calling out to them. Only the rays of light on his hypersensitive eyes brought him back to reality.

It took multiple men from the team to extract Angelo and Matteo from the hole and hours for the men to fully regain their composure. The farmer immediately brought in some food and water for the depleted men. As he was coming out of it but not fully rational yet, Angelo started asking about the men. In what sounded like a drunken voice, he blurted out, "Is everyone all right? Did everyone stay clear of the Germans during the night?"

Everyone stopped what they were doing for a moment and came alongside Angelo. Nini put his arm around him. "Last night? You're a couple hours into the third day cousin! The Tedeschi took their time in leaving the village."

After the initial shock of the revelation, Angelo approached Matteo and kissed his cheek. "My brother, three days dead. Who would believe it?"

In the week following, both men regained their strength and returned to their old selves. They revisited their plans for Geronimo and their new capabilities. Angelo was pleased and impressed at the team avoiding detection in the woods, as well as the comprehensive list of resources the men made during their time there. After reviewing and culling their list, the men all rested and waited for word from Geronimo.

On July 12, just a few weeks after the Allies landed on the beaches of Normandy during Operation Overlord, Geronimo returned, ready to begin a new phase in the evolution of Angelo and the team.

This change would require Angelo and the team to move up to the big leagues. Brushing his beaten clothes, he pronounced, "We train every day, and we look for ways to improve our communications and effectiveness."

Despite the potentially increasing danger and exposure from the relationship, everyone on the team welcomed the opportunity and dismissed the negatives. They were all in and began expanded operational training immediately.

CHAPTER 15

Nowhere to Hide

July 15, 1944
Uletta, northeast of Val Gardena, Italy

Angelo was invigorated to work with his new handler. This was very unlike the opportunity presented by Paolo and the CLNAI. Then he felt there would be a complete loss of control and subordination to bureaucrats on the other side of Italy. He felt the Garibaldis wanted him to essentially be a plug in the central part of the country where the organization did not have many resources. Here, the assessment of the relationship was completely different.

The United States government had taken notice of the team's work and selected *them*. They came to him. This orphaned shepherd boy had created a fighting unit effective enough to be noticed by the largest and most advanced military on earth. Of course, the OSS was working with many other partisan groups, but that didn't stop Angelo from feeling proud about himself and his team. He anticipated learning new techniques and strategies from the "pro team."

The meeting lasted all day and well into the morning of the sixteenth. There was much to cover, learn and assess. Strategies and planning were the first topic of discussion, as Geronimo needed to determine their level of sophistication. It didn't take long for him to be comfortable that the team possessed a high degree of tactical knowledge and professionalism. Satisfied, he quickly turned to communications where Geronimo unveiled his first present: a new PRC-5 "Suitcase Spy Radio" *(see photo reference 15.1)*. The remote portable radio system, weighing about twenty-five pounds in its own suitcase, operated in shortwave and included a Morse code transmitter.

Angelo appointed Nini as his communications man. He would be responsible for the briefcase the rest of the war. Angelo's team would work under many code names, typically changed for each mission to prevent German detection if a message was intercepted.

Geronimo covered proper use of the equipment, its maintenance, and field repair processes Nini picked up on it fairly quickly, and a couple of other men also listened in as backup. A greater amount of time was invested in when they could use it, German triangulation technology used to locate the transmission's source location, and code words and phrases to use. Looking straight at Nini, Geronimo commanded, "Under no circumstances, let this fall into the enemies' hands!"

"Understood," snapped Nini immediately.

Later, Nini confessed to Angelo with a wide grin, "I actually felt like saluting the guy. It's been a long time since anyone gave me such a direct order."

Angelo grinned a sly smile. "I felt the same way."

With comms covered, they turned their attention to weapons training. Geronimo produced an American-made Browning Automatic Rifle or BAR. The weapon was a thing of beauty to the men. Capable of firing up to six hundred rounds per minute and with an effective firing range of 1,500 yards, it was a giant leap ahead of the arms they had been pilfering from the Germans. By utilizing the barrel-mounted bipod, the weapon quickly became a formidable light machine gun. While heavy to carry at nearly twenty pounds, particularly up mountains, it would be perfect to provide suppressing fire while others on the team utilized dynamite, grenades, and higher-accuracy rifles.

When their training was complete, Geronimo simply said, "I believe two for the team should be enough."

Angelo was then offered mortars and other larger weapons. The OSS could supply these and anti-tank weapons, but they were reserved for those partisan groups holding large expanses of land. Most Italian partisans were part of larger organizations like the CLNAI and operated loosely like an army, often controlling towns and small regions. Guerilla groups like Angelo's were atypical and received almost exclusively light arms, ammunition, and rations.

Angelo appreciated the extra capability the heavy arms provided, but the team had always relied on fast exits. They rejected the offer because they didn't want to be slowed down, and they certainly had no intention of trying to hold any land. It was folly to consider holding even strategic buildings or a town since the team was now down to just ten. They had survived on a hit and run protocol, and heavy weapons would have really hindered quick escapes.

They did, however, welcome the addition of new bomb-making explosive agents. Adding new elements like TNT, RDX, powdered aluminum, and others to their dynamite enabled special use bombs for greater lethality and impact. Whereas Rosario had an expertise in deploying explosives, Gianni had developed his own particular talent for mixing the dangerous elements. While most sober people would run from the idea of making concoctions that could go off with even a minor error, Gianni had no such fear. Angelo guessed it had to do with his background. The men didn't discuss it much, but Gianni had made it known that he had spent substantial time in prison before the war.

He had said it was for fighting drunk with the wrong person, but the men suspected something more serious or sinister was the reason. Unfortunately, Gianni became easily enraged and his temper could become alarmingly enflamed. His short fuse didn't help matters. Everyone on the team knew not to cross him, and luckily, he rarely participated in playing cards or wagering of any kind. Anger issues aside, everyone was happy to defer this delicate and dangerous task to Gianni.

Much time was spent discussing airdrops of equipment and cash. The war had been going on for years at this point, and local people had nothing to live on. Between the ravages of war and the depression that led up to the war, there was little semblance of an economy left. The OSS vowed to provide Angelo with whatever cash he needed to buy people's silence or potential intelligence.

Colonel Riepe of the OSS had developed an ingenious method for communicating the partisans' precise location to aircraft making a drop. Geronimo taught them how to dislodge the headlights from the front of a vehicle and point them straight up into the sky. In this way, the light would make a beacon for the aircraft to specifically hone in on. Perhaps more importantly, the light was barely visible from the ground and would not give up the team's position.

Over the course of the war, the OSS eventually dropped over six thousand gross tons of supplies to just the Italian partisan movement. The supply of weapons to the team was proof that the Americans were serious in their support. It wasn't ideological with them; it was pragmatic, and Angelo appreciated that realization.

Lastly, Geronimo produced a contract making Angelo an employee of the United States of America (*see photo reference 15.2*). Angelo had never signed an agreement for anything and neither had anyone else on the team. They all listened intently as Geronimo laid out in detail all the terms and contractual expectations of their relationship.

The agreement would be only with Angelo, as the leader of the team, and the other men argued for their participation. Angelo argued for the others as well, citing how all the men participated in every activity of their work, and what would happen if and when he was killed? But it was to no avail. The Americans didn't want thousands of "employees" running around the European theater of war. They needed a single leader to communicate missions to and to have security-sensitive operational discussions with. If Angelo didn't make it, then whoever would take his place would get a contract. The agreement emphasized the secret nature of conversations, including nondisclosure and loyalty clauses, and stated there would be serious consequences for the misappropriation of any items.

As the official employee of the United States for the team, Angelo's exposure and influence immediately rose. He would be responsible for the cash, weapons, and communications equipment supplied to the team, including full accountability. The Americans would evaluate every strength and weakness of the team, their effectiveness with the resources provided, and he couldn't help to be a bit worried how they would score.

Geronimo also brought news from other areas of the war. One of the younger men, Franco, asked about the area of Tuscany where most his family was from. Geronimo lowered his head and delivered horrifying news. A few weeks earlier, there was a massacre of civilians in the small village of Sant'Anna di Stazzema. In retaliation for partisan activities in Central Italy, the Germans and Fascists had murdered hundreds of civilians.

His report didn't have complete details yet, but he had heard they simply rounded up civilians, including old men, women, and children, and summarily exterminated them. He had heard some were herded up and shot with machine guns; others were put into building basements where they were lit on fire and burned to death. Still others were fortunate enough to have hand grenades thrown into the basements and be blown up. It made all the men nauseated—and furious.

They were all soldiers, but "How could any human do that?" Marco said in an emotional, horrified voice.

"Even in wartime?" Nini responded to the group. Within minutes, the men were up and yelling to each other over how much damage they intended to do to the Germans and Fascists. Each tried to outdo the other with his level of bravado and hatred.

Angelo attempted to calm the men, asking them to remember their humanity and professionalism. But the men turned on him. There was a mob mentality, a feeling of vigilantism growing, and it took some time to abate. Fortunately, Geronimo stepped in. Recognizing his authority and the benefits he brought, the men fell in line, and he helped quell the furor.

As things eventually calmed and the men took to quiet fuming, Angelo noticed Franco alone in the corner. Angelo approached him and asked if he was all right. The young man turned to Angelo with a dejected childlike look. A single long tear rolled down his face and fell into the crack of his downturn mouth. "My cousins are from that village. I have an uncle who has lived there forever and another from not far away."

Angelo couldn't think of anything to say. He simply asked Franco to stand up and then hugged him as hard as he could. At this point, the other men noticed the exchange and came over. The mood immediately changed, and they all became sympathetic to their hurting brother. Franco released himself from Angelo's hold and, in a defeated voice, said that he needed to go there right away.

Each member of the team tried to talk him out of it, but he was adamant that it was his duty to his family. Even Geronimo said it would be crazy to travel south to Tuscany at this time, but Franco wouldn't have any of it. At least several strong reasons against this move were brought forth. Lastly, Angelo argued that he would have to travel as a civilian and not carry a weapon - he would have no means of self-protection. Geronimo agreed that it would be suicide and he should stay with the team and fight. A couple of men empathized, and Gabriel even offered to go with him, but Franco nixed the idea immediately. This was his issue, and nobody else should take the risk for him. Gabriel understood and quietly acquiesced.

With the situation again in hand, Geronimo left with the cover of the night. As he was leaving, he stopped to address the team. "I'm sorry to have delivered such terrible news. But you need to understand that other atrocities are happening all over. Let's concentrate on what we can all do and end this damn war." Providing the secret code name for the planned drop to Angelo, he promised to be back in touch shortly with details and left into the darkness.

The next morning, Franco also bid farewell to the team to face his destiny. There would be no turning back from his new personal mission. One by one, each man hugged, knowing that the odds of him making it were very slim. Franco began to walk away and took one half-hearted turn to see the team. The men waved supportively, but everyone knew it would be the last time seeing their friend. Everyone then went glumly back inside and spoke quietly about all that had happened.

Before lunch, Angelo regrouped the men. It was time to refocus and turn their righteous anger into actionable planning. "Enough!" he said. "Let's get back to work and make the Tedeschi pay."

It didn't take long for Geronimo to come through on his promise. The team received a radio transmission from the US Fifteenth Army Group confirming their first drop. The drop site was about one mile from their headquarters, which was still located in the Uletta barn outside Val Gardena. The delivery was set for August 14 at 3:00 a.m. The nighttime drop was designed specifically for safety. Getting to the drop site would be fairly easy. However, safely waiting for the drop and returning were another story.

Angelo had the entire team show up to the drop site an hour in advance of the appointed time. They were to establish a perimeter, help move the pallets of equipment onto two trucks, and transport them back to their headquarters. Should anything go wrong, they were to stay by the vehicles and provide tactical backup.

Four of the men fanned out to form a loose perimeter around the large field. Angelo nervously realized he could have used eight more men for a perimeter guard in a field of this size. Everyone waited anxiously for the designated communication from the drop craft. When it didn't come at the specified time, they all felt incredibly exposed and vulnerable. But at approximately 3:20 a.m., the message finally came through the radio, and Nini started the truck engine and lights.

This was the most dangerous time of the operation. It would take another five minutes for the drop to happen and about another ten minutes for the packages to land. All the while, there was the chance their mission was compromised and the enemy would surround the field at any moment. Such action would dwarf the team's security perimeter, compromise the men and their contacts in the region, and result in the capture of the valuable arms and cash.

However, within five minutes of sending the receiving signal, the men could start to make out the parachutes from the light of the car headlights and the moon. Even though it took mere minutes, it seemed like the parachutes just hung in the air, taking forever to land. Soon they heard a welcome thud on the other side of the field. Then another closer to them. The packages had fallen safely and were scattered across the field.

Nini cut the lights on the signal truck, and all five men ran to retrieve the contraband now safely on the ground. The men wasted no time loading the two vehicles. The pallets were heavy, and the men had to waste time disassembling them in the field. Using a knife, they roughly cut the heavy strapping and removed individual packages. Still painfully aware of their vulnerability, Angelo released the first vehicle to return to base as soon as it was ready. Within ten minutes, the second followed. The four men on perimeter guard duty stayed back to gather and bury the fallen parachutes and attempt to remove any traces of the morning's happenings.

Once back in the relative safety of headquarters, the team greedily unpacked all the various sized boxes and containers. There was truly an air of Christmas. Angelo kept thinking of how this new equipment would enable them to do so much more. He said to Nini, "Do you think we will ever go through all these grenades and weapons?"

After a moment of thinking, Nini replied, "I'm afraid so, but let's hope not."

One container was noticeably different from the others. Breaking the lock on the sturdy metal case caused it to fall off the table. As it did, piles of Italian lira fell out. It was more cash than Angelo thought he would ever see in his lifetime. He immediately separated it into smaller bundles and piled the bundles next to his personal belongings. He was confused as to how to guard the small fortune he had been entrusted to. Fearing the temptation would be too great on a team member, he had Nini and Rosario keep the cash in sight whenever he was gone.

Taking a sizeable sum, he then left the group and went to the farmer who owned the barn they lived in. Angelo could see the wife of the poor farmer in an adjacent room shedding tears as he paid him handsomely. Angelo felt he not only deserved it but also that he needed to secure the family's future silence as well.

Once back at their headquarters, Nini communicated to Geronimo that they had the goods and encountered no resistance. The men discussed the operation in detail, and Angelo gratefully acknowledged the control and safety of the assets.

With a sigh of relief and acknowledgment of a job well done, Geronimo gave the team a list of targets that needed to be eliminated. A second list included locations where the goal was intelligence only. Angelo and the team knew the local area well enough to recognize all of the targets. All were high profile and extremely dangerous, and the Americans wasted no time in testing the value of their investment.

Wanting to impress his handler, Angelo immediately accepted the two highest value assignments. The first was relatively easy and involved three men developing intelligence on train movements into a series of factories south of them. This was a straight intelligence gathering assignment, which Angelo handed off to Rosario.

He paused for a moment to reflect on his cousin Pietro's keen sense when it came to gathering and discerning military intelligence. He would have been the perfect leader for this mission. But remembering Pietro's electrocution less than a year earlier was too painful to dwell on, so he quickly refocused on planning.

The second mission was more suited to Angelo's skill set. There was a heavily fortified series of factories along the river just north of Trento. The job was to identify the critical areas of the facility and then disable them. Blowing the building would be too large and visible an operation, so he was told to only sabotage the most critical areas. The Germans had built significant antiaircraft batteries around the industrial city, and Allied bombers had continually failed to disable the key installation. Because one of the local men, Gabriel, had some knowledge of the area around Trento, Angelo picked him to do a fast reconnaissance mission to the town and back. The intel gathered would be used to develop the complicated mission logistics.

Prior to departing on this new intel-gathering mission, Angelo pulled Nini aside. "While I'm gone, put booby traps around all the buried stockpiles of cash. I trust the men, but the locals might get wind of it."

Nini didn't feel right about the implied mistrust of the team and confronted Angelo. "Cousin, we have been through so much with everyone. Do we really need to do this?"

Angelo reminded him of his contractual responsibility and shut the conversation down immediately. Nini deferred and spent the next several days secretly placing traps around the cash locations.

Angelo and Gabriel assumed their forged identities and left with only a sidearm, some clothes, and extra ammunition. If anything were to go wrong, at least they would have some defense. The men hitchhiked to Ortisei where they decided to buy two motorcycles from a local shop. The plan was to ride the bikes to Ponte Gardena where they would board a train to Trento.

It is worth noting that neither man had ever ridden a motorcycle and had no idea how to properly handle all that power under their seats. The Moto Guzzi Alce sported a 500cc motor and was the workhorse motorcycle of the Italian army. It had an excellent reputation for its durability and flexibility, and the men thought the bikes would survive the rigors they would need to endure. They didn't know very much about motorcycles, but they knew that if they were good enough for the army, they would be good enough. Not wanting to appear like neophytes and draw attention to themselves, after paying for the bikes, they casually thanked the shop owner and watched as he left them to go back in his store.

Both men stared at the bikes without wanting to ask the obvious. "Have you ever driven a motorcycle?"

Angelo shrugged his shoulders and said, "What the hell, it can't be that hard."

Both men keyed the ignition, and the engine roared to life. So far, so good. Having seen others operate motorcycles in the past, he tried to mimic their actions and released the throttle. The bike immediately bolted forward like an uncaged animal. Angelo managed to be thrown off before it continued down the relatively steep embankment. Angelo wasn't hurt, but this was clearly a bad idea.

Gabriel carefully got off his bike as Angelo brushed himself off. The men wisely decided to pay for a ride and simply abandoned the two motorcycles not far from the shop they came from. They didn't like the idea of wasting money on the purchase, but they also didn't want to draw attention to themselves. Fortunately, thanks to the OSS, money wasn't an issue anymore.

Once on the back of a farm truck heading the proper direction, both men took the time to laugh at each other and the ridiculousness of the situation.

But the laughing didn't last long. Nearing the train station, they gained a new appreciation for what they were up against.

Photo Reference 15.1 –

A PRC-5 Suitcase Spy Radio identical to the one used by Angelo (photo courtesy of National WWII Museum).

Angelo's PRC-5 Suitcase Spy Radio with contents removed and used by him as his sole piece of luggage when coming to America.

Photo Reference 15.2 –

Letter from the OSS acknowledging the employment of Angelo from July 15, 1944 to May 15, 1945.

CHAPTER 16

From Obscurity to Infamy

September 16, 1944
Ponte Gardena, Italy

Angelo couldn't believe the number of soldiers they witnessed milling around the train station. There was also quite a bit more civilians than they expected there as well. Relying on the strength of their disguise and forged papers, the two approached the ticket platform to buy two round-trip tickets to Trento. Slowly they walked across the platform, taking in the people, guards, and their demeanor. Each was quickly profiled and their threat level mentally logged. All the while, both men kept running possible scenarios through their minds. They played out every potential action and the counteraction required. It was speed chess but in a vicious game where a missed move would spell disaster.

Confident that it was business as usual and nothing seemed out of place, Angelo finally felt as comfortable as possible and made his way to the ticket counter. Fortunately, the queue had only two people in front of him, also purchasing tickets. As he waited in line, Gabriel milled about the area and kept watching around the station.

Just as Angelo reached the ticket window, Gabriel grabbed him by the arm and said, "We need to leave now." Angelo knew better than to question him, and they both headed towards the stations platform. As they got close to the stairs, Angelo saw what Gabriel had seen and froze. There for everyone to see was a poster with a rough sketch of his likeness and the following words: BEKANNTMACHUNG! 1,000 RM - Italienisch (NOTICE! $400 - Italian Identity).

The poster had many more details in fine print, but they didn't linger to read it. Angelo knew he needed to read the entire poster, but they didn't want to dally and spend one second longer than necessary. He quickly tore it off the wall as they exited the platform. Being dressed like a Gestapo agent and bearing identity papers, he figured it was worth the risk of someone questioning the poster's removal. He simply folded the poster, placed it in his pocket, put on the airs of someone who had the authority to do such a thing, and began walking.

While that worked in his mind, in reality it drew the attention of a guard on the other side of the platform. Angelo had only taken two steps when the guard yelled for them to stop so he could question them. Turning to assess their situation, Angelo could see a guard with his rifle trained on him. He turned fully and looked directly at the guard, causing the guard to briefly lower his weapon and return the gaze. Seeing as there was at least fifty feet and about a dozen people between them, he instantly concluded that they needed to escape. Seizing the opportunity, they hastily jumped off the platform.

Angelo was modestly confused as to why the soldier didn't take the shot. One reason could be there was a good number of civilians in the way, but that never stopped Nazis from shooting. Their Gestapo clothing and appearance may have also caused the guard to pause just long enough to question himself as to whether it was worth the shot. If he was wrong and shot at a Gestapo officer, it would have meant immediate execution. In the end, it didn't matter. The men made it off the platform and ran for their lives.

As expected, the guards immediately took up the chase. They were instantly joined by two more, and even more could be seen coming. Angelo and Gabriel ran toward a train that was just gathering speed as it left the station. Every rail car that the men could see in front of them had at least some uniformed soldiers. Angelo silently wondered if those guards would exit the cars and chase them or continue along.

Thankfully, one of the soldiers on the train did indeed see them as they approached the moving vehicle but didn't engage. *German discipline at its finest*, Angelo later thought to himself. Their orders were to stay on the train, and that was what they did. They probably didn't dare break orders just to chase two men running away. It wasn't their job.

When they finally got to the train, they both quickly fell onto the ground and rolled under the car to the other side. Misjudging the timing by even a few seconds would have meant being crushed by the wheels of the massive vehicle. Gabriel banged his knee on the iron rail and took a few precious moments trying to get back up.

They jumped up from the safe side of the train and ran as fast as they could to a series of motionless rail cars on the outermost rail line. As they ran, however, a few German soldiers from the train had moved from its interior to the coupler between the cars and fired relentlessly at them. Fortunately, shooting from a moving railroad car does not facilitate accurate shots. The men crawled under one last line of stationary cars and ran beside them along the rail tracks. They ran along the long line of cars for several minutes before some soldiers cleared the stationary cars and began firing on them again. With bullets ricocheting off the train cars, the men finally jumped away from the vehicle's cover and into the woods.

Recognizing that the Germans would immediately have patrols out looking for them, the two kept running for over an hour. Angelo assumed they would think they were heading to a road to procure transportation that could aid in their escape. So, like always, he did the opposite and ran farther into the wild woods, which led to the safety of the mountains. As they made their way up trails forged by deer and mountain goats, they reached the mountain's steep rocky cliffs. Hugging the giant rocks for dear life, they resembled the ibex which seemed a natural part of the cliff face.

Angelo assumed that these posters were at most, perhaps all, local train stations, so hitchhiking anywhere near the city or industrial area would be extremely dangerous. After a night of hiking, they found a small cave to rest inside of and tried to make some sense out of their situation. As the two spoke about their experience and the poster, they had more questions than answers.

Someone they knew had possibly given a sketch to the real Gestapo and ratted on him. Or it could have been the soldiers from one of the earlier train rides. Or, for all he knew, it might even have been from the original printer that made the fake documents for him. The men spent several hours thinking deeply about who it most likely was. They had to try and at least determine if there was a snitch or double agent in the team. While they both knew they would likely never know for sure, for the safety of everyone, they would give this exercise their best effort.

How long would it be till someone relents and turns me in? Angelo thought to himself. Feeling like a hunted animal, he said to Gabriel, "One thing is for sure, we're going to need more cash from the Americans to buy silence." Gabriel nodded in agreement as they continued to try and flush out the truth. Still, they might not get more money. So, as he laid his head in his hand and with a strained expression, he mentally began rationing what they already had.

With no way to determine the source of the poster and its information, the discussion swung to moving into a new territory. The logistics involved would be tricky. There was no certainty they would find local support, and winter was just around the corner.

Angelo's thoughts eventually shifted from fruitless speculation to forward thinking. Nothing he could do now would change the reality that the Germans were onto him. Worse, they would surely be harassing the local population for information. While the people appreciated the team and their sacrifices, life for most people had now devolved into primitive survival mode.

Operating with a bounty on his head was going to rachet the stakes of this unholy game even higher. He would now need to stay hidden from the local population as much as possible and keep using cash to buy people's loyalty.

The men hiked two more days before trusting a vehicle to get a lift toward Val Gardena and the safety of their headquarters. They exited the vehicle and walked the last ten miles so as not to give up their headquarters location. As they entered the hideout at the barn, Angelo was surprised again by yet another new face. This one, however, belonged to an even more unlikely person: a Russian agent.

In late June, the Russian army made a monumental push into the heart of the German lines on the Eastern Front during Operation Bagration. Taking the Germans by surprise, the Russians forced them into a steady retreat which would continue till the end of the war. As the Russians had an interest in any land they could claim after the war, they sent agents into Northern Italy to incite the locals. They focused significantly on the partisans, specifically the Garibaldis, and Angelo's team was one of dozens the agent had met with. Russia had its eye on grabbing as much land as possible for the post-war, and it actively attempted to recruit any fighters it could find that might facilitate its future.

The Russian was a small and nondescript fellow named Dimitri, a person one would never think stood out in any way. He didn't look stereotypically Russian either, with darker skin and rounded facial features. Dimitri spoke short sentences of parsed words in a slow droning monotone. The room developed a palpable chill from just his presence. His Italian, however, was very good, and he had little problem communicating with the team. Dimitri explained how he had been working with Angelo's friend Paolo from the Veneto Garibaldi garrison. Paolo had good things to say about Angelo and his team, and Dimitri tried to convince the team to reconsider joining the Garibaldis. Dimitri saw Angelo's team as a perfect fit to expand into the Trentino area.

Dimitri came off as a tedious cheerleader for communism and offered nothing of real value in the way of resources. Nini asked in several differently framed questions if their team could receive any resources. Cash was king, but grenades, dynamite, and small arms were also welcome. Dimitri dismissed every overture and eventually shut the conversation down. However, his message of anti-fascism, the ultimate power of the masses over the elite, and the pooling of capabilities resonated with some of Angelo's men. It also hit home for most partisan garrisons and oppressed locals, and the region began embracing Soviet-style communism.

Angelo left no room for misunderstanding with his team. They were fighting for a free and independent country and not any particular economic or political system. If the country could be created and the people wanted communism, he was fine with that. But the first and only thing that mattered now was ending this profane war and freeing their homeland.

Dimitri left that evening frustrated that Angelo's team was the only one he met with which demanded independence. He had spent almost all his time in the Veneto region of Italy with Paolo, who had gone "all in" with the Soviets. Paolo was known to spend all his time converting anyone who wanted to take up arms against the Germans to communism, specifically to his own Garibaldi Brigade.

Dimitri was noticeably disappointed with Angelo's stubbornness. Walking toward the barn door slowly, he implied the dangers of going it alone. There was an ominous quality to not only the words he spoke but also the inflection of his voice as well. He made it clear that any of the men who wanted to could find other partisan groups to fight with. There would be no protection for those making their own way. He urged them to leave the team if they wanted to be leaders in the new Communist Italy, which he claimed to be a certainty after the war.

The next day, two of the fighters said goodbye to Angelo and the team. While the very young Alesia was not a critical asset, Gabriel was. Angelo argued with Gabriel not to leave. They had been through so much together and were very close. Angelo vacillated between strategic reasons offered as a fellow warrior and gentle personal reasons offered as a brother. Gabriel listened and they had a conversation, but his mind seemed already set.

It was obvious to Gabriel that the war would be over in the coming year and the Communists were going to run things. He had to think about his future. As a man of thirty years, he had to position himself for postwar life. He told Angelo he was too young to fully understand.

Angelo couldn't argue with the age difference but pleaded that he did indeed understand. "Gabriel, my brother, we need you! The best way to be significant in this war is to stay with this team," he stated.

"You're just twenty-one. How can you know? You're only dreaming if you think that Trentino or the Tyrol will become independent nations. The Russians, Americans, and British are too powerful. Those superpowers would never allow a new country." Given the volatile mix everyone expected in postwar Europe, he certainly had valid arguments.

With heavy hearts, Gabriel and Alessia kissed each of the team members on the cheek and said, "*Buona fortuna, fratelli miei* [Good luck, my brothers]."

Angelo sensed his control slipping away and felt a newly significant weightiness. The Americans had provided vital resources but expected extremely dangerous missions in exchange. The Germans had identified him, and it seemed likely only a matter of time until someone gave him up. And now the Russians were making trouble and meddling with their team.

Gratefully, autumn had pushed aside summer, and it was time to hunker down and let the notorious Alpine winter provide a welcome relief from everything and everyone.

CHAPTER 17

Matteo

November 19, 1944
Uletta, northeast of Val Gardena, Italy

In Central Europe, the winter of 1944–45 was, by all accounts, one of the worst in history. A combination of bitter cold, vast amounts of snow, and few sunny days to dry things out was brutal. While Angelo had hoped for a break in the action, none came. As Allied advances stalled on all fronts, Hitler took advantage and gambled on one last counteroffensive on the Western Front.

Recycling a German tactic from the First World War, Hitler launched his Ardennes Counteroffensive, also known as the Battle of the Bulge. The noose around him was tightening from all sides, and like any cornered rabid animal, he lashed out. Well over five hundred thousand German soldiers attempted to cut off the Americans and their supply lines in the Belgium city of Antwerp. Hitler's hope was to encircle the Americans and force their surrender, thereby taking thousands of prisoners in the process. His irrational mind envisioned a victory which would enable him to negotiate and secure peace terms from a position of strength.

The effort ultimately failed, but it did draw a significant number of German soldiers out of Northern Italy and reduce Angelo's overall exposure. Clearly, the Allies were now focused on Northern Europe, and Geronimo went silent till just after the new year. On the Eastern Front, however, Dimitri had confirmed that Russian forces were not slowing down their advance. Perfectly equipped for winter fighting, the Russians kept a deliberate pace that yielded less daily gain but never gave the Germans a break. He encouraged Angelo to take advantage of the situation and step up his sabotage activities.

Angelo's team set out to do just that. The team analyzed the areas Geronimo had identified and targeted two as high priority. Because of the winter, the number of potential targets was diminished, but there were still some good prospects.

The team planned a formidable operation for December 10 to honor the anniversary of Pietro's capture and murder by torture. After reviewing the options and doing some scouting, they settled on a communications building outside Ponte Gardena. This was perilously close to the rail station where Angelo was certain his picture hung, but it was critical for disrupting the German forces that were preventing the Allies from moving north through Italy.

The building would be seriously fortified, and Angelo now wished he had some of the heavy weapons first offered by Geronimo. Unfortunately, the US had limited planes available, and there was a great need for supplies by underground units all across Europe. Coupled with the rivalries between US service branches that crippled cooperative missions like supplying partisans, the team would not receive another supply drop from the OSS for the remainder of the war. Angelo repeatedly requested more supplies from Geronimo, but it was to no avail. They would have to make do with the resources they had left.

The men strategized the best method of attack on the target. Nini led a contingent which wanted to limit the attack to only the main transmission lines. He suggested they mount the poles and strip or cut the lines. "We've done this a couple of times before, and we know it's fast and safest," he argued.

However, Fulvio fought to take out the main transmission tower. "The lines can be too quickly repaired, and the risk is too great for the limited impact. We need to take out the tower itself."

Lastly, Gianni took the position that they should assault the building itself and blow the entire structure. "If we take out the building too, we'll get some Tedeschi as a bonus."

Angelo noted to himself how the personalities of each person were coming out. Nini played it safe, Fulvio was pragmatic, and Gianni just wanted to blow everything up and kill as many Germans as possible. Each had valid operational concerns and benefits, and Angelo listened patiently as they fought for their positions.

Fearing another situation where the men could be captured and tortured to death like Pietro, Angelo decided on the approach that would inflict the most damage while providing their best chance for escape. They would not go after the entire building because it would be certain to result in significant retaliation. That level of exposure would surely draw more German resources to eliminate the team. But they would destroy the main distribution tower. This action would cripple the enemy's comms capability for months or longer, yet still provide for an expeditious escape. He wanted to do more damage than just cutting lines, which could be quickly repaired, but didn't want to risk a full exchange likely to result in serious losses and punitive reprisals against the townspeople and the team. "This way, we should be able to seriously damage their abilities, take out the soldiers, and still get out before reinforcements can be brought in."

As the date approached, the men were discouraged by a heavy storm that stymied any movement and prevented a major operation. After two weeks, the weather and transportation network finally cleared enough for the operation to move forward. However, since it was almost Christmas, they decided to hold off till January 2.

The holidays brought mixed emotions to the team. There was a real sense that Germany was on its last leg and that the war was almost over. Yet Trentino and the Tyrol's historic lands were still far from liberated, and it had been years since the team had contacted their families. From their headquarters and home, the war continued its brutal punishment on the land and people with no freedom in sight.

Still, sitting around a fire singing traditional Tyrolian songs helped celebrate the season and built back their spirits. They played traditional card games like scopa and tresette. When some of the men ran out of their cigarette wagers, they played for IOUs, which nobody expected collecting. It wasn't that winning was everything; it was the thrill of something riding on their decisions and not wanting the games to end.

They established a relaxed defensive position and spoke about what was on everyone's mind and the minds of most soldiers when in a safe position - girls. There was the usual bragging about girls they almost met or the one that got away or the one they hoped would still be around after the war. Sitting there, grimy, dirty, and huddled around a fire for warmth, Angelo wondered if any woman on earth would ever even look at them, much less engage them in a relationship. Everyone knew it was a long shot, but still, hope in a young man's heart springs eternal.

Enjoying these moments of relative comfort and safety, happily the war disappeared for a precious while. Angelo sat contented and reviewed the faces of his brothers-in-arms around him. Just yesterday, they mirrored a life lived on the dark side of angry. But today, with Christmas and family on their minds, he could see a change and a new determination to end this war and go home.

Thankfully, the weather was clear for the first several days of January, so the men finally set out on their mission a day later than expected. Clutching the cross around his neck that was given to him at his infant baptism, Angelo obtained courage and strength from it once again and led the team of four men outside. Nini stayed back with the remaining two men to monitor communications and recon "easy" targets closer to their home base.

Angelo, Fulvio, Gianni, and Matteo set off at dusk to start the long hike to Ponte Gardena. Because of winter conditions, including massive wind-blown snow drifts, the walk would take about nine hours instead of the normal five hours. Since the winter snows had concentrated the now very seasoned German troops along the roadways, Angelo decided not to rely on hitchhiking or procuring a ride.

The men made it to the edge of the dense forest next to the communications building while it was still very dark. Taking stock of the situation, they were immediately surprised by the number of enemy vehicles they could see. They also spotted a machine gun post near the tower manned by two men, a steel drum containing a fire with three men gathered for warmth, and two additional guards at the building entrance. This was a manageable number of men, but there were enough vehicles to suggest a sizeable contingent of troops either in the building or close by. The men quietly spread in a wide circle to probe the perimeter for any danger and expeditious points of ingress and egress.

With daylight coming in a mere two hours, they had to make decisions quickly. Fulvio argued Nini's position that they should back off and just cut the transmission lines away from the building under safer conditions. Gianni, always the young hothead who loved blowing things up, wanted to attack the building while the enemy slept and take it all. Angelo listened one last time to all opinions and considered them against the new on-site realities.

Despite the assumed large contingent of troops and limited exit opportunities because of the heavy snows, Angelo decided to stick with the original plan and just blow the transmission tower. The wooden tower would be easy to take down. A modest number of explosives placed where the supporting columns met the earth would be enough. They then agreed on the exit. Each man would go in different directions, ultimately circling back off the road network and then proceed back to their headquarters.

The men said a quick prayer and moved out slowly to cover the building and transmission tower. Angelo had the uneasy feeling they were entering this battle holding hands with death and again instinctively clutched the cross around his neck. Fulvio was positioned at the doorway to the small building which housed what they thought to be eight to twelve troops. Gianni provided close tactical support for Matteo who was to place the charges on the structure. Angelo would take the high ground and provide covering fire for the exposed team below.

The three front men silently approached the building first. Keeping low, avoiding open areas, and crawling quietly, they eventually made it to the building. With their knives, they quickly eliminated the two guards at the door. Fulvio stayed behind at the door as a guard while Gianni and Matteo proceeded to the tower. One more German soldier was taken out by Matteo on their way to the target, and a second succumbed to his fate after an extended hand-to-hand fight with Gianni.

Unfortunately, the noise from the fight alerted the men at the machine gun post, and they could be heard readying their weapon to engage the saboteurs. But before they could get a round off, Gianni ran close and threw a hand grenade directly inside their sandbag emplacement. After the blast, he jumped onto the gun's position and finished the enemy off with his rifle. The rage in each of their hearts poured out of Gianni like a vile judgment from the devil himself. Angelo watched in horror as Gianni stood over the incapacitated men and emptied his rifle cartridge into their already limp bodies.

Later Angelo prayed about what they had become. He begged Christ to forgive him and all the men. The fundamental thing that kept him going was the sense of peace he received in those quiet moments of prayer. He long ago convinced himself that God fully forgave him and the men for their blackened hearts and murderous actions. Had he not, he was certain he could not continue.

The noise from the hand grenade discharging and subsequent rifle fire immediately woke the men in the building. Knowing they would be exiting to assume their positions in the firefight, Fulvio prepared himself for the wave of men by falling to a prone position behind a stack of wood. At the same time, Matteo ran to place the charges on the tower. As an experienced saboteur, he expertly placed the charges in a manner calculated to make the tower collapse on or near the building.

Angelo, watching the action through his field glasses, determined that the fight was expanding and moved into position to support the men as they exited. Two men initially appeared in the building doorway, and Fulvio unleashed his BAR. The men fell instantly. More soldiers ran through the door like hornets that had their nest disturbed. Now standing to have a better shot past the bodies in the doorway, Fulvio's automatic weapon continued to unload its fury, temporarily pinning the enemy in the building.

Unfortunately, he had not counted on a shooter to emerge on the rooftop. The soldier ran for a position with cover along the parapet and took aim at Fulvio, who was completely unaware of his presence. Fulvio was shot twice in the chest and, after stumbling three feet backward, fell hard. Barely alive and bleeding profusely, he struggled in vain to move toward a fallen tree for some cover. The next man out of the building put a single shot into his chest, and Fulvio lay motionless.

Angelo put his rifle to its intended use and pinned the German on the rooftop down. With Fulvio out of the fight and the doorway now useable, German soldiers streamed from the building. Gianni shifted his attention to the flow of soldiers and stalled their advance with his automatic fire. Seeing the drama unfold below in slow motion, Angelo considered moving closer toward the action. As he engaged three men who were now on the roof, he hoped to someway get a better shot at the doorway.

Realizing it was too late for that action, he instead scoured the engagement and quickly processed the sight. Within seconds, he attained complete tactical situational awareness and admired his men as each fought with his soul, their weapons merely being instruments.

In the ensuing firefight, Matteo was hit first in the leg. After placing his last satchel of dynamite on the tower, he took a second round in the shoulder. He fell about ten feet from Gianni and yelled in a pained voice for him to run. Not wanting to leave his comrade, Gianni stayed in the machine gun nest and continued the fight. But as even more Germans came out from the building and knowing that reinforcements would not be long behind, Gianni reluctantly made a run for it. He made it to the base of the tower only a few feet from where Matteo lay. The wooden columns of the tower supplied some cover, but a German bullet found his back. Gianni clung to the column for support, but he couldn't overcome the damage to his body and slowly fell. First, awkwardly to his knees and then completely prostrate in an outstretched position on his stomach.

Gianni's face was hauntingly turned toward Matteo. Matteo looked into the eyes of his good friend and saw the spark of life had either left him or was nearly extinguished. He couldn't keep from staring into the eyes of his friend and continued to search for some sign of life. The sound of bullets kicking in the dirt around his position quickly returned him back to his own nightmarish reality.

Realizing that Gianni was likely gone or close to death, and that escape for himself was impossible, Matteo lowered his head and closed his eyes. A mere few second later, he set off the satchel charges and the ground shook from the mighty explosion. The discharge threw dirt and debris for twenty feet, and the bodies of Matteo and Gianni flew like rag dolls with it.

The tower did actually fall and graze the building, likely saving Angelo's life, and Angelo was fortunate for Matteo's expert placing of the explosives. When the tower scraped the building, it took part of a wall and roof with it. The result of the destruction and firefight was now smoke and debris all over the general area and a large plume rising high in the cold, dry air. Angelo used the ensuing chaos to quietly exit back into the familiar woods.

The men had discussed many times that none would let themselves be captured. Angelo was certain that was in Matteo's mind as he blew the tower. The sure torture that would follow capture, like what poor Pietro went through, would almost certainly force them to expose the team before they were finally slaughtered.

But talk is cheap. To actually see Matteo sacrifice himself the way he did stunned Angelo. His position behind some thick brush yielded a better view of the building but also impeded his view of Matteo and Gianni. He saw enough but was grateful that he could not see Matteo's face directly as he made his decision. One less horror to relive later. Angelo vowed to never forget the courage and remarkable sacrifice of his friend. In the days to come, Angelo would be filled first with unthinkable anger but then ultimately intense pride to have served with such incredible men.

Angelo made his way across the woods as the morning sun was just appearing through the trees. Neither fully night nor fully day, he made his way in the slowly gathering light of the early morning. He knew the sun would provide no break from the cold, but he convinced himself to make it through the woods before the day fully broke. From the edge of the woods, it was only steps to the base of the mountain where he hoped to stop for some respite out of the elements.

Finding a small outcropping of boulders that provided an adequate break from the wind, he stopped briefly. Now alone, with his three comrades fallen in battle, Angelo had to start his desperate hike back to safety. Conventional wisdom would have been to walk on the roads instead of through knee-high snow along the mountain.

So Angelo did what he always did and defied what would be expected. He could certainly be tracked easily enough and he knew the Germans got a good look at him. But what soldier would follow him into the wilderness under such conditions? *In the muddy season, we pray for frozen ground, but this is ridiculous!* he thought to himself. With the wind howling and blowing the fresh snow into waist-high drifts, he gathered his strength to face the wall of wind.

CHAPTER 18

The Ultimate Sacrifice

January 4, 1945
The mountains, west of Ponte Gardena, Italy

Angelo didn't have the luxury of time and knew he needed to move on. His adrenaline from the earlier battle had stymied the full effect of the cold and snow. Now taking a break behind the boulders, his senses returned. He felt a cold that could only be experienced during this punishing Alpine winter. Extreme freezing, when paired with the desolate landscape and the loss of close comrades, resulted in a hypothermic loneliness.

After gathering himself, he stepped out from the protected safety of the rock ledge and felt the full brunt of the wind. Cringing, he thought to himself, *This wind attacks worse than any army.* He continued on, certain that the weather and terrain would foil any attempts of following him. Except this time would be unexpectedly different. An entire platoon of *Waffen-SS Panzergrenadiers* did just that. Working under the Nazi military doctrine of *Bandenbekämpfung*, translated as "bandit-fighting" or "combating of bandits," special units of the German army were trained in countering resistance or insurrection behind German lines during wartime. And this one had Angelo in its sights.

The anti-partisan doctrine provided a rationale for targeting and murdering partisan forces like Angelo's as well as the civilians who supported them. The *Führer Directive 46* of August 18, 1942 specifically defined the goal to be "complete extermination." The directive provided immunity from prosecution and enabled the forces to act with "utter brutality." This unique platoon of specialized forces, empowered to exterminate anyone it chose and operate outside the law, was stationed nearby and on its way.

Angelo hiked as fast as he could in the snow and put some distance between him and the now demolished radio tower and station. He climbed to a high-vantage point in an attempt to better assess the situation. As he looked back toward the site, he could see the large contingent of men exiting the woods. He asked himself, *where did these guys come from?* Angelo assumed they were notified by the men in the building that saboteurs were attacking the station. Either that, or the rising smoke from the engagement brought them like the stench of a rotting carcass brings vultures.

Bewildered, he forced himself to rationalize that they would cut the chase off at some point. After another hour of climbing and struggling to move in the engulfing snow, he took a break to gauge his progress and the disposition of the enemy. Laboring to breathe, Angelo carefully uncovered the lens guards of his field glasses. He was immediately struck by his trembling hands, likely the result of a combination of adrenaline once again coursing through his body and the freezing temperatures. From his hilltop location, he could see the platoon, numbering some twenty men, following his tracks now about a quarter mile behind him.

Understanding the urgent need to put additional distance between him and his pursuers, he continued the tortuous hike. There would be no way to hide his movements given the thick layer of snow that covered every surface. Still, he held on to his only hope: that the enemy would eventually give up the chase.

After another half hour, he came to an expansive valley and rested for a few minutes. He could see a church at the opposite side with some welcome wooded and rocky areas that he hoped would cover his escape. The windswept bald and thick woods wouldn't hold nearly as much snow, and he reasoned he could hide his footsteps. His pragmatic mind quickly conquered any panicked optimism; the platoon was gaining on him with every passing minute, and it was inevitable they would catch up.

The Chiesa di San Giacomo was the most beautiful church in the fresh snow, like a postcard he sometimes saw in Genoa's stores (*see photo references 18.1 and 18.2*). His moment of rest passed, and he turned his attention to the enemy which was continuing its relentless pursuit. They were now close enough that he could actually hear them struggling in the distance. While trying to rapidly develop options, he continued to be dumbfounded as to why they kept chasing him under such extreme conditions.

He had hiked the entire previous night before completing their mission to blow up the transmission tower. Now after hiking hours through bitter cold and snow-blanketed terrain, Angelo was near exhaustion. Every step had become a mighty effort as he fought to make it to the church. With resignation, he asked to God in mock disgust, *did you have to make this last stretch an uphill climb and into the wind?* But as he struggled through like a poor animal grasping for its last bit of life, a strange contentment settled over him. He was at peace, believing he could make a final stand with God's watchful eye upon him.

He was only a few feet from the church door when the Germans broke through the forest edge and began firing on him. As he jumped to his feet, Angelo again could not believe these men keeping pace with him. With an adrenaline-fueled sprint, he ran through a small courtyard and reached the church door. Desperately, he flung it open and immediately turned to lock it, all the while developing quick defensive strategies. He was startled by the presence of a priest who had been praying, but was wide eyed at the sounds of bullets hitting the building and Angelo slamming the massive door.

After a second to comprehend what was happening, he ran to Angelo. Observing his weapons and appearance, the priest immediately recognized the look of a partisan freedom fighter. Angelo's panicked demeanor made it obvious he was in trouble and seeking refuge in this holy place. Without flinching, the priest confidently instructed Angelo, "Go up the steeple and hide in the belfry." Confused but without any other plan or ideas, he thanked the priest and complied.

Sitting some forty feet above the land outside, Angelo could see the contingent of Germans approaching. They were deftly walking in Angelo's path; he had done the hard work of making a way through the deep snow, and they were capitalizing on his grueling effort. As the enemy neared, the commander smartly split his force to encircle the church and, using the courtyard wall for cover, precluded any manner of escape.

Angelo ducked into the corner of the exceptionally well-kept bell tower and earnestly prayed. While he felt nearly frozen and close to hypothermic, his mind didn't stop analyzing potential defensive scenarios and options. The bell tower was open on the sides facing the exterior and would enable him to fire down at the men below. Because of the steep angle, the courtyard wall would offer reduced cover for the soldiers. He could also shoot down through the stair access when they would inevitably come to get him. He even entertained the idea of dropping hand grenades down the stair access to take out the men that were sure to come up for him. At least he could maybe even take out a few men below with any luck. It was a certainty that he wasn't going to make it out alive, so he might as well take out as many of the enemy as he could.

Perhaps it was providential leading or the respect he felt in this holy and pure place, but he decided not to do anything rash. *I'm going to die anyway, so why profane the sacred beauty of this church?* he said to himself. He was clear on at least this one thing: he wouldn't damage the building, but he wouldn't be taken alive or go out without a fight either. As he looked out the belfry opening, he considered jumping to his death. The fall was high enough to ensure he wouldn't survive to be tortured. With a thousand scenarios playing in his mind, he was suddenly taken by the beautiful scene. The church tower overlooked a huge valley with the Dolomite mountains in the distance, and he stole a moment of precious peace. Managing a consoling smile, he thought *this place, this homeland, was worth it all.*

With scant few options, he sat back, resigned himself to his situation, and continued to pray for forgiveness and mercy. Certain of his coming demise in that belfry, he didn't even bother praying for a miracle. He just continually prayed for forgiveness. But graciously and when it serves his purpose, God will, at times, deliver a miracle. From his high-vantage point, Angelo could hear, but not see, the following exchange transpiring in the church. He just kept staring at the magnificent view and listening.

Content they had the building covered, the German unit commander banged on the church door, and the priest immediately opened it. The commander and about six men entered the building and brushed snow from their garments. Out of breath and disheveled from the tortuous hike, the commander stood inches from the priest and demanded that he hand Angelo Flaim over to him for crimes against the Reich.

The priest replied that there was no Angelo Flaim or any other person in the building with him. Given the clear tracks in the snow showing Angelo coming in and then not leaving, the German officer demanded again, "We know he is in here. Bring him to us now."

The priest bowed his head and took in several deep breaths. Then nervously, but calmly, he stated again that there wasn't anyone else in the building.

Being drained from the chase and extremely frustrated with the priest, the commander continued angrily brushing snow from his coat. He looked around at the church, perhaps trying to determine the possible location of his quarry or perhaps with reverence to the serene atmosphere. Then with a bark, he demanded, "Look, we saw him enter, and there is no way for him to escape. Turn the traitor in to us, and we will leave you in peace."

The priest now did something that made Angelo freeze in utter disbelief; he took a Bible from a pew, placed his hand on it, and swore to God that Angelo was not in the building. Angelo was awestruck knowing the price the priest was willing to pay for his life. As a Roman Catholic priest, swearing an oath on the Bible, which was a lie, was a mortal sin from which there was no absolution. At that moment, in the priest's mind, he sacrificed his life for Angelo's. He willingly did something that he believed would send him to hell so that this stranger on the run could live; he had truly made the ultimate sacrifice for Angelo.

The German officer took a bewildered step backward. After a few moments of thought, he tried to reason with the priest. "Father, I am also a member of the faith. Are you sure there is nobody in this building but you? You swear to this?"

The priest again breathed hard and meekly said, "As your spiritual father, I swear to God on this Bible that Angelo Flaim and no others are here." Immediately, the priest fell to his knees in front of the commander.

The officer stood dumbfounded for a long moment. He confusedly paced around and stared down at the priest. The contingent of soldiers alternated between eyeing the building for Angelo and staring at the priest in contempt. The minutes passed like hours in the strained silence. Then without another word, the commander ordered his soldiers to leave. The commander convened his troops outside the building and proceeded to retrace their steps. Once they had disappeared across the field and into the woods, Angelo descended from the belfry.

As he entered the chapel area through the doorway that led to the stairs, he saw the priest, still on his knees. Running to him, Angelo picked him up and hugged him strongly. He didn't know what to say but repeatedly said thank you during the long hug. After the extended embrace, he finally released the priest only to see the poor man clumsily lose his balance and drop to the floor upon realizing his fate.

Angelo again picked him up and assured him he would be absolved of this sin, but the priest would have none of it. He simply begged him to leave. Angelo pressed on, trying to ease the tortured man's spirit, but it was of no use. Angelo again hugged the priest, as if trying to absorb some of his pain into himself. These were two men in harm's way: one smelling the sweet fragrance of life, which moments earlier was assured mortality, and the other, the foul stench of death where just before was peaceful prayer.

Angelo decided it's best to quickly be on his way before the German officer could possibly change his mind and return. He hiked another two hours due east, first through alternating woods and rock-strewn terrain and then up a steep mountain incline. The small amount of snow on the rocks quickly surrendered Angelo's footprints to the strong winds. There would be no way to reliably track him for the last hour and a half, and he felt a comforting blanket of peace replace his battle armor.

Continuing this tormenting march, he finally stumbled on a cave cut from a section of shear wall which had a dry floor. Despite his raging hunger, he took the time to pray diligently for the priest and give his unbridled thanks for God's favor upon him. He couldn't help wonder if the priest was aware of him, seen his wanted poster, or if he laid his life down for an unknown freedom fighter. He thought maybe the priest confused him with a different regional leader. In his mind, he hoped that was the case. Could it be that this random priest would just willingly give his life for his? "Who would do that?" he mumbled out loud to no one.

With any semblance of energy passed, he approached unconsciousness. But years of fighting and living in the harsh Alpine winter taught him that without a fire, he would perish, so he mustered his remaining strength to search for firewood. His mind persistently repeated the mantra drilled into him during Alpini survival training: fire, shelter, water, food. While gathering fallen tree limbs and brush, he was blessed to find an animal that had recently frozen to death. He took the gift to the cave, started a warming fire, and cooked his meal.

The echoes of past battles, visions of his fallen family and friends, and now this encounter with the priest pounded the back of his head like a sledgehammer. Angelo had a love-hate relationship with this quiet time between enemy exchanges. He could never fully quell his mind. Emotionally giving up, he heaved several large pieces of wood on the fire and yielded to his exhaustion. An encompassing bitter cold gradually consumed his body once the fire died.

Unsure of how long he slept, he awoke with a renewed energy and hastily made his way out. Throughout the struggle of this journey's last leg, he kept asking himself how the Germans knew his name and why they pursued him when nobody in their right mind would do so. Beaten and depleted, he eventually reached the safety of headquarters. The entire team attended to him after clumsily stumbling through the barn's door.

The result of his obsessive thoughts eventually led to the only conclusion he could rationalize. The German officer retreated without his prize because he would not go against the sworn word of the priest. It was either that, or he knew the war would be ending soon and decided it wasn't worth it. While he was truly grateful for the escape, he was worried about the ramifications of all that had transpired. Ultimately, he came to the frightening realization that one, the enemy knew of him personally as well as his partisan unit; two, they knew they were doing operations in the vicinity; three, they were prepared to pursue them on any future operations; and four, they were determined to eliminate his threat.

Angelo was getting near the end of his rope. Besides himself, Nini, Fulvio, Marco, and Rosario, everyone else had perished under his command. The weight of losing his men, mostly family and close friends, and the experience of the priest's sacrifice left him emotionally spent. He found himself withdrawing from the others and becoming lost in thoughts and memories, which was clearly dangerous in his emotionally fragile state.

For the next month, the men stayed close to their familiar barn, engaging only in minor operations. Much time was spent discussing their new reality and how they could better avoid capture while being hunted. They practiced planning operations from a more defensive posture and worked with Geronimo to employ new specialized tactics.

At the end of the month, they began to get itchy to get back into the fray. Every day Angelo would go out to hunt for food and gather reconnaissance. The afternoons would be spent making snares and laying traps to capture anything possible. The mornings were spent recovering whatever may have wandered into the crude entrapments.

Angelo had become quite an accomplished provider while living on the run. Unable to use weapons or anything that gave off an explosion for fear of exposing themselves, he became fully adept in the quiet ways of the hunter. Snares and cages were deployed to catch rodents, small animals, birds, and the like, but he also scavenged for animals that fell naturally or were killed by predators.

The mountains are a notoriously brutal home for most of the year, and all animals struggled to just survive. The welcome protein ingested from these finds sustained their strength.

In addition to kills or finds that provided meat, he would also forage for berries, nuts, fruits, and plants. He became expert at identifying which types of wild fauna and mushroom would nourish and which would sicken or kill. The winter snow in the Alps was white, beautiful, and silent, and a significant layer of life can be found resting beneath her cloak. Angelo learned to harvest that hidden bounty and survive among that which sustained him.

The team additionally relied on cross-country skis for eased and unseen movement in this extreme season. The snow greatly affected which missions they could do and those that they would pass on or defer until the spring. One day while out, about two days easterly from their base by skis, Angelo came upon a critical mountain pass with the town of La Villa south of its center. Poised between two formidable mountain groups rising to nearly ten thousand feet, the valley ran north–south and parallel to the main transportation line leading from the Brenner Pass.

The main road running through the valley is the Strada Colz. The rural paved road had two lanes, but in complete disrepair. The sleepy town of La Villa rarely saw much traffic in the best of times. Now in the dead of winter and enduring the ravages of war, the road was unable to take heavy traffic of any kind. He stowed his skis in a safe location and headed down to the town to warm up and determine the situation there. A local restaurant seemed ideal to gather information and thaw out with a hot cup of espresso.

The only person working in the small restaurant was an elderly lady that had seen too much in her long life. This area of Italy suffered greatly from the First World War, and now she was trying to survive yet another one. The poor woman had the attitude of complete resignation, and her face rarely looked up to meet another's. Angelo attempted to have a conversation with her, but she just mechanically paced the floor, constantly sweeping unseen contaminants.

Clearly tired of this stranger's constant questions, she slowly stopped, lifted her head, and turned her wrinkled and drawn face directly toward Angelo. Then she spoke without reservation, revealing that the Germans had been coming through more often recently—just troops for the most part, with no significant mechanized units. She did not speak ill of her unwelcome guests, simply that they used her little town as a way station. They typically stayed for a short while and then moved on. Angelo wished her well, left a generous tip, and departed before any trouble came along.

That night, instead of heading back to their base, he spent the frigid night on a mountain ledge overlooking the valley. Prepared for the cold, he settled in and fell asleep immediately. The next morning, he was awakened by the banging of trucks careening from one hole in the road to another. Quickly gaining his senses, he observed a substantial column of troop transports with light artillery being pulled by light duty trucks. Sure enough, the troops dismounted and rested in the town just as the old lady had said.

Over the next few days, he saw another caravan of troops that didn't even have motorcycles or light duty support vehicles. *Why are there only men and no armor?* he thought. There had to be armor somewhere. Working through the puzzle in his head, he finally deduced that the main roads must be used for heavy vehicles and panzer tanks while this parallel back road was used for faster personnel movements. Returning to the barn, he told the men of his find, and they immediately agreed it was time to strike.

Photo Reference 18.1 –

This is the Chiesa di San Giacomo where Angelo hid from the pursuing Germans in the bell tower. This was the view he had from the bell tower, including a good angle down to the courtyard wall that protected the Germans, as well as the Dolomite mountains in the distance.

Photo Reference 18.2 –

This is the exquisite interior of the Chiesa di San Giacomo and the alter step where the priest had been praying.

CHAPTER 19

The Hunters Are Themselves Hunted

February 22, 1945
Uletta, northeast of Val Gardena, Italy

This unique winter from hell wouldn't relinquish its fierce grip, but the men were nonetheless eager to mount a major attack. Regular communications between Nini and Geronimo continued, and they informed Geronimo of a good potential target. Geronimo was adamant that they not damage any roads, bridges, or tunnels. The tide of the war had turned, and the Allies needed the infrastructure to chase the retreating Germans and reclaim the land.

Angelo informed Geronimo that their target was a secondary road carrying mainly personnel, and all tank and mechanized units were using the main road. Angelo had a plan envisioned where the team would work with the US Air Force to deliver maximum damage to the enemy. He then requested air force strafing runs over the troop transports. He deduced that an airborne attack in the narrow valley would scatter the troops where there were few areas for cover. His team could then be waiting to safely pick off targets from positions high above the road. Sadly, all air support was engaged in tying up the main German retreat avenues, and Geronimo had to nix the idea.

Angelo then requested and was granted authority to attack the secondary road with just his team. They wouldn't be restricted by the Americans in their methods because this secondary road was not considered critical. Geronimo followed his approval with an urgent request for the team to take prisoners if possible. The key to shortening the war was solid intelligence on enemy troop's strength and movements. With so much turmoil and confusion in the area, any intel from captured Germans would be hugely beneficial.

The taking of prisoners was something the team had agreed long ago never to do. Particularly now that they were down to just five men, their very existence relied of stealthy withdrawals after an engagement, and prisoners would be too great a liability. They didn't have enough food or even a method to quarter them safely, and the reality of them operating so far behind enemy lines was that there wasn't a safe way to even hand them over to the Americans. Lastly, the men weren't trained in interrogations, and none of them wanted to be a part of it. The idea of beating another person, even a hated German, until they confessed information was something abhorrent to them all. Worse yet, after the poor individual couldn't take any more, murdering the man in cold blood was incomprehensible. They believed that killing in action was honorable, but murder was not.

The men all hated the Germans and what they had done to their homeland, but, in the end, they knew that most were simply soldiers obeying orders. Angelo's experience with the German commander that retreated when he knew his prey was cornered demonstrated that there were some good among the bad. He and the team had no intention of playing judge and executioner. Angelo placated Geronimo and agreed to try and secure prisoners from any exchange, but everyone knew it wouldn't happen. The team tried to execute their war with a semblance of honor and morality. While an impossible task, they relied on their unspoken code to maintain their humanity and spiritual health.

Geronimo was also keenly interested in the alliances the team may have formed with other partisan groups. In actuality, the team was so isolated that they hadn't much knowledge of other underground fighters' activities. Geronimo told Angelo that the Garibaldis were getting more active to the east and south of them. He recommended Angelo not partner with any other fighters and remain independent.

This was surprising to Angelo and raised his curiosity. Geronimo explained that Germany was solidly on its heels on all fronts and the end would surely come soon. He wanted Angelo's small and independent team to be available for operations that they didn't want to give to the official larger partisan organizations. Angelo conveyed his understanding to Geronimo but stayed curious at the interesting request. He considered making the journey to see his friend Paolo for clarification but decided to wait until after this upcoming mission.

The men immediately began their final preparations. Angelo reminded everyone that they had to be especially sensitive to weather conditions. From his recent mission, he knew better than anyone that they could be out in the elements for weeks, so they needed to bring extra clothing, food, and other essentials. The good news was that because of the very rural areas they would be traveling through, they could travel by day when there was at least some thermal value from the sunlight.

The plan was to utilize skis the first day to forge new paths through the deep snow at the base of the mountain ridges. Once they reached the mountain itself, they would transition to hiking and carry their skis and packs over a somewhat protected lower ridge under the summit. Once on the other side of the mountain, they would then ski down to the point of the operation. For the beginning and ending segments of the journey, skis would be the only practical method of movement in the thick snow.

Still, with each man carrying some thirty pounds of supplies on his back, it would be extremely challenging. They would ski in fresh snow, and then carry the skis in addition to their packs and hike the mountain at over eight thousand feet in elevation.

Knowing that the following days would challenge them in every way imaginable, Angelo simply told everyone, "Put together your packs and get some sleep. We're in for a few tough days." The men, knowing the truth in the statement, immediately began packing the items each was responsible for.

With the benefit of a bright, clear, sunny day, the men headed out. Conditions of the first day were better than expected. They were able to ski along animal tracks already cut in the snow, making the effort much easier. Even the climb over the mountain ridge was better than expected, with the wind having blown large segments of the rocky area clear of snow. They made good enough time that they were able to make it to the back slope and ski down. They chose a campsite that enabled them to safely see at a distance the road that was their target. Each man took a two-hour shift staying awake to watch for trouble.

The next day, the men were up at sunrise. While Angelo, Nini, and Fulvio maintained a watchful eye for unwanted visitors, Marco and Rosario readied their explosive charges. They carefully loaded their satchels and checked the detonation devices. That afternoon, the only traffic they saw was a few farmers and hay carts moving food for their animals.

Once evening was upon them, they moved down to the road to set the trap. Angelo, Nini, and Fulvio dug depressions in the road bed where Marco and Rosario then placed the satchels of TNT. Once placed, the men loosely covered the improvised mines from view and ran the igniting wires to a safe area above the road (*see photo reference 19.1*). Rosario was to stay at this lower location and blow the charges at the opportune time. The other men retreated to a higher elevation to fire down a hail of bullets on the troops that they anticipated to be scrambling from the explosions.

Camp this second night saw the men only getting partial sleep because of their site preparations and the cold. There was no fire again that evening because they didn't want to give up their presence and position. Lying on his back, gazing at the stars above, Fulvio pointed out a shooting star. "You ever feel like that's us? Brief lights falling and quickly fading out?"

Rosario thought for a second. "Some of the stars hang around in the sky too. Maybe that's us? Shut up and try to get some sleep!"

Morning came and everyone woke early to watch for German forces to pass below them. The hours wore on, but there was no activity. When night came again without the traffic they anticipated, the men bedded down early and took the opportunity to try and get fully rested.

The next morning was more of the same. Sitting under a mountain ledge in the near-freezing cold, Rosario made a joke about the ice sickles that hung precariously over them. "I don't want to be under these things when the fighting starts. They look more dangerous than a bullet!"

The men laughed and continued to ready themselves by going through the escape plan repeatedly. After extending bipod supports to their BARs for more accurate automatic fire, they strategically placed hand grenades and spare ammunition on the ground behind available cover. While anxiety led to them never being fully comfortable in their readiness, they felt as prepared as possible for the coming hell. Finally, they went out of sight to do calisthenics and stretching. Without the benefit of a fire, getting their blood moving provided a little warmth for their freezing bodies.

As noon came, Angelo was getting worried. They didn't bring enough food to sustain them for an extended outing this long. The men spoke of raiding the town below to get additional food, but the decision was to wait till nightfall. Angelo didn't want to risk getting caught in town when the Germans came through. If they were still stuck in this position at dark, then they would raid the village. Rosario split the remaining hard salamis and unleavened bread called *cha-cha* to help them last as long as possible. Cha-cha can best be described as a hard plain pizza crust. But served warm with melted prosciutto, it was delicious and filling. The carbohydrate, calorie, and fat-rich foods provided significant energy in a very small and manageable package.

Fortunately, at about two thirty in the afternoon, the men heard the unmistakable sounds of vehicles and men marching in cadence. Rosario moved down to his safe spot and grabbed the detonator switch. Angelo quietly took his field glasses and strained to get a good look at the caravan. As hoped, there seemed to be troops without heavy backup. The column consisted of several trucks filled with men, followed by foot soldiers, followed by two more trucks, then more foot soldiers, and lastly another truck. At the front of the line was a motorcycle with sidecar and two men. Nini assessed the total number of men to be in excess of one hundred.

As the lead trucks came within a couple hundred feet of the buried satchels, the team tensed and readied themselves for the coming exchange. Each man prayed silently. Instinctively, Angelo clutched the cross hanging from his neck. Giving it a kiss, he unleashed the potential killing power of his BAR by switching the safety and triggering the weapon. Rosario patiently waited for the lead vehicle to pass over the explosives and pushed the plunger at the most opportune moment.

The explosion was larger than any Angelo had ever experienced. The lead vehicle sprang from the ground as the blast from below blew it and debris everywhere. The vehicle immediately caught fire, and Angelo was horrified to see men running haphazardly, completely engulfed in flames. Every soldier along the column followed their training and leapt for the road's ditches. The next five minutes were a blur as the team poured a barrage of bullets from their BARs down upon the exposed men.

The discharge from the team's weapons could not be hidden in the blanket of snow. Easily determining where the fire was coming from, the German troops immediately began to return fire. Gaining their collective composure, the two middle vehicles from the caravan peeled off and made their way across the frozen ground toward the team. The men concentrated their fire on the vehicles but couldn't impede either.

Immediately, mortar fire screamed from the ditch line and multiple locations along the column. Angelo and the team ducked for cover where possible. Huge boulders blew apart, and the few trees in the vicinity snapped like twigs. Splintered tree segments tore through the area with the same lethality as shrapnel. Maximizing the cover offered by the discharging mortars, two enemy vehicles continued getting closer. As the smoke cleared, Angelo could see regular troops staying in the ditches while a unit of men from the two advanced vehicles quickly dismounted and swarmed their location.

Angelo put his weapon down, reached for his field glasses, and saw that the dismounted troops had skis too. It seemed that it would be the Waffen-SS Panzergrenadiers chasing them again. Remembering the tenacity and toughness of the soldiers from the chase at the Chiesa di San Giacomo church, Angelo immediately ordered a retreat.

Rosario had already begun his move up toward the team from his earlier firing position and was within ten feet of Fulvio when a mortar round exploded near Fulvio. Temporarily losing sight of the two, Angelo and Nini paused their shooting and loudly called out their names. Initially, there was no reply, no movement. Marco continued yelling for his friends. In a strained voice, Rosario said he was hit but able to fight. There was no response from Fulvio. Rosario had taken shrapnel in the shoulder, but Fulvio never had a chance. Rosario could move but was greatly limited in his ability to shoot. Nini and Angelo resumed firing at the enemy. As the scene fully cleared, Angelo issued the order to continue their retreat.

Marco and Rosario made the first move up the mountain as Angelo and Nini held the Germans back with covering fire. The two struggled to climb and evade direct lines of fire, particularly with one man wounded. As they reached their cover position, they began returning fire as best they could. The near continuous covering fire focused on the men from the vehicles enabled Angelo and Nini to follow the path of their teammates and make their way up the mountain slope.

The Germans seized upon the opportunity from the men's retreat and break in BAR fire, and progressed steadily upward. As the team made their way along the rocky trail, Angelo reached a high-vantage point. He paused and looked back upon the position they just held. With an element of shock, he saw that it was now leveled by mortar fire. Where he stood just ten minutes earlier was now mostly gone.

This dance with the enemy continued for nearly an hour. Nini estimated the number of men pursuing them at twenty. With only their four, escape would hinge entirely on exploiting the terrain. The men finally reached the rocky ridge of the mountain from where they had previously skied. At this point in the chase, the advantage flipped to them. Quickly, they set up with their rifles to cut down the pursuers as they made their way up the path flanked by large boulders and the mountain. The narrow path was in some places only a foot wide and created a perfect kill zone. The single line of men would be easy targets, and there would be no chance for the enemy to flank them.

The strategy worked well, and the team was able to eliminate multiple targets while slowing their advance. Crouching behind the huge boulders and occasional tree provided excellent cover. Unfortunately, the enemy had a resource that quickly reversed the advantage. They began dropping mortar shells all around the team's position. With each round striking the ground, more and more rock debris would be displaced. It was not enough for a full rock slide, but any shell hitting the right spot, and everyone would be buried. While the boulders provided good cover from the shrapnel and broken off rocks, it would only be a matter of time until one found its mark.

So again, the men retreated up the rocky mountainside to set up another ambush location at an opportune gap. As the Germans pursued, the men would occasionally stop to hopefully pick off a couple more of the enemy and then begin climbing again. Angelo sought to avoid staying in one place too long, which could provide the enemy an easy mortar target.

Rosario questioned the tactic because the strategy enabled the enemy to gain ground. The deliberately slow process had the team patiently letting the Germans advance until they reached a kill zone, but it also aided them to get perilously closer with every advance. There were only so many perfect ambush sites, and the enemy was ultimately gaining additional critical ground with each. Angelo understood but gave the order to again move up and around the mountain. He resolutely insisted they stay on the move and let the mountain protect them.

As they had done before, they now reached a place for yet another ambush site. Angelo took a position by a large boulder, and Nini set up next to a jagged rock ledge. Rosario laid behind a boulder and examined his wound. He immediately saw that his makeshift bandage was nearly soaked through. The loss of blood revealed the extent of the wound, even if his adrenaline had him feeling only tolerable pain. He rearranged the bandage a bit to try and get a dry spot over the wound. Realizing the futility of this as even the slightest movement of the bandage shot pain to his very core, he recommitted himself to the coming battle. Awkwardly dropping to the ground, he settled into a position that would enable him to fire his weapon.

As the first of the enemy made it to the gap, Marco began firing down from his standing position at the crotch of an ancient tree that had seen its share of fighting men. Unbeknownst to the team, the Germans were able to find another route up the mountainside and found a weak, but ultimately effective, flanking opportunity. Two men had maneuvered into position and fired on Marco. Their aim was off, and he survived the surprise. However, in responding to the threat at his side, Marco inadvertently exposed himself to the troops below. Several men fired upon him, and he took a round in the left forearm.

Nini called out to Marco for him to move back toward him and Angelo. The enemy was getting uncomfortably close, and they would soon need to change tactics. Nini suggested using grenades to put some distance between them and then make a run for it. With only two men able to truly engage the enemy and their ammunition rapidly being depleted, they simply didn't have the firepower to continue the fight. Angelo agreed. The four men retreated once more up the mountain a short distance and came upon a perfect ambush site. Scanning the area, they determined that the terrain wouldn't support a flanking move by the Germans, and this gap would be their final stand.

They only had to wait ten minutes for the German contingent, now down to about a dozen men, to approach the gap. This time, however, Angelo and Nini each hurled two hand grenades into the gap. The four ensuing explosions broke apart and moved many large boulders. The gap that was now shut off to the Germans and would take them hours to clear, if they could do it at all. The team didn't wait around. They immediately moved quickly along the mountain and out of site from the enemy.

When they felt it safe, Nini attempted to dress the wounds on his teammates. He used the resources available to him, like the pristine snow, to first clean the wounds. Then he tore strips of clothing to bandage them. The makeshift dressing was woefully inadequate, but it would help stop the bleeding till they made it back to the barn.

The wounded men, with the additional burden of hunger, lacked the sufficient strength to hike at any reasonable rate.

"I'm glad we lost the Tedeschi in the mountain. We wouldn't stand a chance out here," Nini said to Angelo.

The wounded men were indeed a significant hindrance, but the team managed to keep a slow yet deliberate pace.

After a few hours of hiking, they made it to the open valley. Angry that they had to ditch their skis at the start of the escape, they now had to hike through deep snow to make it back to the base. Rosario and Marco were very weak and in significant pain, and their progress slowed even more. Between their general condition and the need to cut a new path through the snow, it took far longer than they planned to make it back. The painfully slow hike had them all near frozen. As the men approached headquarters, each one collapsed from exhaustion. Nini went to the farmhouse and the farmer's wife came out to properly dress the wounds of both injured men. Gratefully, over time, both men would recover without lasting damage.

Over the next month of recuperation, the team would evaluate many alternatives of how to move forward. The news was everywhere that the Germans couldn't hold out much longer. Given what they had all been through this winter, the men appeared beaten and tired beyond measure. Eventually, they narrowed the options to two. The first was to simply sit out the rest of the war in recognition of their sacrifice and decide it was over for them. The second was to move south and join forces with Paolo. With the resources the Garibaldis had been amassing, they could continue the fight under his command.

While they were resting and building their strength back, a different option surfaced.

Map Reference 19.1 –

This map shows the location of La Villa, and the valley through which Angelo's partisan team attacked. Of note are the two mountains on either side and specifically the one on the left from which Angelo launched his attack. Location 1 is the location of Angelo's team. Location 2 is the attack location. Location 3 is the town of La Villa.

CHAPTER 20

Clearing the Way

April 6, 1945
Uletta, northeast of Val Gardena, Italy

When spring finally arrived in the mountains, it generally came swiftly and vigorously. Meadows that were covered in thick snow quickly became blanketed in flowers and plants of all types. But this tortuous spring brought steady rains and colder-than-normal temperatures. This translated, operationally, into muddy and impassable low-lying areas—a significant impediment to many types of traditional missions.

As the winter had worn on, the war slowed but did not completely stop. The Western and the Eastern Fronts both stalled significantly yet still continued. In contrast, however, buoyed by the addition of the Tenth Mountain Division entering the war in Central Italy, the Allies were making steady progress up the length of the country. The legendary Tenth was a special division trained specifically for mountain warfare. Their training and operational capacities were unique and made the difference in the Italian advance that winter. Geronimo made Angelo aware of the new infusion of talent and capacity soon after they landed at Naples.

But even where Angelo was, in remote areas of the north, the great news of the Allies advance spread like wildfire. In six weeks of ferocious fighting, the Tenth had broken through the German mountain defenses of the Gothic Line and secured Riva Ridge and Mount Belvidere. German troops, once thought invincible to the Italians, were now seen for what they were: a defeated army just marking time until the end. This emboldened Italian populace quickly led to thousands joining the partisan movement, and in the final months of the war, the Germans were endlessly harassed. Hundreds of partisan attacks across the country were frequent and effect.

Geronimo now had new instructions for Angelo and the team. Missions would now rely more on stealth and cunning instead of dynamite and boldness. Angelo embraced the new requests and looked forward to providing the conquering armies whatever information they needed.

At six thirty in the morning, as they have done since the beginning of time, the woods adjacent to the headquarters began their imperceptible brightening. There was a tangible air of finality to the war, and Angelo embraced his new directive from Geronimo to gather intelligence for the Tenth. The training received by these men was very similar to what Angelo had gotten with the Alpi Graie Alpini Division before his desertion. He also recognized that he had matured as a mountain soldier by this time, and he was certain he could add significant value. He and them would share a bond for mountain operations, and he considered it a great honor aiding them in their decision-making.

The Tenth Mountain Division continued to move steadily north with the aim of ultimately capturing the Po River Valley. The Po is a great river that is fed from the massive amount of rain and snowmelt that come off the Dolomites and Alps. It runs primarily west to east and provides a significant natural barrier to taking the north of Italy (*see map reference 20.1*).

So much was happening during the month of April in Northern Italy that the OSS wanted clear and accurate information. Utilizing his forged documents and his bona fide Italian documents, Angelo would be now traveling across the region providing critical information on German and Fascist movements. He traveled in civilian clothes in which he could pass as either a German Gestapo agent or an Italian businessman. He kept his Gestapo papers in his left coat pocket and his Italian papers in the right. Depending on who stopped him, he could pull out appropriate documents which would hopefully corroborate a backstory and facilitate safe passage.

Unfortunately, Marco and Rosario, now fully healed, decided they didn't want to participate with Angelo and Nini in this new mission. They felt the team could be better used by continuing their previous missions. Sabotaging infrastructure leading to the Brenner Pass between Italy and Austria would do far more damage to the Germans than gathering intel.

Rosario, because of his bitter hatred of the Germans, simply wanted to kill as many as possible - personally. "Intel has value for others to damage the German war machine, but I need to kill as many as I can myself. All I ask for is my rifle and as much dynamite as you can give me."

Marco had always respected Rosario greatly as the old man on the team and simply followed his lead. At the age of only twenty-two, Angelo was actually a little younger than most on the team. Yet after all that had transpired since first deserting the Italian army, he felt like the group's old man and a father. Angelo understood Rosario's need to take revenge directly. His family had suffered beyond measure through both world wars. In the end though, war is like rust. It eats away the soul till there is nothing left. The ensuing hate is a powerful and irrational monster. Both Angelo and Nini tried to reason with their fellow teammates, and the four men passionately discussed how to proceed.

Angelo and Nini argued that the Americans knew the best way to use their resources, but Rosario wouldn't budge from continuing the acts of sabotage that had been so significant. Given all that transpired, once the need for revenge got into their heads, it was impossible to change. It takes root like kudzu or ivy that can never seem to be completely killed back.

In the end, the four separated, and Angelo never learned the disposition of his two fellow fighters. That evening, the normally welcomed silence was replaced by a deafening symphony of tragic memories. It would be yet another bad night for sleep.

During the first two weeks of April, intelligence gathering on Axis activities extended across all of Northern Italy. The pace of travel was both exhausting and dangerous. Utilizing the connections made by

Gianni the previous summer, he engaged several trusted sources by both radio and in person. However, the information with the most value came from direct observation and experience. Regular radio communications with Geronimo ensured timely actionable intel on the rapidly changing realities.

The Allies continued their steady advance up the spine of Italy on three primary fronts. The US Tenth Division, who's primary responsibility ran up the center of the country. The US Ninety-Second Infantry Division, also known as the "Buffalo Soldiers Division," moved along the west coast to Genoa, the city where Angelo had grown up, and then ultimately to Turin. Within a week, the Eighth Army advanced northeast toward Venice and Trieste. With the Germans in full retreat, the goal was to eliminate their capacity to retreat back into to Germany. If the Allies could stop the Germans at the Alps, they would have no reinforcements for the fight against the Russians and Americans, both of which were quickly moving on Berlin.

Angelo traveled and constantly recorded critical information. The daily excursions by train or hitchhiking were dangerous, and the stress of constantly being "on" wore both men. During the fourth week of April, he was in the area west of Milan when his sources told him Mussolini was going to flee the area. He also learned that the partisans were going to stop him at any cost. Angelo requested to stay and participate in finding the deposed dictator.

Geronimo concurred that Angelo should stay in Milan and monitor the happenings. Monitor but not participate. This surprised the men, and they reacted quickly. "Why can't we assist in the hunt for Mussolini? We know this area as well as anyone and want to be a part of finding him and getting justice."

But Geronimo had other intentions for the men and demanded they stay back.

With the anticipated fall of Mussolini, the Allied strategy was to have the Italian people rise up and make escape for the Germans as difficult as possible. Angelo, at a minimum, hoped to get to Genoa and let his family know that he and Nini were fine. Geronimo was again adamant. Angelo and Nini were to stay where they were until the downfall of Mussolini could be verified. Even after the dictator had been dealt with, they were to stay and continue to monitor events and report on activities in the region.

Angelo, however, didn't like taking orders from anyone. He had spent the entire war calling the shots for his team and had survived to the end. He and Nini plotted to get away against the wishes of the US agent. Nini took a stronger position than Angelo anticipated, saying, "Come on, Angelo, there's no way that Geronimo, located who knows where, would ever know that we had left. And supposing he did find out, it would only be a day, and what is the worst that could happen? The war is essentially over for us."

But after the initial emotional response to being told what to do, pragmatism took over. Geronimo always seemed to have the pulse of what was going on. Could there be significant action in Genoa or on the way there? What could be waiting for them if they took off on their own? Based on the destruction of Milan, could Genoa have fared better? Ultimately, they fumed to each other before finally capitulating and hunkering down.

The men didn't have to wait long. The next day, on April 25, the CLNAI declared a general uprising. The CLNAI was the large partisan movement Paolo belonged to and the one that tried to recruit Angelo's team earlier. It enjoyed participation from many, if not most partisan groups and brigades. By the war's end, it had become a political force and was extremely sympathetic to Communism, as applied in a very Italian way. Initially, the party was highly aligned with traditional Soviet Communism, but soon after liberation, it became a coalition of the many political factions in the region and developed its own unique Italian bent.

Angelo embraced Communism but primarily as a means to attain his ultimate goal of a free Trentino. As such, his focus was outside the developing constituency, and he was practically unknown to the organized Italian resistance in Milan. He was, however, very well known by many local townspeople. Angelo used the remaining money dropped by the OSS earlier that year to buy security and secrecy from people all across Northern Italy.

Mussolini and his mistress rightly feared for their lives and, aided by German agents, escaped from Milan that day. Two days later, they were captured by local partisans near Lake Como, a mere sixty miles from Milan. In another two days, they were both shot dead and hung in public for all to see.

Unfortunately, throughout this tumultuous week, Italy plunged ever deeper into a state of complete chaos and lawlessness. There was no real government, the remnants of the German army were trying desperately to get back to Germany, the Allies were moving aggressively on three fronts, and anarchy ruled the streets. A general "purge" started almost immediately of any Fascist or German sympathizers. Men were shot without due justice, and women would routinely have their heads shaved in shame or worse. Without any legal system to speak of, it was a prosecutorial free-for-all.

Not being known by the local partisans and authorities around Milan, Angelo desperately wanted to leave. Trying to explain that he was one of the good guys to an angry mob trying to pick out and punish Italians sympathetic to either Mussolini or Hitler would be nearly impossible, particularly if he were caught with his Gestapo papers. But he had no other option than to just sit there and wait. It was a dangerous gambit, and he felt exposed and open to being misjudged. Operating covertly and in league with the American OSS, he would surely be persecuted if he were discovered. Deep in thought, he kept nervously clicking his cigarette lighter over and over waiting for the chance to leave.

But Angelo would not be there to see Mussolini hang or to enjoy the war's end in Italy. On the twenty-sixth of April, Geronimo and Dimitri both sent radio messages to again change his location and focus. Both were concerned for what was awaiting the Allies in Berlin as Hitler was being choked into submission.

There was justifiable fear from both that the outskirts of the city would be mined or booby-trapped. The Allies also didn't have any reliable data on Nazi troop strength or mechanized resources within the city. Even worse, Allied bombing had reduced Berlin's once large brick and masonry buildings to little more than heaps of rubble. It was the perfect place for ambushes or a counteroffensive as a last-ditch effort by a madman. Despite the risks, Angelo's new mission was to go to Berlin and determine these and other strategic items for both governments. While eager to get away from the dangerous situation in Milan, going into the heart of the cornered beast shook both men to the core.

Initially, Nini flat-out refused to go. He argued it was nothing more than a suicide mission, especially now that everyone knew the war in Italy would be over in weeks, if not days. He and Angelo were the only two left from family and friends that survived this horrific experience, and he wasn't going to die now, not at the fifty-ninth minute of the eleventh hour. Nini had become confident the end was imminent and had become lost in dreams of going home and starting over.

Angelo heard the message from his cousin loud and clear and couldn't argue against it. It was hubris to think they would survive, and Nini was right. There were thousands of things that could go wrong and too many unknowns to list. They had no idea where they were going, what to expect when they got there, and a questionable support structure for survival.

Ultimately, they talked themselves into going. They correctly reasoned that there would be tens of thousands of men going into a city completely laid waste. Without reliable intel, there was no doubt many, if not most, would perish. A greater level of intelligence could end the war a day or two earlier and save many lives on both sides. With no illusions of personally surviving, the men radioed both the OSS and Russian Intelligence that they would leave that day. Just one day before Mussolini was captured and only two days before the surrender of German forces in Italy, they left on this last mission, code-named *Meridian*.

Angelo and Nini regretted that they weren't in Italy with family and friends to celebrate the end of the war, but they remained focused on this last effort to gather intel for the fall of Berlin - one last mission. They both knelt and prayed for safety in the most unsafe place on the planet.

Map Reference 20.1 –

This map shows the extent of progress the Allies made in Italy before the war's end. The Allies never made it into the mountains and the Val Gardena region where Angelo operated. He served the entire war, nearly three years, entirely behind enemy lines. The red star indicates the last location of Angelo's operations prior to the Meridian Mission and going to Berlin.

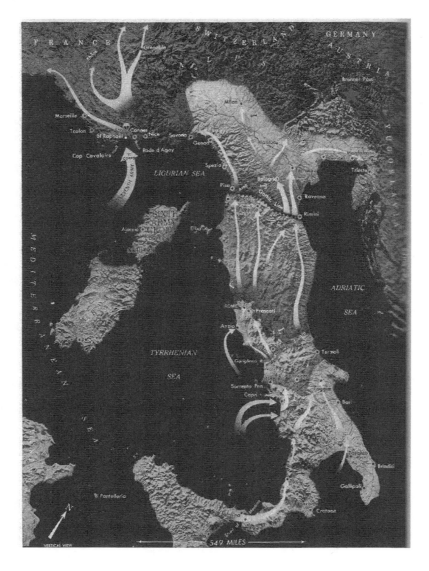

CHAPTER 21

Robbed of V-Day

April 27, 1945
Berlin, Germany

Angelo and Nini were completely surprised by how little difficulty they had getting to Berlin. The war was essentially over, and even the most fanatical Nazi soldiers just wanted to get out of Italy and back home. The ensuing movements by every political faction involved in the war left the transportation network in complete disarray.

The two first boarded a train from Milan to Trento. The ride was nerve-racking, as everybody on the train was suspicious of everyone else being some sort of enemy. Nobody acted on their assumptions though, as they were all praying to just survive the coming weeks. Even so, Angelo and Nini rode with their eyes wide open and *pistolas* at the ready.

Geronimo had radioed detailed information regarding the contacts they should meet as well as the location. When they exited the train, they continued five blocks to a pristine area of the city that seemed nearly untouched by the war. They waited there about one hour till a car with a single driver approached and exchanged the agreed upon code phrases.

"Do you think it will rain tomorrow?" Angelo said first.

"Not here, but maybe in Rome where I am from," the man correctly replied.

Welcoming the men into his vehicle, the driver immediately gave them two sandwiches, some water to drink, and proceeded north. Aside from the initial pleasantries and thanks for the ride, everyone generally rode in silence.

Angelo didn't ask, and the driver didn't offer any name or personal information, which suited Angelo just fine. There was no telling who this individual was aligned with. The ride did, however, give the men the opportunity to reflect on all that had transpired. Angelo fought the desire to remember fondly the men he served with and the achievements they had made for the war effort. Instead, he drove himself to stay focused on the mission. Even so, he couldn't help but look back at Nini in the rear seat and smile a nervous but assured smile. Nini responded by indignantly looking out the window. One more mission - just one more and it would be over.

The next stop was a small town off the autostrada called Vipiteno Sterzing. Once exited from the main road, the driver drove onto a local road. When that ended, he then proceeded off the road for about ten minutes to a barn not on any road or map. They were now just about five miles from the Brenner Pass, which was arguably the most dangerous segment of the journey. In the barn, Angelo was pleased to see that some cheese, bread, and water had been left for them.

The driver instructed them to wait there until another agent would come to take them the rest of the way. Angelo and Nini thanked the stranger once again and anxiously sat and waited. Not knowing how long it might be till their next compatriot made an appearance, they agreed to take advantage and get some sleep. They took one-hour naps with one staying awake to keep guard. They also agreed that they would alternate sleeping on the remaining legs of the drive. The hours passed slowly, and they began to worry that there was a breakdown in the mission. Nini let Angelo know in no uncertain terms that he still didn't feel good about this final mission. "This is crazy. We should be home now." he said. Angelo couldn't argue and just nodded.

After both were able to take several naps, Nini heard a vehicle approaching and woke Angelo. It was a heightened and anxious state when the old rickety wooden door slowly creaked open. The unfortunate driver of their next leg entered to find both men hiding behind equipment with their weapons trained squarely upon him.

The driver instinctively held up his hands. Angelo initiated a new slightly modified code phrase to verify his identity.

"Do you think it will rain tomorrow?"

"Not here, but maybe in Naples where I am from" came the correct reply.

The subtle phrase change was agreed upon with Geronimo and Dimitri at the start of the mission. The difference in phrasing would be used to determine if the previous driver had been compromised.

It was a complete surprise to both men that the driver was German and spoke little Italian. The inability to communicate well just worsened their apprehension over the mission. However, they had little choice but to trust the driver since he knew the code phrase and mission specifics. Being in security-sensitive radio silence, they couldn't communicate with Geronimo once they left Milan. The man provided them with a change of new clothing, and they again departed.

As they approached the Brenner Pass, multiple guards were checking identity papers to grant entry *(see photo reference 21.1)*. Nini remarked, "This area is fortified with more concrete bunkers and artillery than most of Italy!"

Angelo silently nodded in agreement. For a couple of miles from the border and in the mountains leading to the pass, the Germans had built up impressive defenses and avoided relentless Allied air attacks.

Twice the vehicle was stopped by German guards and their accursed dogs. Angelo trembled at the dogs only feet away from him but now understood why their driver was German. Before handing their papers over, the driver spoke discretely with the guards. Their conversations went uncomfortably long, but, in both cases, they were allowed to proceed without incident. Since Angelo couldn't speak with the driver except for a few words, he thanked him at length as best as he could. "*Danke, danke!*"

The appreciation of his guests was easy to see, and the driver just held his thumb up in the universal language of okay.

They drove a long way north. The vehicle first passed through Munich, and Angelo enjoyed a secret smile as he recognized a few spots from him being there in what seemed like an eternity before. During the remaining six hours of the journey, they passed countless reminders of the Allied bombings as they drove a circuitous route and avoided potential problematic areas. The driver was obviously very knowledgeable of the local situation. On five separate occasions, he diverted off the planned route to bypass roadblocks, checkpoints, and other potentially dangerous stops.

Finally, the group arrived in the small town of Ketzin, about thirty minutes west of Berlin. The region around the town was small and nondescript, housing about seven thousand people prior to the war. However, during the war, the population quickly increased to some ten thousand people, with the increase attributed to German support personnel.

The small town of Ketzin would achieve lasting fame as the place where the Russian army completed its pincer move around Berlin. On the morning of April 25, the ring around Berlin closed when Soviet Commanders Zhukov's and Konev's units met at Ketzin. Berlin had become completely surrounded. The Russians were eager to avenge the atrocities of Stalingrad, named after their leader, by exacting revenge on the German capital.

When Angelo and Nini arrived on April 29, they were greeted by a Soviet operative named Maksim. After exchanging basic information, Maksim radioed Geronimo so Angelo could get his orders directly. Their instructions were simple in concept but incredibly difficult in reality: go into Berlin and determine troop strength, mechanized capabilities, and defensive capabilities of the Germans. They needed to assess what the Allies would experience when they arrived and the level of resistance they could expect. The next morning, he, Nini, and a German operative named Lars snuck up to the edge of the once beautiful city.

As the men approached the outskirts of the city that had visions of world domination, all that could be seen were fires and destroyed buildings. This was the third day of massive shelling. People were walking around in a daze, seemingly oblivious to the danger everywhere. Women clutching children would walk calmly through piles of rubble as if going on a Saturday walk in the park. Their numbness and trancelike state surely reflected the emptiness in their hearts and their living nightmare. Even the children didn't cry, as if they understood the futility of tears when their guardians were themselves devoid of any ability to feel.

German soldiers could be seen taking defensive positions without any direct leadership. Angelo witnessed that most were very young and seemed to only want to find a good hiding spot. They were about to be overrun, everyone knew it, and there would be no sanctuary. The ever-present smell of death and suffering hung in the rancid air like smog in a filthy city.

The team proceeded and began their assessments. Because Lars spoke fluent German, he would focus on asking questions and gleaning unseen information. Angelo and Nini each documented infrastructure damage and conditions.

All three would use their experience to discern defensive strategies, heavy fortifications, choke points, and other relevant intelligence. Lars would report directly to the Russians and Angelo to Geronimo. However, it was Lars that was able to converse with the locals to determine specifics, and the men openly shared their observations and evaluations.

Inching ever closer to the inner city, they made their way down a wide, once-elegant parkway. All evidence of the ancient trees that adorned its perimeter had been burned or blown away. Only stumps remained to show their stately once-proud heritage. The fires which raged all around them made the temperature almost unbearable in this claustrophobic hell. The smoke from those fires hung in the air like the fog Angelo was so accustomed to, and often revealed the enemy as shadowy silhouettes.

As the men continued deeper into the tempest, the conditions only worsened. Remnants of bombings littered the streets, with vehicles and animal carts overturned and burning. Concrete dust and the smoke from withering fires were commonplace throughout, making breathing difficult.

Berlin was a sewer of profanity in which the Nazis were now drowning. Buildings that once towered over the busy city streets had fallen as if subject to a catastrophic earthquake that wouldn't relent. Entire wall sections many stories high could be seen leaning precariously over the street, seemingly waiting for the slightest wind or provocation to cause their fall. The men could not believe the extent of the carnage. It was far worse than the damage they observed in Milan, and the very ruins themselves seemed soaked in the blood of the devil.

Angelo and Nini were both terrified of their physical surroundings as well as the obvious danger from the city being shelled. Fortunately, Soviet shelling was concentrated in the heart of the city. Their intended mark was the chancellery, where leaders believed Hitler and his high command were hiding in a below ground bunker. While Lars wanted to get closer inside the city center to see the disposition of the building and hear what he could about Hitler's state, Angelo and Nini refused. The shelling had continued throughout the day, and this was close enough. Being just outside the inner city, occasional errant rockets would regularly fall precariously close. Between the incessant whistling of rockets hitting the target and the sporadic ones landing too close for comfort, the men prayed to simply get out alive.

But it was to no avail. Lars was the only man who could speak the language well enough to get them out of trouble. Despite the near physical altercation brought on by their argument, the men knew their lives were intrinsically tied to Lars's. They had to stay with him, no matter what, and the three ultimately continued their journey into the furnace.

The team advanced through a standing gate which had seen most of its accompanying fence destroyed long ago. Progressing into an alley, they hid behind a truck that had been leveled by a fallen section of building. Body parts of the poor victims caught inside littered the area. They continued on and next took cover behind a bicycle leaned against a pile of rubble. Though there was no wind, its wrangled wheel slowly turned as if from its own dark force. Since there wasn't any room to walk among the debris, they crawled from one pile of rubble to the next.

As the day wore on, they kept moving through the carnage. Despite the danger and nauseating smell of death, the team collected a sizeable amount of intelligence on every critical front. They observed many units of artillery still manned and prepared to fight the invading Allies. Although they thought Lars was crazy to want to go in, both Angelo and Nini later agreed that the intel was invaluable, and the man was a pro's pro. He seemed fearless in the face of incredible danger, all the while speaking with bribed soldiers, frightened elderly civilians, orphaned children, or whoever seemed safe to speak with to assess the defensive readiness of the city.

Entering the city center, they noticed a distinct change. While obviously weary, dirty, and exhausted, the soldiers here appeared far more mature and battle hardened. A surprising number of seasoned soldiers had taken up strategic positions and created many sangers from the rubble around them. Virtually every former building housed snipers just waiting for the final Allied assault. The team agreed that the German high command had put their young inexperienced "soldier citizens" and Hitler Youth in the outer areas of the city to absorb the brunt of the coming attack. The inner city had the benefit of disciplined veteran soldiers to protect its leaders. The Allies would certainly take the city, but based on what they observed, Hitler was determined to make them pay a heavy price.

As the day turned to evening, the men all wanted to return to the relative safety of Soviet-controlled Ketzin. They slowly backed out the way they had moved in, hoping to not stir up any resistance. In the twilight's dwindling light, the men continuously tripped over the endless debris and rubble.

During the two-hour exit process, Lars learned that Adolf Hitler had committed suicide earlier in the afternoon. Suddenly, according to Lars, the men's mission changed; now they needed to secure collaborating information of Hitler's death. Going back to the sources that Lars had spoken with earlier in the day, they tried in vain to get direct confirmation. With the nightly bombardment starting, the men were forced to exit and return to Ketzin.

Looking to the sky, Angelo could make out the shapes of planes dropping their destructive ordnances. The deafening sound of the heavy bombs landing made Angelo long for the solitude of his beloved mountains. Looking back over his shoulder, the horizon was blurred by the incredible amount of concrete dust and dirt in the air. But after each massive explosion, Angelo couldn't help but be taken by the colors produced during the blast. Brilliant reds and oranges would rise high into the sky after each bomb detonated.

Meanwhile, Nini kept pushing to get out fast. "Let's go, let's go!" he prodded. With most of the landmarks in the city blown, there was a legitimate fear that the bombings could easily be off their target of the central city. Nini nagged both men about the danger to be had as death would be raining down well into the night.

When the men returned to Ketzin, they were greeted by euphoric cheers and vodka toasts. Unbeknownst to Angelo, he, Nini, and Lars were just one of four teams the Soviets had sent in to provide situational awareness. Two of the other teams were able to secure confirmation from their sources that Hitler was indeed dead. Angelo immediately radioed Geronimo who reinforced the news that Hitler was truly gone and that negotiations for a complete surrender were proceeding.

Angelo couldn't believe it. He didn't know what to say or think. The dream of making it to the end of the war had somehow come true. After the brief elation of receiving the news, all the emotion of losing so many family members and friends suddenly washed over him, and he broke down. He felt guilty for celebrating when the memories of his fallen brothers were all too fresh.

He stayed with the team celebrating for about fifteen minutes and then went to a private area and prayed. Angelo would sadly realize over time that his war with the enemy was little compared to the war within him.

In this moment of solitude and thanksgiving, he realized just how much he had matured spiritually. At the start of the war, he was like most youth. There were more important things to think about than eternal life and death. He once thought himself invincible. Now he recognized it was God's providential hand that got him through, and he simply couldn't tell his Heavenly Father thank you enough.

Understandably, the men couldn't wait to get back to their families, but it took another three days until May 2 for the Germans to officially surrender in Italy. Because of the chaos in Northern Italy, traveling back home was deemed to be too dangerous, and both men were ordered to stay put. The orders to stay with the Russians and await further orders from Geronimo and Dimitri hurt like a gut punch. Since they had no other option, they tried to make the best of it.

In resignation, Angelo said to Nini, "I'm really getting tired of this vodka. I wonder if Zio was able to hide away any wine from last season?"

Photo Reference 21.1 –

Set of Identity Papers issued December 23, 1944.

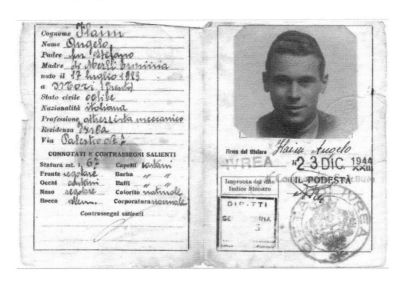

Another set of Identity Papers issued April 27, 1945, the day he left for his final mission to Berlin. Note the photocopy of the above photograph taped onto the forged documents.

CHAPTER 22

Returning Home

May 2, 1945
Ketzin, west of Berlin, Germany

Angelo felt vindicated. It had been a long fight, but he stood there now amid death and ruin, wearing the badge of life. He had flowed down the long foul river of decay that was this war, and now he could smell the sweet ocean waters it had at last emptied into.

Surprisingly, direct orders never came through from Geronimo. Angelo and Nini came to feel essentially abandoned with their Russian counterparts, unable to participate in any significant way. In the race to bring Berlin to its knees in retaliation for what the Germans did to Soviet cities, their revenge was all consuming. The Russian leadership generally provided some input, but left the men essentially on their own.

The glorious day of victory finally came on the second of May when seventy thousand remaining German soldiers laid down their weapons and surrendered Berlin. While expected, the avoidance of further bloodshed was a giant relief to everyone.

"Thank God we didn't have to take all of Berlin," Nini said to Angelo. "Nobody would have survived." Angelo agreed as he hugged his cousin and repeatedly kissed him on his cheeks.

The two participated in the celebrations with their Russian comrades but still longed to return to Italy. However, the days spent with the Russians endeared them to Angelo. He couldn't help but develop a genuine respect for the men and their fighting will. Equally, the Russians were eager to hear of the work Angelo's team had done as saboteurs. A true sense of respect and gratitude grew in each party.

Angelo would remain with the Russians until May 15 when OSS Commander Marcucci provided the paperwork enabling him to safely return to Italy (*see photo reference 22.1*). The men couldn't wait to get home. Their families didn't even know they had survived. They believed all the men from the family had either fallen in battle, been taken prisoner, or perished along the way.

The return trip to Italy paralleled their long trip in, except the last leg was by train. The American military gratefully provided a jeep and driver to take them south to Trento and the improved safety of their home country. Nini confiscated a bottle of locally made wine, and Angelo "procured" some Russian vodka. Together with the American driver who didn't speak Italian, they drank and sang the entire way. In Trento, they bid farewell to their new best friend and rode trains to Milan and ultimately Genoa.

The train rides back were surreal. There were times of exultation, where everyone celebrated the great victory over tyranny and dictatorship. Then during lulls in the revelry, Angelo would take a good look at Nini and become dejected; there were worry lines crisscrossing his young face that weren't there before the war. Nini was physically and emotionally different - aged beyond his years. Angelo wondered if he, too, bore such visible scars.

Both men waded into the waters of remembrance. Angelo tried to make his peace with all he saw and did. Still, he worried about the damage and death he was responsible for. He desperately needed to believe that he wasn't the bad guy.

Angelo imagined the faces of the men he led who were now gone. They reminisced about each one, fondly remembering in detail their idiosyncrasies and personalities. However, neither could bring himself to speak of Pietro. Paradoxically, the sweetest and most gentle person on the team suffered the most horrific torture and death.

The others on the train were also struggling with conflicting emotions. There were times when everyone would laugh, sing, and dance - absolute joy shared among strangers. Then by a strange unseen force, the joy would wane and be supplanted by an eerie quiet. And then again after a short respite, someone would share his grappa or start singing a traditional song, and the train would again erupt into a joyous frenzy. Angelo and Nini rode the manic-depressive waves, first cresting in total elation, only to crash onto the beach of melancholy.

As they approached Genoa, once a beautiful symbol of Italian architecture, industry, and culture, they were struck by its shattered remains. Angelo initially took it in stride; little could surprise him at this point. Every major occupied city in Northern Italy had been bombarded relentlessly in an effort to force the Germans to capitulate. Genoa was no different. And yet actually seeing it up close after being gone for two and a half years, he was shocked at the degree of destruction. It was barely recognizable and alarmingly close to the same destruction he observed in Berlin. The largest buildings that defined the silhouette of the city had all been erased. The extent of the destruction silenced both men. The two silently prayed that the bombings had not reached the northern suburbs and their families.

Before disembarking, they changed into the clean civilian clothes provided by the OSS in Germany. With fresh clothes on and familiar footing, both men stepped onto soil they hoped they would never have to run from again. With great anticipation, they set out to find what remained of the family.

Making their way through the scarred city was painful. Remembering it like a cherished photo, the stark reality shredded the lovely memory. As they walked, occasional gusts of wind would stir grayish ash from the recent fires, giving the appearance of black snow. People everywhere were sifting through the remains of buildings, trying to salvage any building materials that could be reused or repurposed in rebuilding efforts. Unable to let go from what they had become, Nini and Angelo walked slowly and surveyed the piles of debris and broken buildings for enemy personnel. They didn't speak of it to each other, but both men couldn't help the cautionary essence of their saunter. Reflexively, any sudden sound or unexpected movement would cause both to stop and quickly evaluate the source.

After two hours of careful walking, they were only several blocks from their uncle's apartment. Angelo and Nini finally spoke of the devastation and damage evident everywhere. Even standing buildings bore the wounds of automatic weapon fire, shrapnel, and bomb debris. The war made sure nothing would survive without a scar.

Rounding the corner and crossing an intersection provided the men a view of the four-story apartment building they called home. Gratefully, the building and its two neighboring buildings remained intact and only showed relatively minor damage. It was now the cusp of evening, and Angelo's heart skipped a beat in anticipation that the family would be there.

Racing to be the first one home, Nini and Angelo scurried up the three flights of stairs. As Nini had about twenty pounds on his opponent, Angelo was the first to the door and pounded on it as hard as he could. He was immediately rewarded with the sight of his aunt, his Zia Renata, and the smell of his favorite food, polenta, cooking on the stove.

His aunt broke down in uncontrollable tears as she hugged first Angelo and then Nini. Her frail body and diminutive size hid a strength that surprised Angelo. Years of fighting for survival had toned her middle-aged body into a rock. But for the first time in a long time, the rock softened a bit and returned to its humanity.

In just a minute, Zio Angelo came to the door and repeated the scene. Kissing his son and nephew on the cheeks, he whispered, "I didn't know how, but I knew you would both make it."

Angelo shut his eyes hard and savored the incredible moment. As he wiped his tears of joy now running freely, he couldn't help feeling respectful of his elder. There was his Zio Angelo, standing tall and proud, without a single tear. He hadn't changed a bit, still dignified and solid as a rock. But Angelo didn't care at this point. He was beyond ecstatic to see his family again. The intensely joyful episode was broken when Zio asked where they had been. Since all the other men from town had been back for weeks, everybody presumed Nini and Angelo to be dead.

Nini told his father that they were in Berlin and needed special permission to return safely. That and the time it took to make their way back all the way from Berlin. Zio Angelo instantly realized just how deeply embedded the young men had been and told them to be careful with other people. "There are many factions still active here, and it is very dangerous."

Zia Renata interrupted at that point and said with a commanding voice that all this talk would have to wait because the boys needed to eat before the polenta got cold. Angelo couldn't help but grin at the reference to he and Nini as boys. Still, just like boys, the two raced again but this time to the table and their waiting banquet.

*****

That first evening home was an incredible experience for Angelo. He and his uncle planned his future and what he could expect when leaving the safety of the apartment. Angelo learned that it would be as difficult to survive the postwar as it was in the war itself. Thankfully, Zia Renata just kept shoveling heaps of polenta until the two burst at their seems.

The next day, Angelo and Nini faced the most difficult mission of the war, when they slowly and deliberately walked to Pietro's family apartment. It was broken and lifeless. While intact, windows were missing and a section of the top two floors had half of the structure missing. The two carefully climbed the single flight of stairs to the apartment door. Angelo became worried as he surveyed the door to the apartment. It bore the distinctive markings of the doorknob being bashed in by the butt a of a gun. He quietly knocked reverently.

When the door opened, there weren't the tears of happiness like the previous evening. Instead, they found Pietro's mother alone and grieving. She had learned of her son's murder two months earlier and also lost her husband only six months prior. The local partisans attacked a truck carrying Nazi soldiers and killed several of them. In retribution, the Nazis apprehended several dozen local men, including Pietro's father. Going door-to-door, they simply gathered men at random and unceremoniously took them away. Some were tortured and shot while others were taken to work camps where they perished.

After a few weeks, she was informed that her husband died while in captivity.

While every country on the European continent lost huge numbers of citizens, Italy fared among the worst in terms of military and civilian losses. In total, some 70,000 out of 200,000 Italian partisans died; over 300,000 Italian troops perished; and over 150,000 Italian civilians did not survive.

Angelo wasn't sure how to proceed. He was used to leading men in a hostile environment, but was not prepared to comfort and console Pietro's mother. Still, he did what he could. He simply held the poor woman for seemingly hours as she sobbed. When she regained control, they sat, reminisced about Pietro, and prayed together. With all the men dead, she worried out loud how she would survive. Even though he had no idea how, Angelo promised the family would ensure she would be okay.

She demanded details from Angelo and pleaded with him because she had heard her son was taken as prisoner. But Angelo couldn't imagine telling her the horrible truth of it all. He kept the conversation vague and said only that Pietro fell valiantly in battle. Even though she pressed for details, Angelo lied and said he and Nini weren't there when it happened. One day, the truth of his torture and electrocution might come out, but he wouldn't be the one to deliver the news. Not this day. Not any day.

Angelo's war had been like one long extended battle: quick decisions, maddening chaos, continuous sacrifices, dangerous encounters, and finally victory with his return home from Berlin. In the end though, all that remained was the rotting remnants of lives lost. Not knowing what to say or do, the two eventually just quietly left the poor woman.

"Will we ever be normal again?" Angelo asked Nini.

Thinking deeply, he simply replied, "I don't know, my brother. I don't know."

The gloom of the morning continued into the early afternoon as everyone remembered Pietro. But like ice in the sun, the sadness would slowly melt away, only to return during cold, lonely emotional times. Thankfully, later in the day, other friends and relatives came by to see them. Some of Angelo's exploits had made the rumor mill in town, and he was surprised to be treated like a hero, at least for a while.

The Americans quickly terminated their contract with all partisans, including Angelo. Over the next week, they attempted to verify and certify the efforts of those that helped in the liberation of the country. Providing official documentation was critical to "reintegration" into Italian society. There was a particular emphasis on the leadership of the partisan units as they had the most exposure. Angelo was surprised and very proud to have received a hand-signed certificate of appreciation from "Wild Bill" Donovan, the legendary director of the OSS (*see photo references 22.2 and 22.3*).

Unfortunately, it didn't go as smoothly as anticipated for Angelo. Notoriety and exposure didn't sit well with the man who spent every waking minute up to that point trying to remain in the shadows. Slowly, he adjusted to who he had become - a humble hero that lucked out. He needed to transition into the next phase of life. With the depressing morning clouds giving way to a beautiful summer day, he looked to the bright-blue sky and asked the heavens, "Now what?"

Photo Reference 22.1 –

Letter from the OSS at the close of the war granting Angelo the approval to wear US Army clothing and safe passage via US government vehicle to Genoa.

> HEADQUARTERS
> 2677TH REGIMENT OSS (PROV.)
> APO 512, U. S. ARMY
>
> 15 May 1945.
>
> SUBJECT: Angelo Fiain
>
> TO WHOM IT MAY CONCERN:
>
> 1. Subject has been employed by this organization on confidential missions behind enemy lines. It has been impossible to furnish subject with civilian clothing, necessitating his wearing of U. S. Army apparel until such time as subject will be able to change into civilian clothes.
>
> 2. The authority to wear U. S. Army apparel granted in this memorandum will expire 25 June 1945.
>
> 3. Subject has the approval of this office to proceed to his domicile in the city of Genoa. Subject is authorized to travel by U. S. Government vehicle.
>
> ANTHONY MARCUCCI
> 1st Lt., CMP
> Security Officer

Photo Reference 22.2 –

Certificate of Appreciation to Angelo Flaim from the Commander of the OSS, Major General Bill Donovan. While most soldiers received a form certificate, partisan leaders received hand signed and sealed certificates by General "Wild Bill" Donovan himself.

The certificate reads:

This certificate testifies to our gratitude.
Mr. Angelo Flaim

For his selfless help to this office and to the United States Army in the struggle for the liberation of Italy.

The documentation of his efforts and his disinterested sacrifice have become part of the historical archive of the Office of Strategic Services of the government of the United States of America.

Signed, May 15, 1945.
William Donovan, Major General, Director of the Strategic Services

Photo Reference 22.3 –

Closeup of the OSS seal in wax on Angelo's Certificate of Appreciation

CHAPTER 23

The Mayor of Genoa

June 6, 1945
Genoa, Italy

The summer was complicated. The long purge of suspected Fascists and sympathizers was brutal. Anyone who held a government job during the war was sought after, taken captive, and convicted without trial. The fever for revenge and retribution swept the populace like a pandemic, and there was no time or place for deliberations or trials.

At the same time, the Communist party was solidifying its hold on Northern Italy. The CLNAI gained significant power throughout the end of the war. Until liberation and the surrender of German forces, it operated an authorized shadow government in the region. The CLNAI was a political heavyweight, even negotiating cooperative agreements with both the French and Yugoslav Resistance Movements. The left leaning of the organization, never fully trusted by the Americans or the British, became manifest in it's very first statement which contained the following: "There will be no place tomorrow among us for a reactionary regime, however masked, nor for a limp democracy… It will be strong and effective democracy… The government workers, small farmers, artisans, all the Trades Unions, and other organizations of workers will share power."

Because of this power, Ferruccio Parri, the publicly recognized resistance hero and leader of the CLN in Rome, became prime minister at the war's end. In this capacity, he ran the transitional government with King Victor Emmanuel III, who had ruled Italy prior to Mussolini seizing power.

But as the year wore on, the purges ultimately waned. Soon it became apparent that Prime Minister Parri was a vulnerable politician. Forced to resign in November of 1945, he was replaced by the Christian Democratic party leader Alcide De Gasperi.

During these times of great political turmoil, Angelo laid low. He went to work in his uncle's factory for a bit but was completely without a plan. Worst of all, Trentino and the Southern Tyrol was still under control of the United Nations Occupation Force. It was one of two areas in Northern Italy where power was not yet handed off to anyone or any organization. Angelo prayed that the prolonged turnover and uncertainty would ultimately lead to the reinstatement of territorial independence.

It was during this time when Dimitri from the Soviet Union contacted him. Angelo was completely taken aback by the contact, their interest in him, and their invitation to go to Soviet territory to discuss his future. It appeared that the men he stayed with for three weeks in Ketzin were not only impressed by Angelo but were also more powerful than the foot soldiers he had assumed they were.

His uncle warned him though, "Angelo, watch out for the Russians. They are different. I don't trust them."

Having no secure future and hoping the Russians were going to help establish an independent Tyrol, he took his uncle's advice to heart but still accepted their invitation. He had little idea this was actually an interview for something completely different, and his curiosity ultimately won out.

Disembarking the train after the long ride to Lviv, located in Western Ukraine, he was greeted by his old friend Dimitri and two armed guards. After the usual pleasantries, they crammed into a small vehicle and rode to a nondescript building nearby, tucked away among other nondescript buildings. He thought as they rode, *There are a lot of newer properties around here. How did they rebuild so much in so little time?*

Angelo recalled the awful destruction of Stalingrad, already becoming legendary, and expected to find it all across the region. He also noted surprising similarities between the many buildings and artwork of the city with that of Italian architecture. There were intact buildings still standing that would have looked right in place back home in Genoa.

This city, with its similar resemblance to his home, eased his significant trepidation. What would they ask him to do? He had no interest in working for the Soviets, and he certainly wouldn't move anywhere in Russia. After being on the run so long, he looked forward to settling down in Genoa, at least for a while. Now that he was actually here though, he worried what the Russians might want with him and if this was a good decision.

On entering the building, Angelo was ushered into the first room on the main floor. The small room with a large table and many drab gray chairs was a commonly found shared conference room for the floor. As several more men entered, his uneasiness and apprehension multiplied. The men in the room spoke to each other in Russian extensively, but Dimitri only translated approximately one in ten words. Clearly, they were discussing him and looking at documents he assumed were about him, and he wasn't getting much feedback. Angelo's profuse sweating gave away his nervousness.

Dimitri pulled him aside and simply said, "Relax, my friend, everything is good."

Amid his extreme anxiety, Angelo couldn't have been more surprised when the team asked him to become the mayor of Genoa! They told him how they were looking for someone who could carry Communist ideals forward in Northern Italy. They spoke extensively about his work in the war, his creative leadership and problem-solving, and of his popularity with the people of the region. There were moments where he felt himself almost blushing. It was an unusual, albeit pleasant surprise reaction.

Angelo was shocked that they knew so much about him. As they continued, he was extremely surprised when they commented on missions that he had never spoken with anyone about. The idea that they could know so much about him and his life, however, scared him more than impressed him. But this position would be a real honor, and he was flattered into acceptance.

With the Soviets happy that the two sides had an agreement in principle, Angelo asked the big question on his mind: "What was the disposition of the Tyrol?" While being mayor of Genoa was an incredible honor and great place to start his political career, he fought for Trentino and the Tyrol and wanted to know if there were options there for the long term.

That's when Angelo's bubble burst. They told him that the United Nations controlled the region and still considered it an occupied territory. In their opinion though, it didn't seem likely that it would become an independent country. There was still a sliver of hope, but the other regions of what used to be Tyrol had already been snatched up by neighboring countries.

Italy claimed and received the region of Trentino, and Austria received the North Tyrol. Without the two other sections, the South Tyrol had little chance of being independent. Moreover, Stalin was more interested in buffer countries around Russia and ultimately didn't care about the Tyrol as it held little strategic value to the extended USSR.

This was terrible news and made Angelo call into question the net worth of all the years fighting and lives lost. Nearly his entire family and most of his friends were fallen, and for what? He thought to himself, *where's the value in losing Pietro, Ricco, Daniello, Matteo, and all the others if independence is no closer?* He was becoming lost in unproductive memories, but couldn't help himself.

Quietly, he asked for a moment to go to the restroom. There, in the privacy of a dirty toilet stall, his mind wandered to places far away and times not so long gone. He reminded himself to stay pragmatic and keep moving forward at all costs. After what must have been an embarrassingly long time, he emerged with his game face on. He extended his hand out to the senior person and said confidently, "I would be honored to become the mayor of Genoa and continue the growth of Communism in Northern Italy."

The Russians assured Angelo that they would control the election and his position was certain. Unfortunately, it would be at least a year until the national and local elections would be concluded. A few months after that, he would be appointed mayor by the newly elected city council. An appointed mayorship was not uncommon at that time in Italy. Angelo also appreciated that he would have the significant benefit of not going through an election process. The position of mayor would not become an elected position in Genoa until 1993.

Uncertain of what he should do in the interim, the Russian team suggested he should go to the university and study general business administration. He agreed since his new role would require business basics that he didn't yet possess. With Christmas practically upon them, Angelo left Lviv with news nobody back home would believe and the intention of entering college at the age of 23.

Angelo didn't realize how much he had changed until he reentered at school. Whereas he was rarely interested in studies as a youngster, preferring to daydream and skip school whenever possible, he now looked forward to it every day. Relating his lessons learned to his experiences as a leader during the war drove his learning home in a tangible way. He found himself actually enjoying his classes and how they would benefit him in his future position.

As a full-time student, he worked part time for the political establishment in Genoa. He wanted to be more involved to gain a better understanding of the roles and responsibilities he would be required to administer. He had learned the hard way to always gather as much intel as possible before embarking on a mission, and this new career would be no different.

Most of the city jobs were straightforward, and there were many people to fulfill them, enough so that each city employee had only a single task to worry about and execute. The work was significantly easier than him presiding over many dangerous missions with little resources. He lamented that he couldn't find a single person who could do multiple things at once, or show any creativity in solving problems. Worse yet, over time, he became extremely disenchanted by the graft he witnessed. "These people are almost all crooks!" he would say to his friends. The level of inward greed manifested by the outward corruption came to sicken him.

The final straw for him was learning that the CLNAI had horded weapons, ammunition, and cash during the war. Critical supplies which could have saved partisan lives or shortened the war were instead stockpiled in preparation for the vengeful purge they would soon unleash on the people. Angelo's resources had run very tight toward the end of the fighting, and he could have made vitally good use of just a fraction of the lira, weapons, and ammunition stolen by the large organized partisan groups. Many of the partisans who were involved then were now working in or for the city in some way.

By the end of the school year, he came to the conclusion that he couldn't function in this type of work environment. He had worked in the system for a mere five months but had seen more than enough. There were two types of people working for the city: the lazy and the corrupt. Most people merely went through the motions of their boring, repetitive responsibilities. While some could potentially be turned by appropriate leadership, the majority were beyond disingenuous. They used their jobs for personal enrichment, coercion, blackmail, and self-indulgent bullying.

Angelo couldn't identify with any of what he saw.

Once appointed mayor, he envisioned making significant changes to the organization and culture. He didn't know how to do that, but ethically, he could not be associated with the way city government business was being conducted. He worked and studied hard to determine if it was even possible to bring about the change he felt was needed.

One of his trusted professors eventually leveled with him. "An individual can be turned in his ways but a culture cannot."

Sound advice, but Angelo wanted to believe there was some hope.

The summer finally brought the much-anticipated national referendum on the type of government Italy would adopt. The referendum pitted two very different political systems and future for the country. One was a restoration of the monarchy which historically ruled Italy before Mussolini and his Fascism regime, and the other was a democratic republic similar the United States model.

In a very close election, the country voted for a democracy, with the vote split significantly by region. Northern Italy and the regions north of Rome voted overwhelmingly for democracy whereas lands south of Rome and Sicily voted overwhelmingly for the monarchy. The vote only reinforced the two-culture nature of the country, with the north and the south in perpetual opposition. The final tally had the democratic republic winning with only 54 percent of the vote, and the monarchy quietly resigned without any violence or unrest.

Angelo had hoped that the referendum would produce change at the local level, reasoning that new officials would demand new policies. However, the referendum had virtually no impact. With an appointed mayor, not elected, conditions actually got worse over time. Over the course of the summer, Angelo became more and more disheartened.

This was a pivotal season for both Angelo and Italy; the referendum was over, the transitional governments were becoming entrenched, foreign influence was waning, and local elections were still well into the future. Angelo was worried about the significant length of time between his visit to the Ukraine and the anticipated local city elections. He decided to contact Dimitri to discuss their anticipated influence regarding his appointment. At first, he didn't think much of it when he couldn't reach him. But after several days and more insistent attempts, Angelo began to worry about losing the job that he really didn't want anyway.

In actuality, he was more confused than upset. His appointment seemed to be taking forever, and he was perplexed at the lack of communication. He knew that without the Soviet's strong backing, he had no chance of being appointed. With Dimitri incommunicado, few connections of substance in the new city political structure, and unbridled political corruption everywhere, he became resigned to the idea that he would likely not receive his appointment. So it was actually a bit of a relief when the announcement came on December 4 that Giovanni Tarello of the Italian Communist Party had been appointed mayor by the city council. Even though he had determined he didn't want the position, his competitive nature still resulted in his being upset. Clearly, the local Communists saw their influence grow and the Soviet influence wane, so they exerted their political power and chose to install one of their own.

Angelo didn't mourn the lost opportunity. He became unenthusiastic and lost all respect for Communism and politics. Both seemed fake and dangerous to him. He returned to the university to start another year of studies. He had no idea what to expect or what his future would look like, but staying in school seemed the smart move to make. He knew a life plan was necessary but felt frustrated by his inability to control his future. *Something will happen, I just know it*, he argued with himself.

CHAPTER 24

Treading Water

December 20, 1946
Genoa, Italy

Angelo eventually overcame the embarrassment of not getting the appointment, primarily because everyone he knew understood the situation. Nearly everyone was aware of the rampant corruption, and his family and friends knew the position wasn't a good fit anyway. With the end of the fall semester, he continued to wonder where it was all going. His entire adult life had been spent on the singular activity of staying alive, with little opportunity, mentoring, or experience to envision a peacetime future. While he found his classes interesting, he now wondered how they would get him a job or career when he finished.

At the start of the Christmas vacation, he was introduced to another student named Maria. She seemed a vision to him, even though she was more than a few years older than him. Her thick wavy black hair curled gently as it touched her shoulders, and she wore it back in a ponytail much of the time. Angelo loved her in that look because her hair pulled back revealed more of her striking facial features. Her pronounced cheekbones and chin were classically beautiful in the Italian heritage, and he felt he could look into her deep-green eyes forever and never grow tired. "Now this is worth my focus!" he mused to himself.

Maria was a tough gal who survived the war at her family's villa about two hours outside Genoa. She had even been a part of the local resistance supplying intel, food, and safe lodging to the local partisan forces. He was particularly proud of her helping Jews escape to

Switzerland. From her villa northeast of Genoa, the Swiss border was remarkably close, and her family aided hundreds on the risky journey to safety over the mountains.

Angelo had dabbled in dating since the war's end, but no one could understand him or relate to him in conversation. Everyone had their own war stories, but Angelo had a hard time connecting with anyone. Maria was different. In addition to being a beautiful companion, she was sophisticated and possessed a quick wit and sharp tongue - the type who could steal any heart. Most of all, she was a lady, gratefully different from the girls he had dated previously.

For the several weeks they had off during the Christmas break, Angelo stayed at her family villa, and the two were inseparable. Unfortunately, at the start of another semester, he needed to return to Genoa. He was angered that the distance from school to her home would reduce their visits to only once per month, which made a lasting relationship very difficult. Clearly the timing was all wrong.

"How can I have any hope of making this work with such an anchor around my neck?" he lamented to Nini and his Zio Angelo. While he certainly had feelings for her, he also felt she was more than a bit out of his league. He, basically a poor country boy, and she, an educated lady from a wealthy family, just didn't seem a likely fit. Sadly, she admitted having the same realizations. They stayed friends, but both felt they needed to move on in their search for love.

The winter hit hard again and required everyone to stay inside more than Angelo liked. While the time initially helped him focus on his studies and achieve excellent grades in school, he again felt trapped and depressed. He found himself regularly conferring with his uncle and others about what he should do next. Angelo endured his schooltime but openly wondered if it was wise to continue after finishing the current year. He could easily have a career at his uncle's factory if he asked. And when the mood was right, he even second thought himself about moving and settling down with Maria. That itchy feeling that he needed to move on was settling in again, and he uneasily tried to suppress it.

The year dragged on in slow motion as each uneventful week painfully led into the next. With the holidays passing and a new year celebrated, he at least felt his heart fully relieved from the sudden loss of the mayoral appointment. He had finally come to feel good that the whole episode was behind him. With no vision or mechanism to end the extremely common corruption at every level, he was glad now not to be a part of it. That path was closed to him, his ego was restored, and he gratefully focused on a different journey.

Equally unappealing was working at some lifeless machine for his uncle. His memories of working at his factory making bombs was still very fresh in his mind, and they weren't happy ones. Sitting at a machine churning out machine parts didn't challenge or interest him. Certainly, he had a good chance of moving up quickly in the company, but nobody could reasonably guess the economic future for the country or region. Also, losing his job if the economy took another downturn was a distinct possibility. "If this doesn't work out, then what would I do?" he said to himself. It was an emotional and intellectual dead end.

In contrast, he recognized and subversively fed his adventuresome heart. It hadn't been that long ago that he was leading men into battle and crisscrossing the mountains executing dangerous mission plans. Consequently, the monotony of school became overwhelming, and he began conjuring ways to get out. He continued to work hard in his studies but prayed for patience as the spring semester unfolded. Despite his efforts, he grew increasingly frustrated and disillusioned. The months continued to grind like the long marches he was forced to do during military training. It's hard to say if it was the spring fever, only being able to see Maria sparingly, or any number of other factors, but his mood plummeted, and he felt adrift.

On April 10, he slowly shuffled into his classroom with his head down in a droning, trancelike state. Each step seemed a struggle as he made his way to his seat. With unceremonious resignation, he plopped himself down in the usual hard wooden chair and opened his books. Seated next to him was a man he had never met named Luigi. He was a quiet man of large stature that rarely spoke. Luigi's only memorable distinction was the berets he wore daily. Most often gray, with occasionally other colors, he could be counted on every day to show up wearing his beret. Angelo felt bad that he never tried to get to know his neighbor, but he assumed that the man likely had his own war history. It's unfortunately common among veterans to recede into themselves and not feel comfortable enough to speak freely, even among each other.

The room was full like usual when the political science professor began his lecture. In midsentence discussing the previous day's lessons, the professor turned away from the students and wrote "Benito Mussolini" on the chalk board. As he scribbled the infamous name, he announced that today they were going to review and discuss the effects of his dictatorship and Fascism on the country.

As he finished writing, the student sitting directly in front of Luigi spoke out and said there wasn't much to discuss. He pronounced emphatically that Mussolini was a misunderstood savior for Italy and that Fascism would one day again be the rule in Italy. He then explained in-depth as to why the country would have been better if Mussolini had survived. As a partisan, this infuriated Angelo. How could he be so blind as to the ruinous nature of the man and his politics?

However, as the man continued preaching about the glories of Fascism and Mussolini, Angelo could see anger welling up inside Luigi. The more the man pontificated about the greatness of the system the partisans fought and died to end, the more Luigi appeared like a bomb ready to go off.

Surprisingly, Luigi ultimately spoke very calmly and asked, "Do you really believe that?"

The man in front of him quickly turned around and said, "Absolutely!"

Luigi simply smiled and said, "Okay, okay, you're probably right."

The man turned back around and faced the front of the class again, seemingly pleased at having won the argument.

Without hesitation or emotion, Luigi casually pulled a concealed sidearm and shot the man at the base of his head. The man's head was nearly severed by the shot that struck his neck from such close range. The rest of the class instinctively dove for the ground and scrambled to find any cover they could. Angelo had nowhere to run or hide. When Luigi immediately stood up and quietly walked through the classroom door, there was a palpable feeling of relief in everyone.

Once Luigi had left the room, everyone instinctively ran for the door to escape, not knowing if he would return and continue shooting. Angelo followed suit and could see Luigi lumbering down the long hallway as if nothing had happened and he was going to the cafeteria. Angelo quickly broke his observation and ran as fast as he could in the other direction.

He finally had enough. It would never be safe for men with his history to survive in the postwar reality of Northern Italy. During the war, the enemy wore uniforms and could easily be identified. Now everyone wore the same clothes and interacted with each other freely. Determining friend from dangerous foe was virtually impossible. He recognized that while he had made many friends in his adventures, there were still plenty of people who would like to see him eliminated. Emotions of the day ran so high that random killings like the one experienced in the classroom were unfortunately not uncommon.

So it was primarily out of safety that Angelo chose a most unexpected course - to leave for America. Italy had become too dangerous, Russia too ideological, and the rest of Europe was a mess where his past could catch up to him. Plus, he still had a mother in America that he hadn't seen since he was a boy, as well as a relationship with a powerful OSS agent. He couldn't speak the language well, but at least he understood some and wouldn't be going in completely cold.

That afternoon, he contacted Geronimo. Angelo sweat bullets and became emotional as he told his past handler, now friend, of his realities. He just couldn't continue life in Italy and needed to come to America immediately. Geronimo, understanding the value Angelo could provide working for the Americans again, began working out the details. The following day, Angelo received the call from Geronimo that he had arranged transport on the next ship sailing to America.

Geronimo instructed him to go to the port of Genoa and report to ticket counter number 3. There, he would find his ticket on the next ship out, the *SS Marine Shark* (*see photo reference 24.1*). He was told to tell no one of his trip. Geronimo wanted to ensure his asset made it out of the country safely. "Just get here, and I'll be there to meet you," he said.

A mere six days after the classroom incident, on April 16, 1947, roughly two years after the war's end, Angelo was ready to board the massive ship, leaving the port of Genoa and Italy forever. At the dock were the people he loved most: Nini, Maria, Zio Angelo and Zia Renata, and his little cousin Paldo. Zio, Zia, and Maria begged him to give the situation some time and to fully consider his decision; they argued he hadn't given his postwar life a chance. Did he have to leave so quickly? Things would get better. Angelo hated his family pleading with him because he had thought it through and had made up his mind.

Even while standing at the ship's boarding area, each tried in vain to change his mind, but it was to no avail. The decision was made, and he slowly approached each person and said his goodbyes.

Zio and Zia were first. He hugged them and thanked them for never deserting him and for all their help in his survival. Angelo knew that if it hadn't been for Zio, he would likely have never made it through the first winter on his own. Paldo, now just beginning his teenage years, simply smiled and shook Angelo's hand. He barely knew him since he was just a small boy when Angelo had left.

Maria pressed closely and asked him once more to stay, but not a single tear fell from her alluring jade eyes. Even under these incredible circumstances, she remained noble and kept her composure. Angelo looked at her beautiful face, kissed her passionately on the lips, and told her to go find her true love. He was certain this was his only option, and he would not be returning. He knew in his heart that she understood and would quickly move on.

Nini then pulled him aside from the others. Speaking in hushed tones, he lowered his cap over his mouth, leaned into Angelo, and stammered through his tears, "Go, and don't look back."

Nini, special to Angelo in every way humanly possible; Nini, who had shared childhood and youthful adventures with Angelo; Nini, who was the only one to survive the war with Angelo; Nini, who felt a hole in his heart forming as big as Angelo's; Nini - he alone understood.

Angelo looked into his cousin's eyes, now lined and aged beyond their years, and couldn't say a word. He knew there would never be anyone closer to his heart than Nini. Not even a wife could emulate the level of closeness developed through their experiences. He searched in vain for words, something profound to express his love and respect. All he could do was weep uncontrollably.

Hugging his cousin at the plank leading onto the ship, he eventually got some words out and tried in vain to thank him for everything. For being his conscience as boys while growing up. For being the trusted second-in-command throughout the war. For being the close friend he needed when losing Pietro and all the other men lost under his command. For providing an invaluable sounding board and counter opinion on every decision when lives and missions depended on it. For everything.

Angelo kissed Nini on both cheeks and wished him success and happiness. He then grabbed his valise and turned to walk up the plank. After a few steps, he felt his knees buckle, and he was luckily holding onto the handrail or else he would have fallen. As he righted himself, he stood staring at the opening to the ship, the portal to his future. Pausing briefly, he fought the urge to look back. He felt all the power in his heart pulling to turn and change his chosen path. But his mind, strengthened by years of executing impossible decisions, forced him to continue upward to his destiny (*see photo reference 24.2*).

Photo Reference 24.1 –

Angelo's ticket on the SS Marine Shark for his voyage to America.

266 | Through Sacrifice : Freedom

Photo Reference 24.2 –

This is a photo of Angelo on the left, with his cousin Nini on the right, in their advanced years. The person in the middle is Nini's only son, of course, named Angelo after my father.

CHAPTER 25

Turn the Page

April 28, 1947
Ellis Island, United States

Angelo stood in the massive ship's mustering area with thousands of other immigrants. The crossing was over, and they were finally moored where the Upper New York Bay meets the Hudson River. Waiting for the ferries to take them to Ellis Island seemed to take forever. Every person nervously pushed the unfortunates in front of them in a futile effort to escape captivity. After being on the ship for so long, each longed to again feel the stability and security of the ground under their feet.

Slowly, the gathering of humanity flowed into a single line. Angelo made his way from the dark bowels of the cavernous ship to its opening on the starboard side and was momentarily blinded by the brilliant sun. He now understood why it was taking so long to exit. As they moved from inside the ship onto the smaller steamboats that would ferry them to Ellis Island, each had to stop and let their eyes adjust. The older passengers required a particularly long time to readjust from the darkness to the bright outdoors.

When it was finally his turn, Angelo eagerly made his way across the wobbly passageway with anticipation. The passengers were packed into the steamboat ferry like sardines in a can before it slowly traversed the bay. Nearly one thousand people were crowded onto its decks for the short ride to Ellis Island. The painfully slow ride was made worse by Angelo being stuck in the middle of the horde. There was no way to relax, and the smell of hundreds of bodies jammed in together was nauseating.

The boat finally docked, and after a short while, Angelo disembarked. Finally stepping onto land, he made his way to the edge of the crowd and paused. Immediately he was hit hard by the gravity of his situation, perhaps even more so than with any of his military missions.

He had dutifully primed himself for the emotion of this moment, saying plenty of prayers and spending hours in meditation. He had prepared and had executed his plan with the confidence of a man with nothing to lose. He had endured the misery and uncertainty following the war, anxiously waiting for the optimal moment to "drop the plunger" on his old life and execute his new life plan. The resulting explosion, which is always greater than one expects, snapped him into familiar survival mode.

Fight or flight? That was the ultimate decision to be made at the pivotal moment in previous survival situations, except this time there was nowhere to go. Going back was not an option, so he had no choice but to move forward into this new "battle" for his future life. He was grateful but far from cheerful. The first steps into his new paradigm were both frightening and exciting. Like two fighting dogs, he alternated between fear and joy. But ultimately, one dog always wins. And for Angelo, it was worry and anxiety. For the first time in a long time, he began to question his decision-making.

Realizing he had burned the bridge to his past, he allowed his stubbornness to take over. He was on his own again, a lone deserter without a clue. But this time he was deserting family and home, not an easier target like Mussolini's army. Still, the parallel to his past worried his present.

Rejoining the "huddled masses," he slowly slipped back into the fray. Like a drop of water in a river of humanity, he flowed with the massive crowd easterly across a large open grassy lawn. And like his fellow sojourners, he became awed by the view of the New York skyline directly ahead of them. He felt some comfort as everyone pointed at the skyscrapers and spoke in almost reverent tones at the sight.

After a few more minutes, he looked back for a final view of the ship that had forced this hand. His spirit was lifted by the sight of the Statue of Liberty rising behind the silhouette of the ship. He had seen the welcoming monument from a distance the previous day, but its immense size could now be fully appreciated. Before long he found himself standing in front of the enormous immigration building. "Is everything in America always massive?" he said to the person next him.

Both men laughed, and the other responded with a resounding, "Yes! I have been here once before, and the city never ends."

While clearly joking, Angelo couldn't help but be impressed by the sights.

As he entered the building, fear took over again. Law enforcement was everywhere, and the crowd was being dealt with in a strict militaristic manner. One line led to another until they were all finally sorted into long queues on the other side of the great building. The sight of so many armed men in uniform was unsettling and brought to mind the train stations of previous missions. In an anxious state, he instinctively peered to his side, subconsciously looking for Nini. Of course, his cousin was nowhere to be found. None of the other men he had come to rely on were there either. In leadership of a team, he had found courage. Now in solitude, his courage had abandoned him.

He nervously continued forward, staying within sight of the gentleman he had just spoken with. After relying on his team for survival, Angelo was never truly comfortable alone. He had become dependent on close support around him during the war, and now he couldn't help but try to have backup. Pushing and maneuvering through the crowd, he made his way next to the man and started another casual conversation. Angelo couldn't recall what the conversation was about, but it did help consume the awful time waiting in the queue.

Angelo finally reached the table with two uniformed men for what was to be the first of several stops. At this station, the port police checked passports and incoming documentation. There was also a litany of questions asked to determine the "fitness" of the individual to be in America.

Aside from expected questions, like country of origin, name and address, level of literacy, etc., some unexpected questions were also asked. Questions such as the passenger's final destination, if they had a ticket there, if the person had ever been hospitalized, or if they were a polygamist or anarchist. None were an issue for Angelo, except one specific requirement to possess a minimum of $30 for entry into the country.

If one passed that series of questions, then it would be on to a doctor's examination to test for signs of physical and mental weakness. If approved by the doctors, it was on to yet another immigration officer who would verify the interrogative questions from the first officer. If there was any doubt in this officer's mind that the individual was withholding something or was not fit to be in America, they would be pulled from line.

Angelo's fear rose to its highest level over the requirement for $30. He only had $0.25 in his pockets and a few spare clothes in his valise. He didn't speak much English and was worried about being interrogated by an immigration officer over his lack of belongings and money. He worried he would never get through this to even meet Geronimo. He immediately focused and started to pray in earnest. There was no way he could go back. A quick scan of the area revealed many others regularly being pulled from other lines. His mind immediately began developing and discerning potential alternatives on what he could say to get through. With no idea how to offset his detractions, he meekly stepped up to the imposing immigration officer and tried to catch his attention in a friendly, professional manner.

The officer barely looked up to gaze at the next in the long line of immigrants and began his monotone questioning. Angelo answered the questions posed to him as best he could. He was then asked his name and the port of origin. At this, the officer stopped and checked an inconspicuous piece of paper to his side. He looked carefully at Angelo and then back at the paper. Then the officer called over another officer and had Angelo pulled from the line. Angelo was stunned. He couldn't believe he was being pulled so quickly, and his mind buzzed with potential actions.

As his heart raced, it took everything he had to walk calmly with the indifferent officer. The accompanying officer didn't say a word but coolly escorted him to a grand staircase. Angelo's mind sped faster than his heart as he was led to a second-floor room. He opened the steel door and told Angelo to take a seat at a table. After entering the room behind Angelo, he abruptly turned and locked the door.

The two were alone in the room but didn't speak. Angelo asked the officer as best he could what was going on, but the officer wouldn't respond. *How could I have gotten into trouble already?* he frustratingly asked himself. After about an hour, there was a knock on the door, and the officer unlocked it and went out into the hallway.

Angelo's anxiety had reached a level making him think he would burst. After yet another few tortuous minutes, the door opened and a man in a trench coat entered. Angelo instantly recognized his friend Geronimo, who extended his hand, saying, "Welcome to America. It's great seeing you again."

Angelo was so relieved he jumped up, pushed the man's hand aside, and hugged him hard while fighting the desire to cry. After an extended embrace and some normal pleasantries, Geronimo excused himself. "It's going to take about another hour for me to get through your paperwork. Just sit tight."

Angelo had no idea what the expression "sit tight" meant, but there was no way he would move for anyone unless his ex-handler was with him.

Angelo couldn't believe it. Having Geronimo there to help him through the process would surely resolve any concerns. If there were any more issues, he could be counted on to know what to say or who to call to smooth things out. He felt confident that by the end of the day, he would be an American. Time dragged as he waited for Geronimo to return, and the one-hour promise came and went. Angelo just sat and patiently waited.

It was nearly noon, and he was more than noticing his hunger when Geronimo finally appeared and said, "How about we get some lunch?" Angelo again eagerly jumped up and agreed.

Geronimo led him out and down the stairs toward the throngs arriving from other ships. Angelo followed him without question as they walked right past the immigration tables where he was stopped earlier. Geronimo smiled and continued past the rooms on the sides of the building and finally out the far side, saying, "Come on. My car is parked at The Battery in New York." Sensing the mounting confusion in Angelo, he put his arm around Angelo's shoulder and reassured him, "Don't worry. Everything's been taken care of."

As they walked and continued to the ferry station, Geronimo continued to thank Angelo for his service to America. During the ferry ride to New York, they happily recounted the missions that the two collaborated on and lovingly remembered all the men lost while serving under each of them. Angelo told him all about Nini and the men on his team, the incredible support they had been given, and the huge benefit of the supply drop arranged by him.

The men quickly boarded the ferry for the short ride to New York and moored at The Battery. Once in New York, they stopped for a quick bite at a local restaurant. While there enjoying a hamburger, Geronimo issued Angelo all his immigration papers, signed and approved.

Angelo ordered a coffee and nearly spit it up. "The owner of this restaurant should be put out of business!" he declared. "He should not be allowed to water down this terrible coffee." Angelo's first experience with American coffee was not a good one. Geronimo explained the difference between American coffee and the espresso he knew from Italy, but Angelo still thought it a crime to call it coffee.

The men continued to talk over lunch. Geronimo seemed particularly keen about Angelo's time with the Russians and the particulars of his trip to Lviv in Ukraine. But Angelo had the impression Geronimo already knew most of the facts, and he was only confirming what he already knew. With lunch finished, the two walked to his parked vehicle, a one-year-old Ford Tudor sedan.

Angelo asked Geronimo if this was the biggest car in the world. He wasn't joking. The imposing vehicle was larger than the size of a contemporary full size sport utility vehicle. Geronimo laughed and said it was standard issue for law enforcement agents. The men laughed and entered the car. But instead of starting the engine, Geronimo threw his arm over the back of the bench seat, placed his hand on Angelo's shoulder, and made him a pitch to join the OSS.

He explained how the OSS was changing and would soon become a permanent member of the US intelligence forces, primarily responsible for overseas intelligence gathering. Geronimo spoke extensively about the offer and of how Angelo would be a perfect fit. There would be training involved, as well as extensive travel and education. With his command of the Italian language and knowledge of Central European politics and cultures, he would likely be an analyst for that region. Once his studies and training were complete, he could potentially ascend to a field agent for the region. His compensation would enable a comfortable living, and the excellent benefits package would pay for nearly all expenses.

Angelo was shocked as he intently listened to Geronimo's vision for a future that he could never have imagined. When he was done, Geronimo said, "Well, what do you think? This is an opportunity of a lifetime. We are creating a new organization that will be very important called the Central Intelligence Agency, and you could be right there at the ground floor."

Angelo thanked his friend and said he wanted to think about it. Geronimo was visibly stunned and couldn't imagine why he needed to consider the offer. He knew that Angelo had no money or plans for a future, and he couldn't go back to Italy because it wasn't safe.

"What could possibly be in your way?" he asked.

Angelo sheepishly lowered his head and said he had made a promise to a girl he met on the boat to go and be with her. She was in Chicago and that's where he planned on going. Geronimo let out a big belly laugh and said he was crazy. A woman he had just met, located in a city he had never been to, was a recipe for disaster. He again rattled off the many benefits of joining the OSS/CIA like machine gun fire. There were so many that his list took nearly ten minutes.

Angelo couldn't disagree with any of it. This was more than anything he could have ever dreamed of. He told Geronimo that it was indeed a terrific opportunity, but he needed the night to pray and meditate on it. "Can I please get back to you in the morning? It's been a long difficult day, and I really need rest to make the correct move."

Geronimo agreed and drove him to a nearby hotel. Once inside, Geronimo secured a room and paid for the night in cash. He turned to Angelo and said, "Please, my friend, use your head. I'm offering you a career and opportunity to make a difference in the wars to come. More importantly, in trying to avoid any future wars." When done, he paused in thought and continued, "If you want, we could bring Diva here for you."

Angelo smiled and said, "I believe I understand fully. Please, let me just think on this tonight, and I will have an answer for you in the morning."

Geronimo turned to exit the hotel lobby. After taking a couple of steps, he paused and said, "Sleep well. I will be back at nine tomorrow."

CHAPTER 26

Go (Mid) West, Young Man

April 29, 1949
New York City, United States

Angelo rolled around in his comfortable bed and eventually woke from a night of rather contented sleep. When he entered his room the night before, he anticipated hour upon hour spent in agonizing decision-making. But instead, he slept very well. He knew it didn't make any sense, but his decision was made. The bona fide offer from Geronimo was generous and the greatest opportunity he would likely ever get; it could be the perfect start to his new life.

It did, however, have a few powerful negatives. Angelo had enough of guns. At the war's close, he turned in his weapons and vowed to never pick them up again. Even after all he had experienced, he still could not easily take another's life, particularly up close, man-to-man. And even then, he could only take a life when it was necessary to save his or others' lives. Geronimo said this new life would require significant arms training, and Angelo reasoned, "The only purpose for that must be they know we will need to use them a lot." The thought of even holding a weapon again was bringing back bad memories and was something he just couldn't see doing.

He also questioned whether he wanted to spy on his former friends and colleagues in Russia and Italy. While he renounced Communism after getting a good taste of it, the Russians had treated him well considering everything. The idea of spying on them and the new Italian government just didn't sit well. Plus, he saw a significant difference between intelligence gathering during war, and spying during peacetime. Finally, the thought of asking Diva to move to New York was ridiculous. They had only shared the better part of one day together in their entire relationship. No, he had to somehow get to Chicago, win her hand, and create a new life there.

The previous evening, he was so spent he went to bed without dinner, so he awoke with a strong appetite. But this morning, he still had only twenty-five cents in his pockets so it appeared there would be no breakfast either. He thought, *Maybe I can talk with Geronimo over breakfast before giving him the bad news. He'll be mad, but at least I'll get to eat.*

Angelo went down to the lobby at 8:45 a.m. to meet Geronimo and sat in a chair facing the door. Exactly fifteen minutes later, right on time, Geronimo arrived. He extended his hand and said, "Good morning. What is your decision?"

Angelo was momentarily taken aback by the abrupt exchange. He began to explain why he needed to say no, but Geronimo cut him off and calmly repeated, "So what is your final decision?"

Angelo swallowed hard and said, "I'm sorry, but I must refuse."

With a saddened face, Geronimo pointedly stated, "I am sorry for that, Angelo. Know that I will never be able to help you again. You will be nothing but another immigrant. Your life will be harder than you can imagine. We can bring Diva here from Chicago to be with you. I have checked with my superiors and they have no problem arranging her transport here. I have to ask you once again. Please, think carefully. Will you please reconsider?"

Angelo simply replied, "Thank you, but I need to get to Chicago."

As Geronimo was leaving, he again shook Angelo's hand, smiled, and said, "Please never contact me again, my friend. This was a one-time offer good only for today."

Angelo nodded his understanding. As he turned to go, he wished Angelo well and told him to never discuss his background with anyone. "If you are ever contacted by someone who could have been tied to Germany or the Fascists, tell them your name is…I don't know…Bob. Just don't give them your real name."

Angelo thanked him and asked if he could have some money for breakfast. Geronimo laughed and said if he would stay with him, it would be an expense covered by the government. Angelo shook his head with a determined no. Then Geronimo reached in his pocket, gave him $10, and walked out of his life forever.

Angelo sat in the hotel lobby for some time thinking of his decision and what to do next. But his new life had already started, so the moment of introspection was brief. He returned to his room, took a shower, grabbed his valise, and headed back down to the lobby to ask for help. He didn't recognize the older man working the front desk and wearing a tattered and filthy vest and shirt. Angelo wasn't very impressed, but perhaps this man could help, so he approached with a smile.

The man laughed contemptuously and told him he should have thought about what it would take to get to Chicago before coming here. "That's the trouble with all you immigrants. You come here with nothing and then expect something from us."

Angelo apologized and turned to walk away. Fortunately, another older gentleman was checking in and told him about Travelers Aid International, a nonprofit organization which assisted travelers in trouble and which had representatives at the train station within walking distance. Angelo thanked him and immediately left for the train station.

Grand Central Station was less than three miles from the hotel, and Angelo thoroughly enjoyed the one-hour walk. Passing Washington Square Park and marveling at the architecture of Lower Manhattan, he progressed to the train station. Again, Angelo couldn't believe the majesty of Grand Central Station. The towering structure bathed in natural light was breathtaking. Oddly, the structure reminded him of the mountains he loved back home. Both were awe-inspiring in their majesty. *But surely all of America can't be like this?* he thought to himself.

Finding a police officer, he enquired about Traveler's Aid and was introduced to one of their agents. Angelo told her his story, and the kind lady listened intently. Unfortunately, she informed him that while she sympathized with him, their mission was to protect lost white girls from being coerced into prostitution or taken advantage of. Their mission was very specific, and there was simply nothing she could do to help.

Discouraged but knowing this was his only chance, he again pleaded for assistance. He was only trying to get to his mother in Pennsylvania, not even all the way to Chicago. The woman took pity on Angelo and walked him over to a ticket station and said, "Please give this man a one-way ticket to Revloc, Pennsylvania."

Angelo's mother lived in a tiny town in the western part of the state, about sixty miles east of Pittsburgh. Angelo was handed the ticket, paid for by the nonprofit, and then the lady reached in her wallet and gave Angelo another ten-dollar bill. "Here, you will need this to get some food."

Angelo nearly fell over himself in gratitude. He had never heard of a thing like nonprofit charities and thought it's wonderful that they existed in America. Thanking the woman one last time, he promised to be a good man and that he would pray for the lady and the organization. Angelo immediately went to a local vendor for a bite to eat and then used some of his money to call his mother. She was thrilled he was in America, couldn't wait to see him, and would be at the station to meet him when he arrived. Overwhelmed with excited anticipation and gratitude, he boarded the train for the trip westward.

The trip was uncomfortable because to save money, he was given the least expensive ticket possible and didn't get the luxury of a sleeping car. He had to stand or sit on the floor in an open car the entire ride, but he didn't care much. He was just grateful to be on his way first to reunite with his mother and then with Diva. He had money for food, and he would soon be with family.

As he pulled into the little country station, he looked out and saw only a few people waiting there. That was fortunate because all he had was an old photo and old memory of his mother, and he was scared he wouldn't recognize her. But Erminia was easy to spot by her constant waving. Slender and modestly tall, she looked just like her photo. Happily, there was no mistaking who she was.

Angelo leapt from the train, dropped his valise, and ran to give her a huge hug. She stepped back a bit because she initially didn't recognize him. While she had changed little over the years, Angelo was now a grown man and very different from the boy she left. Realizing it was him, she returned the strong hugs and wept tears of joy.

She finally stepped back and looked at him hard, taking in every feature of his face and body. Her examination ended with a piercing look into his eyes. Like only a mother can, she knowingly recognized the boy she loved and had to leave behind. They both separated a bit and returned to each other a content and grateful smile. It was then Angelo saw the others there with her.

First, he was formally introduced to Erminia's husband, Angelo's "new" stepfather, Carmine Poeta. Carmine was a butcher in Revloc, who ran his own humble general store. He was a strong imposing man who had come from Italy some forty years earlier.

Carmine and Erminia introduced their two girls first, named Tini, short for Valentina, and Nella, short for Antonella. Next, came Tony, who was just six months younger than Angelo. Tony had his own war experience piloting Higgins boats during amphibious landings in the war with Japan. Being so close in age and fellow veterans, the two quickly became very close. They shared a strong bond, and Angelo gratefully had someone he could confide in. Tony could never replace Nini, but the two always remained best friends.

Angelo settled into country life slowly, which was such a change from Genoa. Erminia enrolled him in Saint Francis College with Tony so he could learn the language better (*see photo reference 26.1*). Tony regularly found it a good sport to tell Angelo the incorrect words so he would be embarrassed by saying something inappropriate or off-color.

After one particular experience, Angelo had enough. A professor called on Angelo and asked him a question about the American Revolution, for which the correct answer was Boston. Angelo didn't know American history or the language well yet and awkwardly hesitated. Sitting behind him, Tony immediately recognized the opportunity and whispered "Boob City" in his ear. Angelo sat straight up in his chair and authoritatively announced his answer.

Everyone in the classroom roared with laughter, but the professor wasn't amused. Both men were reprimanded and took from the experience a significant amount of additional homework. When the school day was complete, Angelo took Tony to task. After a bit of roughhousing, he playfully pinned Tony on the ground. "No more. Agreed?" he commanded.

"Okay, I give," Tony replied through his shortened breath. Both men laughed it off, but Angelo would never again be embarrassed like that.

In addition to his studies, Angelo worked part-time as a laborer for Tini's husband, Fred Parisi, at his factory in Brockway, Pennsylvania. An extremely small town of only a few hundred people, it was located about one hour north of the college (*see photo reference 26.2*). He and Fred developed a considerable amount of respect for each other, and Fred recognized an opportunity in his newly arrived relation. Northern Italy was world renowned for accordions, and Fred thought there would be a good market for them in the US.

Angelo and Fred formed a new company to import and sell these very valuable accordions. The idea was for Angelo to contact the manufacturers he knew in Italy and handle importing requirements, and Fred would do marketing, sales, and the business side of things. Angelo leaned upon his instincts and the decision-making skills that had kept him alive for years and jumped into the venture wholeheartedly. He had little understanding of business but was a voracious learner.

Angelo dutifully contacted a friend he had at the Giustozzi Accordion company in Castelfidardo, Italy. The manufacturer was eager to develop a new sales channel in the United States and enthusiastically entered into a relationship. Fred developed the marketing materials and began selling to regional stores that sold musical instruments. While sales did not take off significantly, they did manage to sell enough to keep their interest up.

Unfortunately, Fred's manufacturing business grew and took most of his time. The meager accordion sales couldn't compete, and Fred chose to dedicate his time to his traditional business. Within a year, the enterprise was closed. While the accordion business was a failure from just about every measure, the effort gave Angelo a taste of business and was an opportunity to learn much from Fred. He came to realize the income he could make and the independence he could enjoy by having his own business.

Throughout this time, Angelo remained focused on his prize still waiting in Chicago. He and Diva each wrote weekly, and through their love letters, Angelo slowly paved the way for a relationship. But there were still many obstacles to overcome in their budding romance. Taking advantage of this time in Pennsylvania, he diligently planned overcoming strategies with the same exigent focus as any of his previous military missions.

Angelo was from Northern Italy, and Diva an Etruscan. The Etruscans were an original society in Central Italy that gave rise to the Roman empire and civilization. They considered themselves the true Italians, not diluted or conquered, but of the original Italian culture. The land of Tuscany where her farm was located was known for vineyards and rich farmlands, giving rise to virtually every type of crop imaginable. While best known now for fine wine, the farm Diva was raised on produced exceptional cigar tobacco for Toscano Cigar Company based in nearby Lucca.

To Central Italians, Northerners were considered second class, particularly Angelo's Tyrolian culture. The Tyrol's roots were in Austria and its Germanic traditions. To this day, most of the lands comprising the old Tyrol still do not speak Italian and maintain a dual language society and unique dialect. Travelers today experience street signs in their German dialect, with the Italian translation in small print below. Nearly everyone speaks the Austrian flavor of the German language. Its mountainous region is best known for winter sports, sheep, and equine ranching, completely unlike the farms of Tuscany.

Worse yet were the Sicilians or Southerners. They had been conquered and controlled by the Moors from North Africa and had little in common with Central Italians. The reputation of the southern Cosa Nostra and Mafia spawned in the nineteenth century were well known and feared throughout Central Italy. Even their fishing-based society and traditions were considered foreign to Central Italians.

Everything from heritage, culinary traditions, language, and dialect was different between the three celebrated regions of Italy. With thousands of years of history as fertile soil, the roots of bigotry and intolerance ran deep, particularly in the rural farmlands that Diva's family came from.

The distinct three-culture nature of Italy is legendarily humorous yet politically serious. It manifests itself even in current times and would unfortunately play out significantly for Angelo and his relationship with Diva.

Diva's mother, Maria, was not happy or exited by a relationship with Angelo. He was not only a Northerner but also a partisan. She deeply resented the partisans because the Germans executed severe punishments on local civilians for partisan activities. She suffered tremendously because their farm was located along one of the German defensive lines running across Central Italy. They lived for many months in a literal war zone which frequently changed hands between the Germans and Americans. Maria had come from Italy to America very soon after the war to escape the political chaos and danger of postwar Italy. She regularly endured nightmares from the hardship inflicted on her family and friends because of partisan activity in the area. Like all hatreds born from warfare, time may ease its intensity, but the feelings simmer under the surface like lava waiting for any opportunity to erupt.

Angelo, being both a Northerner and a partisan, registered two strikes even before meeting Maria. Much of his courting efforts would in fact be aimed toward Maria. Going to Chicago unprepared would potentially be the third strike, and he refused to strike out in this, the most important mission of his life.

But in the coming years, he did indeed become prepared. He learned English, did well in college, saved some money, became acclimated to life in America, and kept the relationship with Diva moving forward through his weekly love letters. Finally, he felt ready. He could approach the family as a bone fide suitor. It was time to say goodbye to his mother and Pennsylvania family. It was time for the scariest mission of his life, going to Chicago and winning Diva.

Photo Reference 26.1 –

This is the first known photo of Angelo in America, taken at his entry into St. Francis College and published in its school newspaper.

Photo Reference 26.2 –

This envelope and mailing address provide a clue as to how small the town of Brockway actually was. No street address was needed. Diva would simply send the letter to the town and Angelo would get it.

CHAPTER 27

Red, White, and Blue Collar

May 30, 1949
Revloc, Pennsylvania, United States

Once again, Angelo was on the move to a place he had never been. But he prayed that this time would be his last. He was incredibly grateful that his entire new family in Pennsylvania came to the little train station to say goodbye. This was one aspect of small town living he relished. It seemed the entire town showed up to wish him well. Slowly, everyone gave him a last hug and kiss on the cheek.

Tony punched him hard in the arm and said, "Now you have to come back to get me back." With everyone laughing, it was impossible to not see or recognize the excitement in Angelo's voice and tenor.

The last to wish him farewell was his mother, Erminia. For the months leading up to this moment, she tried to selfishly get him to stay. After a decade of separation, the last two years together had been the best of her life. Angelo dreaded the moment of goodbye with her, but she bravely held back her tears and smiled, saying, "Go, find your future. Now that you are here in America, we can see each other with just a train ride."

Angelo appreciated her strength and resolve. He responded with a silent hug and tears of gratitude.

So once again, Angelo stepped onto a vehicle symbolizing separation from family and friends. He instinctively paused. Turning back, he waved to everyone and took in the magnitude of his decision.

It had been just over two years since going through the same miserable experience when leaving Italy. *Lord, let this move be my last*, he silently prayed.

He picked up his valise, this time full of clothes, and boarded the train for Chicago. Finding his window seat, he never stopped waving and smiling at all those who waved and called from the platform. Through the commotion on the train car and the engine's roar to life, he tried in vain to discern the screams of support coming from the crowd. Slowly the massive vehicle pulled away from the platform. Angelo kept waving until a turn of the carriage hid his well-wishers from sight. Angelo smiled to himself and did a careful review of his compartment. Peering blindly about, he saw everything and registered nothing. Finally stowing his suitcase in an overhead compartment, he plopped into his seat with an exhausted thump.

Looking around the train car, he was taken by the similarity to those he had ridden in Italy. During wartime, the cars were badly beaten up and unkept, just like this car. He slowly rubbed his hand over the dull gray upholstery and pondered how those rides shaped his life and how lucky he had been.

He remembered the dangerous rides and his brethren who were badly injured or didn't survive them. Like the surprise of the screaming engine whistle, the memory of losing Pietro sprang forward in his consciousness. Instantly, the screams of his cousin coming from within the castle walls were as fresh as the night it happened. Also front and center was his feeling of impotence at not being able to do anything to save him.

Agonizing over the loss yet again, unable to stop its debilitating repetition like a scratched phonograph record that relentlessly repeats, he questioned how it was that he survived. Several of the other men were better fighters than him and certainly more skilled in weapons use. They were even far more eager to use those skills whenever possible. If anyone should have died, it was him, and in these quiet moments, he fought the invisible antagonist of survivor's guilt.

Why me? echoed over and over in his mind. *Why should I be lucky enough to still be alive?* He tried repeatedly to focus on Diva and his anticipated new life. But it was to no avail. The more he tried to force the past out of his mind, the stronger it came back. In these sacred times of solemnness, the train car became a confessional, and he held imaginary conversations with all his men. Trying to cheat judgment, he playfully attempted to remember the joyful moments with each. But soon the monster he had created in his mind roared back and demanded the self-defeating emotions that sustained it. Clutching the air like it was a friend's arm, he begged them for forgiveness.

Angelo had only one significant consolation: he had done his best. He knew in his heart that he couldn't have done anything more to safeguard any of them. He also reminded himself of his own involvement in virtually every mission. The men were never subject to any danger that he himself had not experienced with them firsthand.

Finally, he thought himself fortunate that these quiet moments didn't present themselves often. When he got to Chicago, he would make sure to stay busy and be with other people. "I will not be a slave to these destructive thoughts anymore!" he declared to himself. "God has brought me here for a reason. He has put Diva in my life for a reason. I survived for a reason. I'm sure I'll never understand that reason, but I'm done questioning it. I'm going to get the freedom I fought so hard for!"

He finally broke the chains of destructiveness one more time. Closing his eyes and focusing on prayer, he centered himself on his destiny in Chicago with Diva. This regular practice always eased his soul and quieted the demons. Expressing his gratitude, he began to feel more at ease once again. He knew it unlikely that he would ever experience full peace, but falling asleep amid the commotion of the fast-moving train was a welcome start.

Angelo awoke a few hours later when the train came to a full stop. He looked at the scenery and smiled; this time his perspective was different. He felt almost a calling, a reassurance and sense of comfort that he was doing what he should be doing. Anxious at the thought of seeing Diva again, he smiled broadly and nervously tapped his fingers. Biting his nails in angst until they bled, he wondered how they would get along. Through their constant letter exchange though, he felt comfortable that he knew her as well as anyone.

And he was prepared. He was donning a fine suit and had taken some college classes and received excellent grades. He also had a respectable amount of money saved and in his pocket and could speak the language well enough to communicate with anyone. Her family would *have* to accept him. He committed himself to meet any demand her mother or father would make of him. He was in this for the long term. No more relocating and the regular need to start over. No more uncertainty over his chances to succeed. No more danger. Just a simple life of honest work with the woman he loved.

Angelo's small-town experience in rural Pennsylvania was diametrically different to what he encountered as he approached the mammoth city of Chicago from the east. He could not believe its size. It was like the country changed in an instant.

After traveling through mostly small towns, he was astonished at the scope of the first major facility they came upon, the US Steel Works in Gary, Indiana. It stretched for miles, and the train traveled directly through the middle of it. The small factories he had seen while working for his uncle in Italy and then with his friend in Brockway were dwarfed by what he saw. The sprawling complex was block upon block of interconnecting buildings and overhead bridges. Many were multistory giants with chimneys rising to the skies that belched out smoke in every imaginable shade of gray. *Surely I can at least get work in a place like that. There must be thousands of people working there*, he thought to himself.

Beyond the initial US Steel behemoth and after sailing through a virtual sea of factories, he felt confident he could provide for his future family. As the train pulled into Chicago's Union Station on track 29, he could barely contain his excitement. He grabbed his valise and waited impatiently while the locomotive took an excruciatingly long time to finally stop. At last, the conductor barked his instructions, enabling the passengers to exit, and he hastily disembarked and ran through the crowd to reach the main station where Diva and her family waited.

Once through the doors of the giant station, he momentarily worried that he wouldn't recognize her. After all, he only saw her for less than one day, and that was over two years before. But scanning the crowd left no mistake. He spotted her almost immediately and started walking briskly toward her. In a short while, she saw him and also made her way through the crowd toward him.

Angelo couldn't believe it. She was even more beautiful than he remembered. And at last, here she was pushing through the crowd to get to him. When they finally met, the crowd and the world disappeared as he passionately kissed her and hugged her. He felt like his entire life had eclipsed into this single moment. The two were still embracing and lost in each other when a man stepped up and jokingly said, "Diva, you know this guy?"

Like a car hitting a wall, Angelo was suddenly brought back to earth. He separated from Diva, and she composed herself, saying, "Angelo, this is my father, Augustino, my little brother Angelo, and my mother, Maria."

Angelo eagerly shook the hands of her father and brother and thanked them for coming to get him. He then turned to hug Maria, but she abruptly extended her hand for a handshake. *Okay, this may take some time*, he thought to himself.

But nothing could quell his enthusiasm and excitement. There would be time to win everyone over. The most important thing was that Diva was clearly "all in." The love that grew from the long-distance relationship was genuine and strong. From this he could build upon and they could certainly overcome any obstacle.

Diva had arranged for Angelo to rent a room in a home only a few blocks from where she lived. The family continued exchanging pleasantries as they drove to it. Augustino spoke at length about the beautiful architecture of the buildings they drove by and all the wonderful things about the city. Angelo feigned interest, but his eyes never left Diva.

That evening, Diva had Angelo over for dinner, and she introduced him to friends and extended family. Everyone had a million questions and were eager to finally meet Diva's man of mystery. While a modest and humble man, Angelo couldn't help feeling prideful as Diva showed him off.

That night, as he collapsed on the mattress of his small room, he dreamed of his future with Diva and gave thanks for God's safe deliverance to this moment. He reminisced about family and friends and the long road he took to arrive at this moment in time. At just twenty-six years of age, he felt he had lived an entire lifetime already, and yet he was still very young and starting a new life afresh.

The next day was a welcome one with nothing to do but visit the city with Diva. She showed him all the sites, and they spent every moment together. As the day waned, they stopped for coffee and spoke seriously. Both recognized they hardly knew each other and agreed to date like a "normal" couple. Their exclusive relationship would enable each to be certain of the marriage they envisioned and would give Angelo time to "sell" himself to the family.

As long as Angelo could be with her all the time, he had no problem with any of it. Slowing down and simply enjoying each other's company without the pressure to marry was actually welcome. Besides, he needed to find a job and save some serious money if he was going to start a family with her. The next day would begin that search, but for now, he simply basked in the moment, her gaze and embrace.

*****

Getting a labor job was not as easy as Angelo thought it would be though. There were many American men who had qualified for the GI Bill and were taking most of the available good jobs. At the same time, many women were also staying in the factory jobs that they took on during the war. The makeup of the American workforce changed forever when women after the war continued to occupy many of the jobs traditionally held by men.

Worse than the job market was the underlying negative feeling toward Italians by many in Chicago. It was only a decade or two since Chicago police were owned by the mafia who had ruled the city through intimidation and violence. Anyone of Italian heritage was immediately suspected of being a part of it. Worse yet were the men that had returned from the war in Europe with a hatred for Germans and Italians. Anyone who served, no matter their internal strength or character, couldn't help but be changed from the experience. Even those that didn't serve had a father, son, brother, or friend that had lost their life in the European Theater of war. Angelo understood this as well as anybody.

He had only been in the city for just under a week when he was assaulted on the street. As he waited for a bus with a friend, they carried on a conversation in Italian. His parents, too, had immigrated to Chicago from Italy just before the turn of the century. When the bus pulled up and everybody moved to get on, a large man turned and spit on him. "Get the hell out of here!" he yelled.

Shocked by the unexpected assault, Angelo immediately replied, "What's wrong with you?"

The man, becoming more enraged, put his finger in Angelo's face, shouting, "I lost two brothers fighting you dagos. Go back. Nobody wants you here!"

Angelo grabbed the man's hand and pushed it away from his face. Turning to speak to him, he saw three other men coming to the man's aid. Some pushing and shoving ensued, and it looked like Angelo was going to take a beating.

Fortunately, two beat cops were walking down the street and ran to the bus stop to end the fight before it started in earnest. The police told the men that instigated the altercation to get on the bus. "Don't worry, we'll take care of these two."

Once the bus pulled away, it was just Angelo, his friend, and the two police officers. The men explained what had happened, and they did nothing to bring on the quarrel. The cops warned Angelo not to respond to provocations, avoid potential conflict, and to leave at the first sight of trouble. They then continued their neighborhood patrol, and Angelo got on the next bus.

Angelo thought a great deal about the exchange. *Aren't all these people either immigrants or descendants of immigrants?* What would he say the next time? Geronimo had instructed him not to tell anyone of his work with the Americans. He felt like he was handcuffed in a boxing match.

Angelo longed to tell people that he and his family and friends suffered greatly and gave their lives to reduce American casualties and shorten the war. But he couldn't. He wanted to tell people that he was a partisan fighting for freedom, but everybody associated the Italian partisans with Communism and the Soviet Union. As the Cold War with Russia was beginning to "heat up" in earnest, this would surely infuriate people even more.

Ultimately, he settled on a story that he hoped would minimize bigotry against him. He told people an abbreviated version of the truth: that he had never fought for the Italian army and that he was an independent person mostly hiding and fighting the Germans when required to stay alive.

He also conjured up a lie in an attempt to gain acceptance, telling people that he spent time fighting with the French resistance known as the Marquis. Because the French underground was not motivated or associated with Communism or the Soviet Union, they were generally held in high regard by Americans. There was an almost romantic association with the work of the French resistance, and Angelo hoped to glean some of it for himself.

Angelo hated telling this lie, but he needed to protect himself. Actually, he maintained a significant level of disdain for the Marquis. For a short time toward the end of the war, the Marquis had crossed the border and claimed a significant part of Northwest Italy for France. It was just another land grab from the defeated Italy, which Angelo understood. Still, he despised the butchering of Northern Italy. Throughout his life, he always resented France trying to steal part of his beloved homeland and the French resistance in general.

As the weeks passed, he experienced luck avoiding confrontation, but no luck finding a job. Unfortunately, it wasn't long before his good luck came to an end. Angelo knocked on the door to a factory that had a sign looking for laborers. The secretary brought him to a small room where a gentleman came in to conduct the interview.

Within five minutes, the man asked him about being an Italian immigrant. He said he had the perfect job for him working on the loading dock. "Come on out to the back, and I'll show you around."

The man hurriedly walked him through the factory and to the loading dock. The shop seemed to be doing general machining work like he experienced in his uncle's factory, and Angelo was certain he could quickly move up from his start on the loading docks.

"Just wait here a minute. I have a couple guys that will want to talk with you." Angelo stood on the loading dock, grateful to have finally gotten this far in his job search. Loading trucks was hard labor and beneath his education and ability, but it would be a start.

Ten minutes passed, and the man returned with three more men. Angelo reached to shake hands with one of the new men when he suddenly grabbed his hand and bent it backward. The pain shot from his hand to his entire body as he fell to his knees. Then without a word, the four men proceeded to punch him repeatedly. One particular blow to the stomach sent him reeling backward, and he fell off the loading dock. He landed on the concrete pad below with a thud, but fortunately was not injured badly.

Angelo composed himself and ran to the street. Making his way back to his room, he questioned everything. *Maybe I should go back to Pennsylvania. I know I can get my old job back.* But he and Diva had not had enough time together. There was no way she would leave with him. He needed to stick it out for at least a couple of years to win her and her family over. But at least it was worth a try. *She knows how I've tried, and she has to at least consider it.*

Angelo proceeded home to clean up and change his torn and bloodied clothes. Washing the blood from his face, he looked into the mirror and thought of every possible thing he would tell her. He had logic on his side. He had his broken body to show his level of effort in trying to make it work. And he had a secure and safe future in Pennsylvania to bring her to. His mood improved at the thought he might pull it off.

"No." That was the simple and direct reply to his long dissertation detailing the reasons they should move to Pennsylvania. "I'm sorry, Angelo, but we haven't had enough time together. I just got here from Italy myself, and if I leave now, my parents would never forgive me."

Of course, Angelo understood. After all, it was the most reasonable response possible, and he knew she was right. Still, Angelo had gotten used to miracles being afforded him in impossible situations and thought he at least had a chance for another.

Augustino was shocked by the treatment Angelo received while trying to find a job. He knew many people who had no ill will toward Italians, and the poor boy was simply running into bad luck. He put it upon himself to get the word out and see if he could help. The following Sunday when Angelo joined the family for Mass and Sunday supper, Augustino told him he had asked around and knew of someone Angelo could speak with about finding a good job.

Two days later, Angelo met the man who apologized for the treatment Angelo had endured. He told him that even though many people hated Italians, there were still many, many more who didn't, and he should not give up. He gave him two names to follow up with and wished him luck.

Angelo immediately went from the man's office to the first factory. The man listened to Angelo and asked him if he had a problem doing janitorial work. Angelo said certainly not, as long as he could have a shot at working on a machine if he did a good job. The employer agreed and made him an offer at the most minimal wage possible. Angelo didn't bother going to the second place and immediately accepted.

Sweeping floors and cleaning restroom facilities was humbling, but it was work. Angelo used the opportunity to better understand the American workplace. The way people spoke, gossiped, and related with each other was very different to what he was used to. After about nine months, an opening for a machinist came up, and Angelo got his chance.

The months passed as he worked machining metal pieces, and finally things began to fall into place. Angelo was able to save some money and go to night school for trade classes. He developed a close group of friends, and the issues he had when first arriving dissipated like smoke after a fire. He was a blue-collar immigrant, but his manic life was settling down.

Most importantly, he had won over Diva. When he proposed marriage on a cold, clear Christmas morning, Diva agreed immediately. Augustino respected Angelo and what he had gone through to win his daughter and wholeheartedly approved the marriage. Even her brother Angelo had become a good friend despite their thirteen-year-age difference. Diva's mother, Maria, was the lone exception. She never fully got over her prejudices and negative feelings about Angelo; Maria would never be an ally of Angelo or the marriage. After a nine-month engagement, Angelo and Diva got married on September 12, 1953. Angelo was thirty years old and ready to begin their life together (*see photo reference 27.1*).

Photo Reference 27.1 –

Diva on her wedding day. This was the photo Angelo carried in his wallet their entire life together.

CHAPTER 28

Freedom at Last

September 20, 1953
Chicago, Illinois, United States

Like all newlyweds, Angelo and Diva entered their marriage full of hope and happiness. They had even saved enough money to rent a small home in a great neighborhood on the northwest side of the city. While inexpensive, it would provide the perfect nesting material to start their family and get them closer to their family goals.

It took some time to outfit their new home, as Angelo and Diva would only purchase items when they had enough cash saved. Angelo hated the idea of paying interest for items other than a home mortgage. Fortunately, frugality ran deeply within both of them. They slowly amassed all the basic necessities of a comfortable home. Diva had her modest kitchen with all the appliances available at that time, and Angelo had a small workshop from where he would tinker and repair any item in need.

Within two years, they had all the essentials covered, and they felt it was time to start a family. The couple welcomed the birth of their first child, a strong boy. Angelo wanted to name his first male child Steven after the father he never knew, Stephano. Diva agreed wholeheartedly, and Angelo was both elated and terrified. A healthy child was his greatest wish come true, but he worried about how to be a good father. Having not grown up with his biological father and him spending most of his life on his own, he prayed that he would not fail at this most important responsibility. Two and a half years later, came their only other child, Thomas, and Angelo now had the family he had always dreamed of.

But with two small children and the cost to outfit and maintain a home, money was always tight. As was not uncommon, Diva stayed home with the young children while Angelo slaved away. Even though working as a machinist was physically draining, Angelo sought and was able to get overtime work on Saturdays. The extra income helped greatly but understandably left little time for Diva or the children.

Within a few more years, Angelo determined that he had enough experience to warrant moving on in his career path. His company loved the work he did and regularly commended him on his skills and punctuality. No matter how he felt, Angelo never missed work or came in late. He felt ready to progress from a machinist's position to that of a tool and die maker and hoped to find a job where he could make more money and not have to work weekends or overtime.

That led him to a tool and die maker position at a small shop in Harwood Heights, Illinois, named Ansan Tool (*see photo reference 28.1*). Angelo had been attending a local junior college in the evenings, and his natural self-confidence ensured he was fully prepared to move up.

Unfortunately, his assessment that things would get easier was naive. Work as a tool and die maker was gritty and physically taxing. Large raw pieces of metal are constructed to make precision tools and forms called dies. These are then used to cut, shape, and form metal. In the process, he would have to also make jigs or whatever would be needed to hold the metal down while it would be bored, drilled, or stamped. The heavy original stock and subsequent tools and dies were needed to be carried and moved around. Adjusting the raw material to precise locations required significant strength and concentration. The exhausting work was a step up, but draining.

The significantly higher pay did, however, enable the family to purchase and move into a new home only blocks from the factory. The new bungalow in the northwest Chicago suburb was a tight fit, but it was a great place to raise a family. The home was only a block from the Chicago city limits, and Diva appreciated still having access to city amenities. The local school was within walking distance, and a Chicago Transit Authority bus stopped only a block away. Since Diva still had not learned to drive, the bus lines were critical for her mobility. The small suburb was a safe and stable place to grow the family.

However, within a year of getting his new job, Ansan Tool announced a significant new contract which would require specialized employees with experience like Angelo's. Everyone was grateful for the job security and welcome bump in overtime pay, but it came with a catch.

The company had utilized every inch of the factory floor and couldn't expand the facility, which necessitated Angelo working double shifts three days a week. These were grueling days that took a toll. The first shift went from seven in the morning to three in the afternoon, and instead of going home, he would continue working till eleven that same evening. The sixteen-hour days in the dark harsh factory were almost too much to handle.

Because Angelo was tired and unavailable most of the time, Diva had the chore of taking care of the home and raising two small boys as, essentially, a single mother. This led to a terrible tension in the relationship. Diva understood and tried not to burden Angelo with the hardships she endured, but the work and strain were clearly visible.

Angelo did his best to calm Diva's understandable angst. "I'm sorry, my love, but I have to do this till the project is over. We just need to see it through. Trust me, everything will work out." Diva reluctantly had no option but to put up with the situation and do the best she could.

Diva suffered terribly during this time. She not only had to assume virtually complete responsibility for raising the children, caring for the home, and managing the daily finances, but she had few friends and was stuck at home all day. On occasion, she would find herself commiserating with her mother-in-law, Erminia, on raising a family as a "single" woman. Even though the circumstances pushed them to the limit, the extra overtime pay was exceptional, and the family managed to save significant money.

Most of the other workers at the factory slowly quit from the punishing strain and time-consuming work schedule. But after about one year, the schedule was cut back to working five ten-hour shifts and then finally normalized with single eight-hour shifts and an occasional Saturday.

Even though he was an exceptional employee and gifted in his craft, in reality Angelo's position and reputation in the company moved up just from simply showing up. Eventually, this led to him getting the "good" projects that required less physical exertion and provided more time at home. Angelo relished the opportunity of finally being a proper husband and father.

Understandably though, the stress of Angelo's life was catching up to him. It seemed nearly every minute was lost in a hurricane of work and typical family needs. At just thirty-nine years of age, his receding hairline and loss of thick black hair revealed the underlying pressure of his struggle. A lifetime of sacrifice was clearly taking its toll. Still, reaching deeply into the depths of all he was, he continued to labor with gratitude and optimism.

The family's two boys were now seven and four and a challenge to handle by any measure. During the period of extended overtime work, Angelo barely had any time with them. But now it was different. He finally had his evenings free to play with the kids and pursue other activities. With just a small amount of outside work around the house required, he found himself with most of Saturday and all-day Sunday to modestly finish the basement of their humble home, focus on Diva and the children, and rest and recuperate.

He invested a portion of that free time in returning to night school at a local college. His studies centered around two topics that he found fascinating: investing and business. He had studied business basics in Italy and was introduced to entrepreneurship in Pennsylvania. He maintained a keen interest in both and wanted to learn all he could. He was particularly interested in stock trading and the process of evaluating potential buys.

Never one to fear risk, he soon began investing seriously in the stock market. By buying quality stocks when he had the cash and then holding onto them, he eventually grew a sizable portfolio. Joining investment clubs and spending time at the college library, he put the same amount of time and energy into stock purchases as he had his military missions.

Angelo set aside a small area of the basement for his investing and creative work. He built a very large adjustable drafting table that served well as his place to lay out strategies and ideas. From there he would plot out his stock analysis. Using only hand calculations done without the benefit of even a calculator, he charted stock prices, price-to-earnings ratios, and other relative investment factors.

Angelo's financial decision-making proved to be excellent, and his investment portfolio grew rapidly. The extra money provided for long-term savings and enabled the family a fair amount of discretionary spending. For a person without the luxury of extra money, Angelo never developed any expensive vices except perhaps food, specifically imported Italian food.

The family were regular customers at the local Italian food store, habitually splurging on imported prosciutto, wines, chestnuts, olives, oils, vinegars, and virtually everything the family ate. Diva had a well-recognized magic in the kitchen that all the ladies in the neighborhood grudgingly acknowledged. Making homemade pastas like ravioli and lasagna, she would lovingly construct everything completely from scratch. Her paper-thin layers of lasagna, borne from hours of kneading, would make any culinary chef jealous. Even the filling in her ravioli was specially made, combining rare ingredients like wild mushrooms and fresh spinach with a pork and ground sirloin base. Even though she only wrote down the basics of her creations, her recipes were sought after by many, even non-Italians.

While fresh pastas were made a couple of times every week, fresh bread was made most every morning. Every day the children would walk home from school to the intoxicating aroma of freshly made warm bread. After the bread was made, she could always be found canning something. Anything fresh or in season was fair game, including tomatoes, Bolognese sauce, pickles, vegetables, jams, and marmalade. Angelo would proudly tell neighbors, who on occasion benefitted from a family feast, "It's okay to be a peasant, as long as you can eat like a king!"

One of Angelo's great social outlets was the local Trentini Club, whose membership was limited to those who could trace their lineage to the Trentino region of the Tyrol. Surprisingly, the club maintained well over a hundred members, and the group met regularly. Angelo loved the comradery. It was a sacred place where he could go to enjoy grappa or homemade wine, play Italian card games like scopa and tresette, and get competitive over a game of bocce. Every Christmas, Santa would be there giving gifts to the hundreds of children, and everyone felt right at home.

But even among these paisanos, he would never speak of his past in the Italian underground. These folks were all of the same heritage, but it was entirely possible that many fought for the Italian army or were Fascists. He was not alone in this concern, as nobody in the club ever spoke of the war or their possible involvement. Fortunately, most of the members had been in America for several generations, and the subject was rarely brought up.

They did, however, dream aloud about the desire to create the state of Trentino or of the Tyrol. No matter the season or how unlikely, by the end of the night, everyone was debating Trentini independence and ways to bring the country back. Angelo was vocal in his support and on current events but strategically fell silent about the missed opportunity at war's end.

Angelo had settled into a quiet and comfortable life. He would sleep well at night, and the terrors which had previously invaded his rest virtually disappeared. He was free to go to work every day, watch his kids grow and play sports, continue his education, and have many friends. The restless soul came to be contented and grateful for what he had and for his unique take on the American dream.

The only exception to this was December 10 every year, the anniversary of his cousin Pietro's torture and electrocution. Every year on that date, after work, Angelo could be found in the "front room" of the house staring blankly out the picture window. He didn't want to be disturbed and the family knew to give him privacy. He simply suffered in silence with something only he could understand and pondered what might have been. Pietro's horrific death became to be the black hole gravitational center which drew in all the other losses. It was the one event that occurred every year, but freed him from memories the rest of the year.

Contrary to what one would suspect, Angelo had found his freedom in the very things that constrained others. While others felt they were slaves to their jobs and families, Angelo finally found his freedom there. Some of the men would spend their days complaining about their wives; Angelo would simply smile and be resolutely grateful for Diva. Others would complain about the sacrifices they were making for kids that didn't seem to care; Angelo was the happiest when he could spend even a few precious hours with his. Almost all complained about the company they worked for and the conditions they worked in; Angelo felt indebted to the company and country that welcomed him and gave him a chance. Others reminisced about bygone days when they were big shots at high school or rebellious youths; Angelo considered himself lucky to have even survived to this point. Sure, he was playing the game of life with chains around his ankles, but his spirit was finally free. His life of sacrifice had yielded the new life of opportunity and freedom he had dreamed of.

One of the things Angelo really appreciated about working at Ansan Tool was their annual vacation time. Their policy was to close the factory for the last two weeks of July every year for equipment and facility maintenance. Angelo looked forward to this time off like most children anticipate Christmas. Every year was spent somewhere other than home, and he relished taking the family on the road.

In the summer of 1968, he was particularly excited about visiting the Canadian Rocky Mountains, which he had heard were like his home in the Dolomites. He missed the majestic mountains badly. Whenever his thoughts would return to Italy, it was always the mountains first. Besides, the 1965 Chrysler Newport he had purchased the previous year still hadn't had its first major road trip, and Angelo was anxious to "open it up."

The pale blue land boat had four doors and a cavernous interior. What it lacked, however, was air-conditioning or a radio. The three-day drive to the northern edges of British Columbia was brutal on the kids, now ten and twelve. The unrelenting heat and the imprisonment of the kids had friends and family laughing at the thought of such a trip. In a friendly conversation, one of the neighbors jokingly told him to pry his wallet open for plane tickets. "Are you nuts? I can see half of America on the drive out!" was his quick reply and honest feeling.

Undaunted, Angelo felt the pull of the mountains and insisted they go. Without distractions and hour upon hour of driving, Diva had her hands full keeping the two boys separated and out of trouble. Their boredom and incessant fighting brought the vehicle to a stop many times when the patience of the front seat reached zero from the squabbling in the back seat. When the vehicle stopped, the kids knew they had gone too far and immediately fell in line.

The only distraction available to the passengers, aside from the unending farms and fields they crossed, was a small miniature AM/FM transistor radio (*see photo reference 28.2*). The radio's limited reception and station options had Angelo and Diva enduring the torture of repetitious 1960's "Top 40" music in a futile attempt to placate the kids. Occasionally, they would stop at famous places, like the Dakota Badlands, to take a quick break and stretch their legs, but the assiduous driving through desolate areas was hard on everyone.

Yet somehow, they made it to the mountains where Angelo was finally at peace in familiar terrain. Whether it was climbing to a waterfall or driving up and down steep mountain roads to make it to the next small town by sunset, he was happier than Diva had ever seen him. There was no such thing as slowing down, and he kept pushing to take in as much as possible.

The sites of the pristine mountains, particularly the hidden lakes and off-road wonders, were heaven to Angelo. He found the mountains similar but also different in many ways. The Dolomites were craggy and feature many sheer cliffs and rock faces while the Rockies were majestic but more spread out and vast. They were also at a lower elevation than the Dolomites or Alps, so they possessed substantially more tree growth.

The entire family was taken by the huge expanses of untouched land. In Europe, the mountains soar higher, but they don't have the sprawling valleys found in the Rockies. The family never stayed in any one place long, as there was always something new to see "just a few miles ahead". Angelo was also enamored by the mountain people they encountered - always friendly and accommodating but generally rough-hewn and fiercely independent.

Unfortunately, with only two weeks off, they reluctantly started the brutal three-day drive back to Chicago sooner than they would have liked. Knowing he might never return to the Rockies, he made the family stop at many places that they had missed on the drive up. Consequently, the return trip was even longer than their outward drive, and was rougher still on the kids and Diva. The small portable transistor AM radio could only entertain the kids for so long.

But Angelo was a changed man on the trip back. He maintained his calm and seemed absorbed in thought. As kids will do, they pushed every button imaginable. Diva did her best to keep the peace and prevent major warfare from breaking out in the rear seat. Yet through it all, Angelo maintained a quiet tranquility that surprised even the kids. Instead of explosions from their father, he would simply pull over and let everyone walk off a little energy. Angelo had finally found serenity. Amid the roughhousing of young sons, returning to a career of hard work and nothing of certainty except his family, he found freedom. While others ran from their lives, Angelo couldn't be restrained from enjoying his.

Finally at the end of the last long day of the trip, the car pulled into the garage. Steve, who always found a way to sleep while driving, was still in a deep slumber when they arrived. Diva lovingly woke him and took him up to the small bedroom he shared with his brother. Tommy volunteered to help Angelo empty the car, but realizing the sizeable effort would take hours, Angelo asked him to instead join his mother and brother in the house and get ready for bed.

As he exited the garage, Angelo turned to him and said, "Hey, Tommy, how about you and I go for a fishing weekend up to Wisconsin some time?"

"Just me and you, Dad?" his suddenly bright-eyed son replied.

"Yeah. You know your mom and brother can't stand fishing," Angelo continued.

"All right!" said his excited son.

That first fishing trip occurred only a few weeks later. When Friday finally rolled around, Angelo rushed home from work. Tommy had already carefully surveyed and pruned the tackle box. Lures which may have been fine in previous years had to be replaced with new ones. Anything that didn't make the cut was replaced with whatever sparkly new thing looked promising. Diva had made enough food to last a week and packed the meals into many bags. With their fishing gear and bags of food, Angelo pulled the car out of the driveway and directed it north. Neither father nor son could wait to get started on their three-hour excursion to Fox Lake, located about a half hour northeast of Madison, Wisconsin.

The primitive cabins which would be home for the next two evenings welcomed them with the quaint patina of age - the kind that never quite appears clean no matter how many times they were scrubbed. Angelo parked under a tree by the cabin entrance and let out a long, exhausted sigh. An all-consuming anticipation had prevented them from stopping on the way up, so Tommy headed straight to the rest room.

Angelo walked to the trunk of the car and stopped for a moment. Turning to view the lake with the moon shining on its rippled surface, he breathed in the sweet night air. The thick scent of pine filled his lungs, and he was instantly transported to wartime days on the run, specifically remembering the morning when he rested by a beautiful lake just like this one after a long night of evading the chasing enemy.

The quiet moment was shattered by the sound of Tommy yelling from inside. Angelo dropped a bag and ran to see what the matter was. Flinging the restroom door open, Tommy had been terrified by the largest spider he had ever seen. Angelo, wanting to exhibit strength in front of the little man, calmly took a piece of paper and held it close to the spider. Moving the paper closer to the spider, it eventually stepped onto the paper and Angelo transported it outside. Tommy was impressed but couldn't help but notice that his dad held the paper as far from his body as possible.

Angelo returned to the car, unloaded their belongings, and lit the small stove for warmth. They heartily ate Diva's reheated pasta and enjoyed some California produced Chianti. While imported and homemade wine was saved for special times, California wine was just fine for daily consumption. After cleaning their dishes, they got "caught up" on the week's happenings over a friendly game of cards.

"This is such a cool place. I can't wait to go exploring tomorrow!" Tommy exclaimed.

Settled in and content with full stomachs, the two decided to go to bed early. "The best fishing is first thing in the morning," Angelo declared, and they agreed to get up at sunrise. Both were so excited, sleep was evasive. Finally, after a stretch of concerted quiet, they both fell into a deep sleep.

About nine thirty on Saturday morning, Angelo groggily stumbled to Tommy's bed and woke him. They both laughed, embarrassed by how late they slept, and vowed to get up early the next day. But for now, there were fish ready to be caught, and Tommy jumped out of bed. He quickly bolted out the door and ran to get the rowboat into the water. Angelo grabbed some dried salami, a loaf of Diva's bread, and canned drinks for lunch. The two rowed out to a spot halfway across the small lake.

"This looks pretty good," said Angelo. "Let's try our luck here."

The two tried several different lures but nothing was hitting. Moving to another spot, they experienced the same bad luck. Refusing to give up, they changed lures every fifteen minutes or so, trying to find the right action, shape, or color to trigger a bite. Angelo couldn't believe their luck but was grateful to be out on the water on a perfect day. Glancing at the bright sun, Angelo suggested a break from their efforts for lunch. Since Tommy had forgone breakfast to get out on the lake quickly, he eagerly agreed.

Angelo told Tommy to return his line to the boat while he took out the salami. Cutting off a large chunk, he gave it to the boy who immediately dug into it. Next came a sizeable portion of bread and a can of soda. The two zealously ate and simply enjoyed their time together.

After they had both had their fill, Angelo suggested they switch to live bait for the afternoon and see if it might trigger some action. Angelo watched as Tommy carefully baited his own hook and slowly released it into the water. Angelo was very impressed by Tommy's patience with fishing, which was polar opposite to his normally manic self.

The first hours of the afternoon passed and still no bite. Tommy kept his line in the water, refusing to give up. Angelo sat back in the boat, basking in the sunshine. His mind drifted to his youth spent growing up next to a mountain lake. He couldn't count the number of times he had thrown some worms into the water, trying to catch anything that would bite.

As he watched his son patiently trying to catch a fish, he recalled the several times he had to use grenades to stun and harvest fish for dinner. The war had returned to his consciousness but, this time, in a cathartic manner. This time the experience felt purifying instead of traumatizing. His life had come full circle. He was content. He was at peace.

Angelo smiled slightly and asked Tommy, "Have I ever told you how I used grenades to catch fish during the war?"

Tommy put his pole down. With eyes the size of saucers, he turned and said, "No, Dad. How did you do that?"

Angelo grinned broadly. After a few seconds of trying to process the idea, Tommy shifted closer, "I want to know everything."

*****

I'm not sure what it is about fishing that opens people up, but I'm eternally grateful for it (*see photo reference 28.3*).

Photo Reference 28.1 –

This is an early undated picture of Angelo, approximately twenty-nine years old, at his first tool and die job just prior to his marriage to Diva.

Photo Reference 28.2 –

This is the original small transistor radio that was the only source of entertainment and distraction during the long family vacation drives.

Photo Reference 28.3 –

Angelo the summer before his death, fishing with his oldest grandchild. He never had the chance to sit in a row boat on a still lake and tell his grandchildren his incredible life story like he did with me. Hopefully this book is the next best thing.

I'm not sure what it is about fishing that opens people up, but I'm eternally grateful for it.

Epilogue

Angelo continued working at Anson Tool for another decade before changing jobs for another tool and die position at Duo-Fast Fasteners. After retiring from there, he spent his time happily with family and travel. He would regularly journey back home to Italy with Diva and visit Nini and other extended family members. His other travel passion was cruising, and he visited virtually every country in the Caribbean Sea and Latin America. When not traveling, he enjoyed donating his time to Meals on Wheels, driving meals to shut-ins and those less fortunate.

Both were blessed to see the marriages of Steve and Tom, as well as the births of four grandchildren. Never boastful, he nonetheless delighted in telling anyone that would listen about his progeny, and his greatest pleasure was any time spent among them.

Angelo lived to be seventy-five years of age and Diva seventy-two when they died together in a head-on traffic accident on January 1, 1998. On their way to an Italian food store, a driver lost control of his vehicle on an icy 55-mph road segment, crossed the median, and struck them at full speed. While tragic, Angelo would have been grateful to go the way he did, in the blink of an eye and with Diva by his side. They are buried next to each other at St. Joseph Catholic Cemetery in River Grove, Illinois.

Acknowledgements

Words cannot express the gratitude I have for those who contributed and collaborated stories for this book about Angelo Flaim, my father. I thankfully acknowledge those who provided insight into the events occurring before my time. With many relatives and friends aging, their detailed remembrances were helpful beyond words. Their efforts have made this novel as true and accurate as possible.

I am blessed beyond measure to call myself the son of Angelo and Diva, brother of Steve, husband of Sue, and father of Spencer and Tyler. My mother, Diva, and brother, Steve, have always supported and loved me unconditionally and could easily support remarkable books of their own. Steve selflessly covered for me in the business we have owned together for decades, enabling me the considerable amount of time needed to research and complete this work. My wife, Sue, the love of my life, didn't flinch when I told her of my desire to write this book, even though my first book took me from home far too often.

Lastly, Dave Narey and Matthew Bullard for their continual support and guidance, and Sidney Bullard for her incredible editing. May God continue to bless you all!

Made in the USA
Columbia, SC
17 March 2024

33190459R00176